TEA

A JOURNEY IN TIME

Dedicated to the pioneer planters
– who started something

Charles Alexander Bruce 1793-1871, East India Company officer, was the pioneer of the tea industry in India. (*Etching, executed in Calcutta c.1850, courtesy Mrs. Jeanette King-Harman, great, great grand-daughter of C.A. Bruce.*)

MAP OF

MUTTUCK, SINGPHO,
and
the Country West of the Booree Dihing River

Shewing all the Tea Tracts that have hitherto been discovered, by Mr C.A. Bruce, Superintendent of Tea Culture to the Hon.ble East India Compy in Assam.

Jypore 1st June 1839.

A drawing from this map is shown in Chapter II

TEA – A JOURNEY IN TIME

PIONEERING AND TRIALS
IN THE JUNGLE

John Weatherstone

Illustrated with fine colour plates, drawings, engravings
and photographs from the past and present

Front jacket

Above
The arms of the Honourable East India Company.
(*By permission of the British Library.*)

Below
Steam transport on the Ganges. Troop-carrying duties
during the mutiny c. 1857
Printed by Day and Sons, lithographers to the Queen.
(*Chromolithograph, Science Museum
Science & Society Picture Library.*)

Back jacket

Above
Shoots of the tea camellia – Golden Tips.

Below
With feet firmly on the ground! Mohan, an elephant
employed for work on Hunwal Tea Estate. One cannot be
certain about his age because birth certficates are not
issued in the jungles of Assam.
(*Photo 2004, courtesy Williamson Magor, Kolkata.*)

The illustrations, except where individually acknowledged,
are from the author's own collection.

In some cases it has proved impossible to trace the copyright holder; in these instances the author offers his apologies should any rights be inadvertently infringed.

Copyright © 2008 John Weatherstone
First published 2008

Jacket designed by John Weatherstone

Published by
JJG Publishing
Sparrow Hall
Hindringham
Fakenham
Norfolk
NR21 0DP

ISBN 978-1-899163-85-4

Printed in China through Colorcraft Ltd, Hong Kong

In John Weatherstone's previous book *The Pioneers* published in 1986 he has included an account of the life led by British tea & coffee planters covering the period 1825 to 1900. The book is well illustrated with engravings, photographs and drawings. India and Ceylon (since re-named Sri Lanka) were the areas in which British planters concentrated their efforts to establish tea and coffee growing estates and the book records their endeavours with considerable accuracy and with great interest for the reader.

The foreword for *The Pioneers* was written by Sir Percival Griffiths who mentioned that he hoped the author would continue his study of these matters and give us a sequel dealing with the life of the modern planter.

Mr. Weatherstone has indeed continued his studies which have concentrated on the development of the tea industry in many countries. These studies are now condensed in this, his latest book *Tea, A Journey in Time*.

Since 1900 the tea industry has developed out of all recognition with changes taking place in practically every aspect of plantation operations and the way of life led by the planters. Tea estates are now firmly established and it is no longer necessary to bear the physical hardships and overcome many of the problems experienced by the British planters of the past. However, it can be recorded with pride and satisfaction that those early pioneers were responsible for the initial ground-work which has since developed into a huge industry and given tea drinkers of the world much pleasure. If those early planters could be told that in 1900 the production of tea in India and Ceylon was collectively under 100 million kilos and in 2000 the production was in excess of 1150 million kilos their delight would undoubtedly be a reason for celebrations at the Club bar.

Inevitably the management on tea estates is now in the hands of nationals and has been for a number of years. It is indeed praiseworthy to record that in India this somewhat gradual hand-over has been achieved without any problems and the estates continue to flourish and improve as in the past.

John M. Trinick

Contents

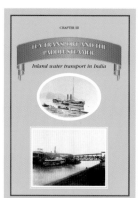

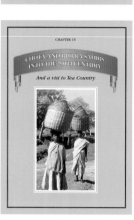

Preface

The customer who selects a packet of tea does not pause to consider the extraordinary history of its contents. But what is known of the industry that produces the tea that so unfailing appears on the supermarket shelf?

Tea was first consumed as a medicinal drink about 5000 years ago by the Chinese, who tended the tea camellia wherever it grew throughout much of China, making tea from an infusion of its leaves. Then, in the 12th century, Buddhist monks brought the tea plant from China to Japan which, like the former country, tended the plant on countless small plots of land where the bushes were numbered in dozens rather than acres.

From that distant past we take up the story in more modern times – from the early part of the 19th century when European entrepreneurs started to take an interest in the cultivation of the tea camellia.

It is hoped that the first six chapters will hold the interest of the reader, in that they are a blend of diverse and, hopefully, interesting facts connected with an industry in which hardship and adventure, for those involved, went hand in hand with the development of a great industry; first in the wilds of the North-East Frontier region of India, in the Dutch East Indies in Java and Sumatra, and then in Ceylon. Today, the tea plant is cultivated in many countries throughout the world.

For the reader, whose only close encounter with tea comes when selecting a tin or packet from the supermarket shelf and then at home when 'drinking the cup that cheers', the last Plantations chapter provides an opportunity of seeing – from the comfort of a chair and without having to journey to far distant countries – some of the tea estates that provide that very welcome drink. Importantly, it also shows the conditions under which those who bring us our tea live and work at the beginning of the 21st century.

The year 2000 was the 400th anniversary of the founding of the English East India Company, and this provides an excellent opportunity to include within the confines of this book just two of the Honourable Company's great achievements: the commencement of a new Tea Industry in British India, in 1835, and the introduction of an Inland Water Transport System on the great rivers in that country, at about the same time. From that point in time we shall journey on to the present day.

One might wonder why reference should be made to the paddle steamer. This quaint looking engine-driven craft looked almost as ungainly on a river as did Orville Wright's aeroplane in the sky. The paddle steamer is included – not only for nostalgic memories of these splendid vessels, that once provided a way of life for all those who lived along the great Indian rivers – but more importantly because the new tea industry – struggling to get on its feet in a remote region far up the Brahmaputra – came to rely heavily upon this new mode of transport.

In the year 1834, Lord William Bentinck put forward recommendations that would lead to India becoming a tea producer in her own right. In sending her officials, first to China to procure tea seeds while enticing that country's tea artisans to India, then by her bold planning of a truly remarkable RIVER JOURNEY (which is told in the second chapter), the East India Company laid a well prepared plan to introduce tea growing into India – thereby ending China's monopoly.

How can one describe, at the beginning of the 21st century and without appearing to dramatize the situation, the hardships and perils that were an everyday occurrence for those engaged in opening out hundreds of thousands of acres of mosquito-ridden jungles to plant the tea camellia? One thing is certain and that is, however improbable these conditions might seem to the reader today, it would be safe to assume that in real life they were a good deal worse. For the European planter there were no hotels at which to put up for the night, no shops, no hospitals, no doctors and many of the early tea men lived off the land – wildlife was plentiful and the rifle was an essential item of his meagre belongings.

To a man who lived in a hut in which snakes,

leeches and scorpions held equal rights of possession - and where for long periods he could not dry out the clothes he stood up in - a year would seem like a long time. This scenario was typical of countless others throughout the jungles of India, Java and Ceylon during the early 19th century, all in the name of plantation crops such as tea, coffee, cacao, cinchona - and rubber, somewhat later.

Let us leave, for a moment, those dank and unhealthy jungles and contemplate our local supermarket, where, if there was so much as a single cockroach there would be hell to pay. The statistics show that we in the United Kingdom drink more tea than any other beverage and that 90,000 cups in a lifetime is normal. That's an awful lot of tea!

So, without more ado, and especially when you next throw a tea party and do some serious drinking, be sure to have a copy of this book close by to impress, or otherwise, your guests, for your fine porcelain tea service and family silver teapot are simply not enough on their own.

Once again my publisher, Jeremy Greenwood and his team, have had the unenviable task of getting to grips with my manuscript and making sense of it. We hope you will enjoy this book about TEA - for where would we tea drinkers be without the cup that cheers?

Lastly, my wife Carolyn deserves a mention in these dispatches as it was she who, in a way, instigated the writing of this book by saying one autumnal morning, 'Bearing in mind you cannot write for toffee, why don't you do something useful during the winter months?' Now, having played second fiddle to the blessed book for quite some time, she deserves something better – like a trip to a tea estate somewhere - as if she hasn't seen enough already!

Writing and researching for this book during the winter months, when the garden has been put to bed and the badgers are asleep in their setts, is not half a bad occupation. As will readily be seen the pictures play a prominent part, for I agree entirely with every word Alice said:

... " and what is the use of a book,"
thought Alice,
"without pictures."
Alice in Wonderland - Lewis Carroll

There are no camellias in this lovely garden but a few million in the surrounding tea fields! The garden of the present manager's bungalow on Leesh River Tea Garden, Dooars, India. (*Photo by A.S. Hobbs, courtesy Goodricke Group*).

Acknowledgements

I should like to acknowledge gratefully the help received from a number of sources. In particular my thanks to John Trinick, known far and wide as 'Mr Assam', for so kindly agreeing to write the foreword to this book as well as reading and correcting parts of the manuscript relating to the chapters on India; also for the Plantations chapter. Like a good slip fielder, nothing gets past him! Long passed the age of retirement, having been nearly 60 years in tea, he is still an out and out tea man, visiting Williamson Magor's estates in Assam three or four times a year as Tea Taster and Manufacturing Adviser. Each time, upon arrival at his bungalow, he is welcomed by the company's elephant, whereupon he instantly feels at home; who would not! Also, a personal thank you to another tea man, Charles Brooke-Smith, ex-Visiting Agent and planter in Ceylon (Sri Lanka) for 36 years, for reading and checking the chapters relating to Sri Lanka and to the Plantations chapter, and, most importantly, for encouraging me to press on regardless while I still have enough puff to blow out the candles on the cake each year. These two gentlemen have generously given much of their time, providing some expert knowledge relating to the world famous tea camellia and its cultivation.

I am very pleased to be able to include the picture of THE pioneer of tea in India, Charles Alexander Bruce, ex-Royal Navy, gunboat Commander and East India Company Officer: I think you will agree he looks every inch a pioneer – solid in character, strong and capable. For this picture we must thank the courtesy of Jeanette King-Harman, great, great grand-daughter of C.A.B. and Col. A.L. King-Harman, OBE, DL.

A great number of super photographs and much other information have been freely given by ex-planters and those in the tea industry and provide us with the many different aspects of plantation life for those who live and work in tea. Also, my special thanks to the wives of planters who have provided photographs and anecdotes from their long years in tea: to Joan Turnbull, behind my venture from the beginning, when it was just a fleeting thought; to Joan Gottelier and Frances Salveson, who also provided photographs and some interesting and unusual reminiscences. Others I remember are the late Trevor Moy, OBE, and Brian Womersley; Elizabeth and Alan Sharp-Paul, who were among the first to answer my jungle telegraph requesting pictures, when a bundle of 17 photographs arrived out of the blue from Australia – that was the start of this undertaking. Others are Bill Atkinson, A. Clark, John Benest and Chris Greenhow.

Also mentioned in dispatches are present-day Sri Lankan planters who have found time to assist me while running their estates: wonderfully helpful to me has been Maithri Liyanage, Manager of Great Western Tea Estate, Talawakelle, for going into 'field and factory' with his camera and taking some great photos on the estate and then dispatching to me – all within three weeks. Other working planters were Ralph Callander, late of Lellopitiya Estate, which was in his family from the days when Alexander Callander arrived in Ceylon from Scotland in 1899, until the Government nationalized the estate in 1975; Bryan Baptist, Director of Bartleet & Co., Tea Brokers, Colombo, for his help during my 'collecting' period and not forgetting N.V.B. Johnpillai, Manager of Poonagalla Group.

Great assistance has come from REICHMUTH VON REDING, Hanspeter Reichmuth, Switzerland, in the way of photographs of tea estates in the hills of Darjeeling and South India, taken while on his travels in 'tea country'. These views – together with those taken by Jayaram Thangavelu, Manager of Havukal Estate – provide a most interesting insight into planting conditions today in these widely separated regions of India.

Also remembered are David Manners for the photographs of his pioneering great uncle, Oscar Lindgren, Assam planter for 45 years in the hard, tough days when 'opening out' meant only one thing – JUNGLE. Also Kim Dodwell, planter, and Tony Andrew; they have all helped the tea story along in different ways by providing the flavour of planting life led by the early tea men.

For the coverage of Tea in Africa, very many thanks to Jane Moncreiff and Rick Tilley. Photographer Jane Moncreiff has provided us with photos of yet another tea growing region in the world, South Africa, by going out into field and factory on Middelkop Estate; in fact rather more than we have been able to show in this book. Rick Tilley, of Eastern Produce Ltd, Blantyre, Malawi, purposefully went about having photographs specially taken on the pioneering tea estate, Lauderdale, which celebrated its 100th anniversary in tea a few years ago. I also acknowledge the help of Andrew Brooke-Smith; G.H. McLean of Sapekoe Estates and K.W. Tarplee of Linton Park PLC and Frank Johnston of Central Africana Ltd for coverage of Malawi.

I would like to thank the following companies and individuals in the tea industry who have made a positive response to my requests for tea-related material and for their help which has allowed me to put together the final chapter about Tea Plantations of the World. Commencing with those on the other side of the world: Australian Geographic, NSW, Joanne Diver; State Library of NSW, Jennifer Broomhead; Nerada Tea Pty., Andrew Weavers; Glen Allyn Tea Estate, Queensland, Tristan Russell; Madura Tea, NSW, owners Stephen Bright, Larry Brown and Ron Ford; Bill Addison and particular thanks to Rod Taylor, ex-Nerada Director, for taking the very interesting photos showing the original tea plants that were put out in 1883 at Bingil Bay in North Queensland; The National Institute of Vegetable and Tea Science, Japan, Dr. Hitoshi Yoshitomi; the Secretariat of World Green Tea Association, Japan, T. Atsumi; Matsumoto Kiko Co. Ltd; The New Century Corporation, Y. Shimomura; Indorub Sumber Wadung Tea Plantations, Indonesia, Jocelyn Rigby; J.A. Russell & Co. Sdn. Bhd. Malaysia, Tristan Russell; Tocklai Experimental Station, Jorhat, Assam, Director M. Hazarika; The Tea Research Institute of Sri Lanka Dr. M.T. Ziyad Mohamed.

Williamson Magor & Co. Ltd., Kolkata, Chairman B.M. Khaitan for some very solid all round assistance; Giri Sodhi, Visiting Agent for WM, and Estate Manager Sanjay Batra for supervising photography on Hunwal Estate and for background statistics; Tetley GB Ltd, Giles Oakley; R. Twining and Co. Ltd, Angela Smith; Lawrie Plantation Services Ltd., Sevenoaks, Kent, Chairman Peter Leggatt MBE and Alan Hobbs; Duncan Brothers (Bangladesh) Ltd.; Goodricke Group and Linton Park plc, Maidstone, Kent, Alan Perkins; Inchcape plc, Gemini Patel; Estableciemento Las Marias, Argentina.

I am grateful to the Honorary Secretaries of: The Koi Hai Directory, Cathie Campbell; The Ceylon Association, Richard Doudney; The Friends of Sri Lanka Association, John Carpenter, for sending out to their members – by way of the jungle telegraph – a synopsis of this work in their quarterly Bulletins.

Last, but by no means least, I would like to express my thanks and appreciation to all those in the many museums who have helped me in my researches with their advice, particularly the British Library (Oriental and India Office Collections). The Library has been extremely helpful and generous by providing many of the lovely colour plates that enhance this book; Oxford University Press, Anna Zawadzki; the National Maritime Museum, Greenwich, London, David Taylor; The Mariners Museum, Newport News, VA U.S.A.; The Royal Botanic Gardens, Kew; The Royal Geographical Society London, Justin Hobson and Joy Wheeler have provided some of the best early tea pioneering photographs from its fine collection.

The willingness to help is half the battle

Finally, had it not been for the support so generously given by Williamson Magor, a tea plantation owning company first established in India in 1869 – and its Chairman – to help with the high production costs involved in printing such a well illustrated book, the story of *Tea, A Journey in Time* might never have been told. Certainly, one cannot get far in this world without the help of others. So, let's lift up our cups to Williamson Magor.

A Ceylon planter's talipot palm shelter.
(*Watercolour by S.R. Fever 1984.*)

CHAPTER 1

THE TEA CAMELLIA AND THE CHINA CUP

Tea Pluckers in China. Lithographed plate drawn and hand-coloured by Elizabeth Twining, grand-daughter of Richard Twining, Tea Merchant. She was an excellent artist, dividing her time between travel, botany and philanthropy, and was the founder of Bedford College.
(*The Plant World by Elizabeth Twining, published by T. Nelson, London, 1866.*)

The Tea Camellia and The China Cup

Next time you are in the supermarket pause for just a few precious moments and survey the wealth of different teas on the shelves. Many tea drinkers will think only of the 'old' tea producing countries, China, India and Ceylon (now Sri Lanka) who together produce approximately 60% of the world production. Nowadays a lot of the tea we drink comes from the African continent: Kenya, Malawi, Zimbabwe, Tanganyika, Tanzania, Mozambique and South Africa; these countries collectively produce almost 14% of world production. The world's major tea producers blend many different teas to produce the unique and consistent taste of their product.

From the foregoing we are all aware of China, Indian and Ceylon teas, after all it is writ large upon the packet that we buy, and anyway we constantly see on television that the best monkeys drink it. Perhaps to be more accurate, I should say chimpanzees, for the close evolutionary links between them – the chimps and us humans – is not doubted. However, that is as maybe and is sometimes expedient to forget. So whichever way you look at it, if you are one of the millions who drink the 'cup that cheers', it is only natural that you should be forever grateful to the men, past and present, who planted and tended the wonderful tea camellia.

People who live in the western industrialized world drink mostly black tea, whereas green tea is favoured by the people of Asia. India, Sri Lanka, Indonesia and Africa are the major producers of black tea, with China exporting a small amount. Japan and China are producers of green tea. The United Kingdom is still the biggest tea importing country in the world.

Whatever tea one drinks, the average consumption in Britain is 3½ cups a day (over the age of ten), or some 90,000 cups of tea during the normal life span. As a nation this amounts to approximately 175 million cups a day. We drink tea every day and the packet is thrown away without further thought, other than to remember to buy another one. Tea bags are now used to brew 80.6% of all cups of tea in the United Kingdom and it is still the most important drink by a significant margin. Those of us who drink tea are not alone, for half of the world's population do likewise – from Mongolia to Egypt and from China to Australia.

Today, the tea camellia is grown in many countries around the world, the five largest producing countries being India, China, Sri Lanka, Africa and Indonesia; other small growers include Turkey, Japan, Taiwan, Formosa, Korea, Thailand, Malaysia, Papua New Guinea and Georgia in south Russia. Should the reader be wondering where else the tea plant is grown – and from the foregoing it would seem practically everywhere – South America too should be mentioned. On this vast continent Argentina, Brazil and Peru all now grow tea, the former having increased its production greatly in recent years. Also, it is not generally known that tea is grown in Australia, along the east coast in Queensland and New South Wales, where it was first planted, as seed-at-stake, in 1977, on a run-down dairy farm in NSW, to form what is now Madura Tea Estate. Not included so far is the only commercially grown tea in the United States (land of the Boston Tea Party) on the Charleston Tea Plantation on Wadmawlaw Island, off the coast of South Carolina.

But what of this very special camellia and the men who have cultivated it, from the Chinese and Japanese

A Mongolian with his tea caravan in the streets of Peiping.

in the distant past to the British pioneers who, in the late 1830s, went out to fever-stricken jungles of India and against all the odds started a new tea industry and introduced an entirely new way of growing tea – THE PLANTATION SYSTEM – in competition with China.

Home of the Tea Plant and Past History

The commercially important tea plant comes from the large family of evergreen camellias, some 80 varieties of which are grown in our parks and gardens for the vivid display of their flowers, set off against dark shiny leaves. It is very probable that the reader has one or more of these varieties in his or her garden. The tea plant that is native to China (*Camellia sinensis*) is small leafed by comparison to its close cousin from north-east India, the larger broad-leafed Assam variety (*Camellia assamica*). The tea plant is indigenous to the forests of south-east Asia, including much of China, Burma and Siam, where, in its natural state, it grows into a tree some sixty feet in height.

The origin of tea has its roots in mythology. The Chinese have made good use of the leaves of the tea plant, first for medicinal purposes, then as a beverage for a very long time. Chinese legends ascribe the discovery of tea to the Emperor Shen Nung, who lived in the third millennium BC. The earliest written record of the tea plant was published by the Chinese in about 493 BC. It is known that they were drinking tea in the 6th century AD, but how and when they discovered that an infusion of the leaves of the wild tea camellia, if carefully processed, produced a most palatable beverage is not known. The first authentic account of the manufacture of tea was written by Lo Yu about 780 AD.

It is said that the Emperor of China and his court drank a special tea which was harvested from truly wild tea that grew so tall the leaves could only be picked by monkeys. Each season some 200 pounds of Imperial Monkey-picked Tea was produced.

By the end of the 8th century China had become an exporter of tea which was at first carried by porters into neighbouring Tibet and Mongolia, then towards the latter part of the 17th century to Russia, along the legendary route taken by the tea caravans. These consisted of between two and three hundred camels each laden with four chests of tea, and travelled from China's western border along a trail that crossed 800 miles of inhospitable Gobi desert, passing through Ulan Bator and on to Irkutsk when it turned west over the great plains of Russia. The round journey took in the

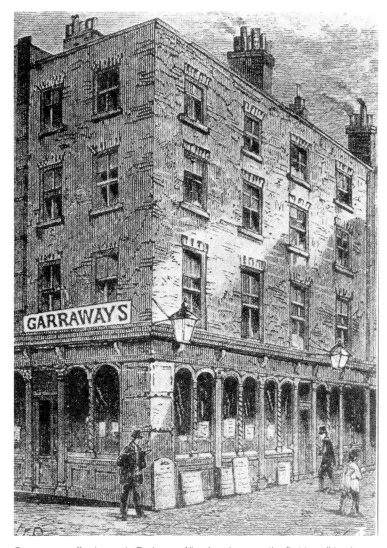

Garraways coffee house in Exchange Alley, London, was the first to sell tea in England in 1657. (*Drawing by permission of the British Library.*)

region of three years.

According to Japanese sources (NIVTS) the first tea seeds were brought from China to Japan in the 12th century and for many hundreds of years thereafter the industry – like that of China – was an occupation, where every villager owned a few bushes.

Tea reaches Europe

The first China tea reached Europe in about 1610 and was carried in the merchant ships of the Dutch East India Company, to Holland; almost contemporaneously it appeared in France and Germany. It was not long after that the first supplies were received in England, by way of the Continent. Its cost in those days was about £10 per pound.

The English East India Company, 1600–1858, was somewhat slow to recognise the importance of the China Tea Trade, and it was not until about 1663 that its merchantmen brought tea directly to Britain.

During the 1650s coffee houses began to appear in London and it was in one of these, Garraways Coffee ▶

Carrying tea-chests to the ship. (*Sketch published by the* Illustrated London News *in 1888.*)

Tea Auctions in London 1679-1998

From the days when we knew only China tea to the final auction on 29 June 1998, when a 44 kilo chest of Ceylon tea sold for £24,420, or £555 a kilo!

A tea broker's clerk taking samples from a chest of China tea. (*Detail from drawing 1878, Illustrated London News.*)

From a contemporary aquatint of an auction in East India House, London in 1808. This was before the days of Indian tea and only China tea was sold at that time. (*By permission of the British Library.*)

London Tea Auction, 1967. (*Print by permission of the British Library.*)

Managing Director of Bettys & Taylors of Harrogate, Jonathan Wild, paid this prodigious sum (see opposite page) for this last chest of tea to be auctioned in London, as a 319-year tradition ends. Various tea trade charities benefit from the proceeds. The normal price is £8 per kilo. Producer countries now have their own auctions and with new technology business is conducted directly with estates through the Internet. (*Courtesy P.A. Photos.*)

▶ House, in Change Alley, London, that China tea was first sold to the general public, in 1657.

The price of tea in Britain, 1657 to 1995

These charts show how much 1lb or 450gms of tea cost from 1657 to 1995. During the 17th and 18th centuries the price of tea varied because the government put taxes on it. The East India Company's monopoly meant that they could charge whatever they liked for the tea. The very high prices led to smuggling of tea and adulterating it. By the 19th century, when the taxes were removed and the East India Company lost its monopoly in 1833, tea prices fell.

Year	Price of 1lb (450gms) of tea	Price in today's currency
1657	16/- to 60/-	(80p to £3.00)
1700	10/- to 36/-	(50p to £1.80)
1756	10/- to 12/-	(50p to 60p)
1784	16/- to 50/-	(80p to £2.50)
1839	6/6d	(32.5p)
1910	3/-	(15p)
1985	45p	(£1.80) per quarter of lb

* 1/- is a shilling or 12d which is equivalent to 5p

Year	Average weekly earnings of a man
1700	12.5p
1870	51p
1985	£140

The above facts are from 'Victorian India, Tea Garden of the World'. (*By permission of The British Library and published by the Library.*)

Thomas Garraway's famous coffee house was the meeting place for the rich merchants of the City. In the stifling atmosphere, heavy with smoke from clay pipes, oil lamps and candles that flickered and burned in the gloom, City men would sit discussing important commercial transactions over, not only tea and coffee, but a glass of punch or brandy. Many would have arrived by horse, or carriage, bringing with them the healthy smell of the stable, and this, in a confined space, mixed freely with the odour of stale sweat, passing quite unnoticed by those present. With wood planked floors and sawdust to mop up the mess below tables, Garraways was one of the more exclusive places in the City.

Thomas Garraway understood the necessity of good advertising, especially when it came to extolling the virtues of tea. On his bill board was the following:

An Exact defription of the Grovvth Quality and vertues of the Leaf Tea

It maketh the body active and lusty

It helpeth the Headach, giddiness and heavyness thereof

It removth the obstructions of the Spleen

It is very good against the Stone and Gravel, cleaning the kidneys and uriters, being drank with Virgins Honey instead of sugar

It taketh away the difficulty of breathing, opening obstructions

It vanquisheth heavy dreams, easeth the brain and strengtheneth the memory.

Only part of the original is quoted, but from this one can feel sure that, by drinking tea, we are, to use a modern idiom, fireproof. And so they were in those days – they had to be! Garraways remained in business for just over 200 years until 1861.

In 1706 Thomas Twining opened a coffee shop in London's Strand which, remarkably, is still there today, trading as R. Twining & Co. Ltd. This old established family business of Tea and Coffee Merchants celebrated its 300th anniversary in 2006.

By the 18th century tea houses and tea gardens had begun to appear in and around London, where they made ideal meeting places for society to meet and gossip over a pleasant cup of China tea and light refreshments. These tea gardens were often situated away from the smelly town areas.

Tea soon ousted coffee as the national drink in the British Isles, but in America the reverse was to happen when tea was replaced by coffee.

America turns from Tea to Coffee – The Boston Tea Party

Early British immigrants to North America brought the habit of tea drinking with them and later it became a popular pastime with the upper-class families of Boston and Philadelphia. The 'swells' would entertain their friends to afternoon tea when, as a symbol of their social success, they would bring out their fine porcelain tea services and silver tea-pots, for, as anyone knows, China tea is best drunk from a porcelain cup. By the early 1770s a third of the colonies' population drank tea regularly twice a day.

Tea first reached America in about 1640 and, as mentioned, soon became the favourite drink; that is, until the Boston Tea Party, in 1773. Some six years earlier the British Parliament had imposed duties on certain exports into its American colony, and in 1770 these duties were lifted - except those on tea.

There had been much agitation in the country for the removal of the monstrous tax on tea. The final straw for the colonials was the arrival in Boston Harbour of three East India Company merchantmen, carrying cargoes of tea, which in all amounted to just under £10,000 worth of China tea, in some 340 chests. By the autumn the East India Company had shipped approximately half a million tons of tea into Boston Harbour alone. The three ships were *Dartmouth* and *Eleanor*, each carrying 114 chests of tea, and the Brig *Beaver* with 112 chests in her holds.

The first of the tea ships, *Dartmouth*, under the command of Captain Hall, put into Boston Harbour on 28th November 1773, and some three days later lay warped to Griffin's Wharf: she was followed by the ship *Eleanor*, Captain Bruce, which also proceeded to Griffin's Wharf, on December 2nd. The patriots, who ruled Boston's streets and waterfront, immediately put an armed guard on the two ships, to thwart any attempt to land the tea. The original intention had been to force the tea-ships to return with their cargoes of tea to London. Meanwhile, on the 7th, the Brig *Beaver* lay off Boston, for clearing and smoking, as some of the crew had smallpox. A week later, on the 15th, she too proceeded to Griffin's Wharf, joining *Dartmouth* and *Eleanor*.

The Townsend Act levied duty on all teas imported into American colonies. In this case the deadline for payment on the teas 'landed' was 17th December.

A notification in a form proper to inflame the good people of Boston and surrounding towns was posted up calling upon them to assemble:

Friends! bretherin! countrymen! – That worst of plagues, the detested tea, shipped for this port by the East India Company, is now arrived in this harbour – the hour of destruction or manly opposition to the machinations of tyranny stare you in the face. Every friend to his country, to himself, and posterity, is now called upon to meet at Faneuil Hall, at nine o'clock this day, at which time the bells will ring, to make an united and successful resistance to this last, worst, and most destructive measure of administration.

With the oncome of darkness on that fateful evening of 16th December 1773, the silhouettes of the vessels were clearly seen by those standing along the town waterfront. Bright moonlight illuminated the scene.

Earlier, a band of sixty Bostonian citizens 'true' had disguised themselves as Mohawk Indians, wrapping their bodies in blankets and, with blackened faces, they waited in three separate boat parties, with axes at the ready.

Rally, Mohawks, bring out your axes
and tell King George we'll pay no taxes
on his foreign tea;
   His threats are vain and vain to think
to force our girls and wives to drink
his vile Bohea!
   Then rally, Boys and hasten on
to meet our chiefs at the Green Dragon.
   Our Warren's there and bold Revere
with hands to do and worlds to cheer,
for liberty and laws;
   Our country's 'braves' and firm defenders
shall ne'er be left by true North-enders,
fighting freedom's cause!
   Then rally, boys and hasten on
to meet our chiefs at the Green Dragon.

The Boston Tea Party, Griffin's Wharf, December 16th 1773. (*From the collections of the Mariners Museum, Newport News, Virginia.*)

The Green Dragon was a tavern frequented by Warren, Adams and Revere, and was used as a meeting place by the Massachusetts Radicals who planned the Tea Party. It was a Tea Party to end all tea parties.

The Boston patriots, some of whom were members of the Sons of Liberty, as well as many others from neighbouring villages, swept down the streets to Old South, into Milk Street and finally onto the Griffin's Wharf, where, with much excitement, they shouted 'Hurrah for Griffin's Wharf', 'Boston Harbour a tea-pot tonight', and 'The Mohawks are come!' The scene was set for the Party.

After the sailors on board the three vessels had been forced ashore, the Mohawks, fifteen or so in each boarding party, went about their work in organized silence: tea chests were hoisted from the holds to the decks where others hacked them open and shovelled and poured the tea overboard, heaving the empty chests behind them. The tide was so low that the tea soon began to build up in the water which was only three feet in places.

It was all over in little more than two hours, and by nine o'clock the harbour was awash with tea chests – ripped asunder. A crowd of onlookers stood on the wharf side cheering wildly.

A Royal Navy squadron, under the command of Admiral Montague, rode at anchor in Boston Harbour only a few hundred yards out, and a regiment of troops, under Colonel Leslie, remained at Castle William, close by. Yet the order to intervene was never given. Admiral Montague, who had witnessed the night's work from a house close to Griffin's Wharf, said the following day: 'I could easily have prevented the Execution of this Plan, but must have endangered the Lives of many innocent People by firing upon the Town.'

Back in England King George III was furious and various Acts were quickly passed including the Boston Port Bill; the intention being to blockade Boston Harbour until the value of the tea was recouped.

From having been a favourite drink tea became the hated symbol of oppression, and the refusal to drink it was thereafter

Admiral John Montague (1718–1792), 4th Earl of Sandwich was in command of a Royal Naval squadron on the fateful night in Boston harbour. His name was given to food and our much loved sandwich, which he reputedly ordered to avoid having to leave the gambling table. As First Lord of the Admiralty he promoted Lieutenant James Cook, R.N. to the rank of Captain after his second voyage of Discovery, encouraging him to volunteer for the third and last of his voyages. (*Oil painting by Thomas Gainsborough, R.A., 1727–1788, courtesy National Maritime Museum, London.*)

regarded as the mark of a true American patriot. It was a fateful night in British and American history, for that night of action was to prove the final straw, the most significant spark, that was to lead to the Lexington Skirmish, the battle of Bunker Hill and the American War of Independence.

Clippers and the China Tea Trade

After those early sailings during the 17th and 18th centuries when the slow, strongly built and cumbersome merchant ships of the Dutch and English East India Companies had brought tea to Europe and Great Britain, a new sleek vessel, the tea clipper, came upon the scene. The tea clipper was the 'Elegant Lady of the Sea', just as the 'East Indiaman' was the 'Aristocrat'.

During the 1860s a succession of fine looking sailing ships were launched from shipyards in Scotland, specifically for the China Tea Trade. The fastest of these oak- and teak-built clippers immediately cut the passage time from China to London from six months to almost three.

The clippers, on their outward passages, usually carried cargoes of raw materials and goods manufactured in Britain. Between the arrival dates of the clippers at the tea ports in China and the loading of the first teas of the season, they would be mainly employed in the Eastern coastal trade, carrying cargoes of rice. After trading up and down the coasts, the clippers would make their way to the tea ports in plenty of time to receive their cargoes of tea.

In China the tea plant is dormant throughout the long winter season, but towards the end of April the bushes throw out new leaf, which is then plucked. After this first spring 'flush' of leaf had been taken and the manufactured tea sent down to the tea ports, a further four or five pluckings were taken at monthly intervals during the summer, the last in September. From the first plucking, with its tender leaves, the very best grades of tea were

The tea camellia (*C. sinensis*) is indigenous throughout much of China, and has probably been cultivated for about 5,000 years. This pastoral scene shows leaf being brought in from a tea field, beyond which are junks of the type that carried the tea, after manufacture, downriver to the tea ports. The picture also shows part of the process of manufacture, using charcoal burning ovens.
(*Early 19th-century drawing, by permission of the British Library.*)

made, and from the last a poorer grade of tea. It was the first crop that was so important to get back to the London docks as quickly as possible, for it always fetched the highest prices in Mincing Lane.

Generally the first teas came down the Min River in sampans and junks to the Pagoda Anchorage at Foochow towards the latter half of May. It was then taken on board the waiting clippers and stowed away carefully by Chinese stevedores, who worked day and night until the vessel was fully loaded. The chests of tea were packed closely with wood and matting dunnage, so that the cargo would remain 'tight' throughout the long and dangerous voyage to England. The tea clippers often encountered typhoons during their passage through the China Sea, and every year one or more vanished without trace. During the five or six days loading and stowing away some million pounds of tea, there would be little sleep for anyone on board until the hatches were battened down and the ship cast off.

By the end of May, or early June, the crack clippers had taken on their cargoes of tea at ports such as Shanghai, Canton, Macao and Foochow and had embarked upon a race that would take them three-quarters of the way around the world.

In the Victorian era the annual clipper race from China to the London docks with the first teas of the season caused as much interest to the general public as the Derby. There was always great competition

between the owners and captains of the fast sailing ships employed in the China Tea Trade. Every year the ship that landed the first teas of the new season at London docks received a premium of ten shillings (50 pence) per ton of tea.

In the great race of 1866, no less than sixteen famous tea clippers were assembled at the Pagoda anchorage, waiting for the first teas of the new season to come down the Min river from the tea growing provinces. Three of the clippers, *Ariel*, *Taiping* and *Serica* completed loading, all leaving on the same tide, and after 99 days at sea all three arrived on the same tide at London docks. The premium of ten shillings a ton, and the special prize of £100, was divided between *Ariel* and *Taiping* as joint winners. *Serica* was a very close third, getting into West India docks a few hours later.

During the 1870s there were between 35 and 40 sailing ships engaged in the tea trade, each carrying cargoes averaging over a million pounds of tea.

Sadly, the beginning of the end was in sight for the clipper ships. The cutting and opening of the Suez Canal, in 1869, caused an immediate drop in the tea carried by the clippers, the days of which were in any case numbered by the introduction of steam. Some of the Glen Line steamers, using the new route through the Suez Canal, could do the passage in a matter of 44 days, as against the 100 days or more by the faster clip- ▶

This fine painting by Montague Dawson depicts the Tea clipper *Thermopylae* leaving the Pagoda anchorage, Foochow, China. Considered by expert seamen to have been the fastest sailing ship ever built, this sleek green-hulled beauty was once the admiration of every seafaring eye. Built at Walter Hood's yard in Aberdeen, Scotland, in 1868, she had a displacement of 1970 tons at load draught and was of composite construction, with an iron frame, wood planking of elm from keel to topside and East India teak for her decks. Her biggest tea cargo carried from China to the London docks was almost one and a half million pounds of tea. which, together with 250 tons of ballast, gave her a mean draught of 2l feet 6 inches.

At 5 on the morning of July 3rd 1869, *Thermopylae* moved slowly out of the Pagoda anchorage under tow with her first ever cargo of tea battened down under hatches. After a voyage half way around the world, passing through the dangerous South China Sea, where typhoons were not infrequent, on through the Sunda Straight across the Indian Ocean and then round the Cape of Good Hope, *Thermopylae* arrived at London docks 9l days later. (*Courtesy of Felix Rosenstiel's Widow & Son Ltd., London on behalf of the estate of Montague Dawson.*)

The transport of tea from the East

In the tea growing regions of China chests of tea were loaded into junks bound for ports such as Macao, Canton and Foochow for shipment to the other side of the world.
(*Permission of The British Library*)

East Indiamen

Tea was first brought to Holland from China during the first part of the 17th century in merchantmen of the Dutch East India Company; supplies from the Continent reached England shortly afterwards. Tea was then brought direct from China to the London docks by the merchantmen of the English East India Company; these ships were called 'Indiamen'.
(*Courtesy National Maritime Museum, London*)

Tea clippers

From the mid 1860s tea was carried in British built clippers such as *Cutty Sark*, *Ariel*, *Taiping*, *Thermopylae* and many others. These fast sailing ships could each carry over a million pounds of tea.
(*Courtesy The Cutty Sark Trust*)

Steamers

The *Glenartney* was just one of the many fast screw steamers owned by the Glen Line. This ship was first home with the new teas of the 1874 season, and her time for the passage from Woosung to the London docks via the Suez Canal was 44 days, which included stops to take on coal.
(*1874, from The Illustrated London News*)

Duration of passage from China to London

1630s	By 'East Indiaman' around the Cape of Good Hope	6 months
1860s	By Clipper around the Cape of Good Hope	3 months
1880s	By Steamer through the Suez Canal	6 weeks

Tea chests being unloaded from the *Louden Castle* at London docks in the year 1877. In the vast holds of the ship were 40,000 packages of tea amounting to two million pounds in weight. Brokers' clerks – dressed in top hats – can be seen taking random samples out of some of the tea chests, after which they would hurry away with their samples to the offices of the tea merchants.
(*From a drawing in The Illustrated London News*).

T INDIA DOCKS, FROM THE SOUTH EAST.

West India Dock from the south-east. Long lines of ships, amidst a forest of masts and yards, lay along every wharfside of the East and West India Docks, their cargoes continuously swinging overhead from ship to wharf, while a busy hive of porters loaded and carted all manner of goods away to the warehouses. A rich aroma of tobacco, coffee, tea and tropical spices came from the casks and mingled with the pungent and grassy smell of horse dung.
(*Lithograph by W. Parrot, courtesy Guildhall Library, Corporation of London.*)

▶ pers, battling their way around the Cape of Good Hope. By the late 1870s most of the tea clippers had been forced out of the China Tea Trade by the steamers, and some went into the Australian wool trade.

The London Docks Scene

(Illustrated pp14-15)

The first teas of the season started to arrive at the London docks in the early part of September, building up in quantity until the end of October, when the market in Mincing Lane was at its busiest. Tea did, however, continue to arrive in London up until January, depending upon how late it was received and loaded at ports in China.

Unloading tea at East India Docks. This drawing, made in 1867, shows a wonderful bustle of activity. Though the markings on every tea chest are depicted in Chinese, chests of Indian tea had been arriving for almost 30 years; the attitude of the general public, and the artist, was still of China tea. However, China's monopoly of the Tea Trade was slowly slipping. (*The Illustrated London News, 1867.*)

The unloading of the tea clippers and the warehousing of their cargoes along the wharves of the East and West India docks always provided a scene of great activity. All the China tea discharged from the long lines of ships was received and prepared for the London market by the dock companies. In 1844, 2000 labourers were employed in the London docks on any one day, handling tea, coffee, cotton, sugar, wines and spirits.

China's Monopoly at Risk

Tea drinkers in the western world had been drinking tea that came from China for almost 200 years; then, for the first time, China was to receive some unwelcome competition - from the East India Company, no less.

In China, methods of cultivation and hand manufacture had remained unchanged for centuries, with little or no capital being ploughed back by the peasant farmers on their small plots of land. The stage was set for an entirely new, more enterprising, way of planting and growing tea: the *Plantation System*, a most efficient form of monoculture, was about to be introduced into British India.

As Empire grown teas started to enter the world markets, slowly at first, then like a tide, China could not compete.

After the loss of much of her great leaf trade with Britain, and other countries to a lesser extent, China still carried on a quite considerable trade with Russia, mainly in the form of brick teas. Poor quality tea, compressed into bricks, had over the centuries been exported to Mongolia, Siberia and Tibet, being carried into those countries by porters and in tea caravans; this trade continued.

Tea drinkers throughout the world had, up until the late 1830s, become used to China tea in their cup, but as Empire grown tea from India and Ceylon began to storm the market, preference for these developed. Here then is the story of that great enterprise.

CHAPTER II

THE HONOURABLE EAST INDIA COMPANY TAKES THE FIELD

The East India Company Tea Pioneer Extraordinary

Top: The Arms of the Honourable East India Company. (*By permission of the British Library.*)
Bottom: First Timers, Darjeeling District. (*Photo c 1863, courtesy Royal Geographical Society.*)

The Honourable East India Company Takes the Field

The English East India Company, known more familiarly as John Company, was the most powerful concern that has ever existed – a colossus to which combined power of many of the largest present day companies would be small by comparison. Properly speaking the Company were only merchants but its fleet of over one hundred vessels, known as 'Indiamen', were as heavily armed as ships of the Royal Navy and its army and political power was all powerful in the East from 1600 to 1859.

By the 1830s the demand for tea was growing rapidly. The import of tea from China to Europe, Great Britain and America had been in the hands of the East India Company, and while enjoying the complete monopoly of the tea trade with China, the Honourable Company was interesting itself in the possibility of growing tea in British India. When, in 1833, the British Parliament abolished that monopoly the Company was ready to go into direct competition with China as a tea producer – a bold step considering the Company's officers knew nothing about tea.

For the Honourable Company, with power over vast territories and continents, which it ruled on behalf of the Sovereign and British Parliament, nothing was impossible, and so it was to be with the great tea enterprise.

The bustling streets of London were a far cry from the unimagined jungles of the East; no man in his right mind would go there unless he went as a soldier with a gun.

In 1823 King George IV was on the throne of England. Five thousand miles away in India the government of that country was in the capable hands of the East India Company. The average Englishman at home would hardly have known the whereabouts of Assam – had he thought about it at all – and the North-East Frontier smacked of fever-ridden jungle and war-like tribes – an assumption not far from the truth.

Discovery of the Tea Plant in Assam

In that same year, Robert Bruce, a major in the Bengal Artillery serving in Assam, was told by native chiefs of the existence of tea plants growing wild in the jungles around Sadiya, in upper Assam. Robert's brother, Charles Alexander Bruce, a lieutenant in the Royal Navy, was in command of a flotilla of H.M.'s gunboats at Sadiya and, as such, was one of the first Europeans to penetrate the forests in the region. These vessels, like the steam gunboat *Diana*, were sail-assisted craft and mounted a 12-pounder gun.

News of the discovery of the tea plant was conveyed

Burma War. Conflagration of Dalla on the Rangoon river, 1826, showing the steam gunboat *Diana* in the foreground. Later, C.A. Bruce commanded this gunboat at *Sadiya*, in upper Assam. (*Artist J. Moore, engraved by G. Hunt.*)

H.M.S. *Dolphin*, Tahiti, 1767. In this view of Matavai Bay, One Tree Hill is seen on the right, while Venus Point – the name given by the astronomers to their headquarters, where the astronomical observations were taken – is about half a mile to the left of the native dwellings. Mount Orohena is the tallest of the Island's mountains, at 7321 feet. (*Engraving from Captain Cook's Voyages around the World.*)

by Robert Bruce to his brother Charles, who, in 1824, sent specimens of plant, seed and flower to David Scott, Agent to the Governor-General; these were eventually received at the Royal Botanical Gardens in Calcutta for identification. No formal recognition was made of the discovery, for it was thought by the Superintendent, Dr. Nathaniel Wallich, that the specimens were of the same family of camellia, but not the same species as those in China from which tea was made. The specimens were, however, those of the true tea plant.

This startling discovery was forgotten for almost ten years until a Lieutenant Andrew Charlton, of the Assam Sebundy Regiment, found, in 1834, similar tea plants growing wild in the forests around Sadiya. Once again specimens were dispatched down river to the Botanical Gardens in Calcutta. This time Dr. Wallich was able to identify and confirm to the Court of Directors of the East India Company that the specimens did indeed belong to the true tea plant of commerce - in this case *Camellia assamica*. Had a valuable ten years been lost?

The Quest for Plants and Seeds of Commercial Importance

During the 18th and 19th centuries many missions of botanical and scientific importance were made to strange and exotic parts of the then known world.

Both before and after the East India Company's initiative in its quest for tea plants, there had been others. The eminent botanist, Sir Joseph Banks, unofficial Director of Kew Gardens for many years, had long considered the possibility of transporting the breadfruit plant from Tahiti to the West Indies, and this was successfully carried out - at the second attempt, in 1791, after H.M.S. *Bounty's* fateful voyage when the infamous mutineers cast adrift Lieutenant William Bligh and loyal members of the crew in the ship's boat.

Joseph Banks was born of wealthy landowning parents, in 1743, and went to two famous schools, Harrow and then on to Eton College, where his interest in botany began. As early as 1788 he had reported to the Director of the Honourable East India Company the possibility that the tea plant might be cultivated in India, in the region bordering the Himalayas.

It was at the Royal Botanic Gardens, Kew, during the 1850s and 1870s that cinchona and rubber seed - brought at some peril by plant collectors from the jungles of South America - was germinated and the resultant young plants sent to India and Ceylon in Wardian cases.

Plants that grew in the forests of South America would, without hindrance, grow at similar latitudes in any part of the tropics: on the African continent, India, Ceylon or Malaya. Consequently it did not take long for the prying eyes of Westerners to discover these treasures and to use them to their own advantage – rubber, cinchona and cacao from the South American continent and tea from China. In spite of the fact that, as everyone knows – even those who are not musically minded – 'there is an awful lot of coffee in Brazil', *that* particular plant is native to Africa.

There can be little doubt that plants and seed were, in every sense, as valuable as gold and essential to the continuing development and prosperity of the British Empire.

To return to the transport of plants of commercial importance and to the breadfruit in particular:

During a voyage around the world to make new discoveries, particularly in the South Seas, Captain Samuel Wallis, R.N. – in command of H.M.S. *Dolphin*, together with the 14-gun Sloop of War *Swallow* and the Store-Ship *Prince Frederick* – discovered and landed on the island of Tahiti in the Pacific, in 1767. While there he found many useful plants and fruits and one of these was the breadfruit – a large football-shaped fruit with a high food value to the millions who live in the East and in the South Sea Islands. This discovery was to lead, some years later, to the transport of the breadfruit plant from Tahiti to the West Indies, for the consumption of those working on the sugar plantations – though when

The Queen of Otahette taking leave of Captain Wallis.

it was eventually planted there and flourished it was agreed that the West Indians preferred bananas!

After a first hostile encounter, when Tahitian boatmen greeted *Dolphin* with a shower of heavy stones, Captain Wallis and his men were to establish excellent relations with the islanders; so much so that upon their final departure from the island, Queen Oberea of Tahiti implored Captain Wallis to stay. This friendship boded well for James Cook and William Bligh, both of whom would follow Wallis in the succeeding years.

At one stage, early on, a group of Tahitians clambered on board *Dolphin*, having first thrown several branches of the plantain tree on board as a peace offering. It was then that Captain Wallis's pet goat played its part in this first close encounter with the natives of the Island. In the words of the day:

> A goat belonging to the fhip, having run his horns against the back of one of the Indians, he looked with surprise, and feeing the animal ready to renew the attack he fprang over the fhip's fide, and was inftantly followed by all his countrymen.

The replenishment of the ships with water, plantains, coconuts and apples went on daily:

> On Monday the 22nd, the natives brought hogs, poultry and fruit to the fhip, which they bartered for knives and other things, fo that the whole crew was fupplied with meat for two days, by means of this traffic. The boats having been this day fent for water, every inducement was ufed by the inhabitants to perfuade them to land.

These were happy days for all concerned. It is hard to imagine how apple trees came to be on a Pacific island and where they came from. However, mention is made of the way the Tahitians planted their crops and fruit-bearing trees: '… the breadfruit and apple trees were fet in rows upon the hills, and the coconut grown upon level ground'.

Captain Wallis had returned to England in 1768, after two years circumnavigating the globe searching for the conjectural Great Southern Continent which early scientists believed must lie somewhere in the Southern Hemisphere balancing the land mass in the north. Having received Wallis's glowing account of the most favourable conditions of Tahiti, and Matavai Bay in particular, as a safe anchorage, the Admiralty and Royal Society believed the island would make an excellent base for the proposed astronomical observations that were planned to be carried out during Cook's first Voyage of Discovery, from a place to be aptly named Venus Point.

Though discipline had to be maintained aboard Navy ships, trust grew between seamen and the islanders and bartering became rife. From Captain Wallis and his officers more exotic presents were given to Queen Oberea and knives and axes were given to her chiefs, while from the seamen came baubles, pieces of looking glass and nails by the thousands which were pulled from the ships' timbers in different parts of the vessels, when no one was looking. 'The price of a female's favour was a nail or two'.

Certainly the island of Tahiti was to become, for ships of the Royal Navy a little under 250 years ago, an important stopping place in the Pacific Ocean.

After their return, Wallis and not yet ranked Captain, Lieutenant James Cook, R.N., anchored *Endeavour* in Matavai Bay. Nails were still in demand for one reason or another. This time the British were known and revered friends and this friendship would later be extended to Lieutenant William Bligh, R.N. when he too anchored H.M.S. *Bounty* in the lovely sweeping bay. After the observations of the Transit of Venus had been accomplished, in June of 1769, Cook opened his secret orders which were to drop south and west to search for the illusive Southern Continent - New Zealand and Australia - *Terra Australis*.

Bligh was Master in H.M.S. *Resolution* on Cook's third and last Voyage of Discovery. By the time Bligh had embarked upon his mission to transport the bread-fruit from Tahiti to the West Indies, Captain James Cook, R.N., F.R.S. was dead, killed with four marines by natives in Kealakekua Bay, Hawaii, on February 14th, 1779. Later, upon retirement, Bligh was made Governor of New South Wales, and he died in 1817 a Vice Admiral of the Blue.

Breadfruit from Tahiti to the West Indies and tea seeds from China to Calcutta, the strongly built and well-armed merchantmen of the East India Company and ships of the Royal Navy were everywhere on the high seas.

Tea - Competition with China

Background to an incredible passage up a mighty river

In 1834 Lord William Bentinck proposed to the Council of the East India Company the setting up of a Tea Committee to investigate the possibilities of grow-ing tea in India with the idea that, should it prove a fea-sible proposition, the Honourable Company's tea lands, such as had been established, could then be handed over to private enterprise for future commercial devel-opment. This in turn led to the departure, in June 1834, of the Secretary, G. J. Gordon, on the sailing ship *Water Witch*, to China. His mission was to procure tea seeds and Chinamen skilled in the cultivation and manufac-ture of tea, and if that meant by devious means then so be it.

While Gordon was away the Tea Committee had received the news that the camellia which had been found growing in the forests of the Muttack region of upper Assam was the true tea plant. By then it was too late to recall Gordon; his mission to 'steal' or procure tea seeds went on. In January of 1835 the Port of

Calcutta was the scene of the arrival of 80,000 tea seeds, which were sent to the Botanical Gardens for germination, under Dr. Wallich. This was a quite remarkable feat on the part of Gordon at a time when Europeans visiting China stayed mainly around the ports and did not venture into the interior. Some ten months later the East India Company had 42,000 healthy young tea seedlings with which to start its tea enterprise in India.

This bold initiative by the Company to go into direct competition with China as a tea producing country, thereby breaking that country's monopoly, was to have far reaching effects upon one of the world's important plantation crops.

From the original consignment of 80,000 seeds, the resultant 42,000 young plants were to be distributed between three trial regions: Assam being allocated 20,000, the Kumaon, in North India, 20,000 and the Nilgiri Hills in South India were to receive 2000.

It was ironic that while these well laid plans were taking shape, the tea plant, albeit a larger leafed variety, *Camellia assamica*, had been discovered growing wild in the forests of upper Assam, on the North East Frontier.

In March 1835 the Tea Committee had recommend-ed to Government that a Scientific Deputation be sent to upper Assam to see, at first hand, the tea plants that had been found. They were to get conclusive proof, by positive identification, that the species was indeed the tea camellia of commerce. All that had been seen before were the specimens which had undoubtedly taken a considerable time to arrive at Calcutta, and in consequence were probably not as fresh as they might have been.

Those nominated for the deputation were Dr. Wallich, Dr. McClelland, a geologist, and Dr. William Griffith, a botanist. The Deputation left Calcutta on 29th August 1835, proceeding first to Cachar and then overland to Gauhati, the final part of the journey being made by country boat up to Sadiya.

Dr. Wallich had been appointed a member of the Tea Committee by Lord William Bentinck. It was on Wallich's recommendation that Lieutenant C. A. Bruce, R.N. was made Superintendent of Tea Culture to the East India Company, in February 1835, having in his charge all the Honourable Company's experimental tea lands in upper Assam. As the great grand-daughter of Bruce said:

> Never before could he have altered course to a greater degree. In every respect he had guts, and for the work that lay ahead of him perhaps, in the circumstances, this was the most essential qualification.

We will look first at the then wild, war-torn region bor-dering the North East Frontier, where the indigenous tea plant had been found and where in little more than three decades a thriving new tea industry would be firmly established and working in full swing. It was in ▶

The Scientific Expedition

During the 18th and 19th centuries missions of a scientific and botanical nature were often carried out by ships of the Royal Navy.

The scene depicted is of Matavai Bay, Tahiti, in the year 1769, and shows H.M. Bark *Endeavour* at anchor, with One Tree Hill at right and Venus Point out of the picture at left. Our view is from the foredeck, looking aft. Standing on the quarter-deck by the port side rail, Lieutenant James Cook, in command, is seen talking to the botanist Joseph Banks, whose dog is beside expedition artist Sydney Parkinson. *Endeavour*, a former collier, was 106 feet long and 29 feet broad and included 94 officers, seamen, marines and scientists, as well as four servants and two large dogs belonging to Joseph Banks, and a pet goat which had previously been around the Pacific with Captain Wallis on H.M.S. *Dolphin*.

Banks had lobbied the Royal Society and Lords of the Admiralty to include him on the astronomical expedition together with five other men including Solander and Parkinson – all engaged at his own expense. The Astronomer Royal, Charles Green, was also on board with his Transit Instrument. The expedition brought back nearly 1000 drawings of plants painted by Parkinson and these are now in the Natural History Museum, London, and at Kew Gardens. Endeavour was away for almost three years during which time 38 died, including artists Parkinson and Alexander Buchan. (*Oil painting by Sidney Fever, 1974.*)

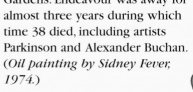

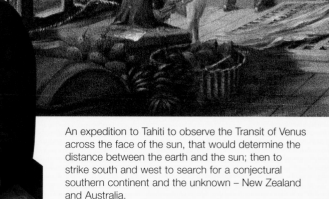

An expedition to Tahiti to observe the Transit of Venus across the face of the sun, that would determine the distance between the earth and the sun; then to strike south and west to search for a conjectural southern continent and the unknown – New Zealand and Australia.

Captain James Cook, 1728-79 by Nathaniel Dance (*Courtesy National Maritime Museum, London.*)

Matavai Bay, Tahiti, proved a safe anchorage on the other side of the world for ships of the Royal Navy:
Wallis, 1767
Cook, 1769, 1773, 1777
Bligh, 1788, 1791

Lieutenant James Cook precedes Captain William Bligh to Tahiti. 'Breadfruit Bligh' anchored *Bounty* in Matavai Bay close to where Cook anchored *Endeavour*.

The eminent botanist Sir Joseph Banks (1743–1820) from a painting by Sir Joshua Reynolds.
(*Courtesy of the National Portrait Gallery, London.*)

The Botanical Expedition

The Quest for Plants and Seed of Commercial Importance
1791	Breadfruit plant, from	Tahiti to West Indies
1826	Tea plants	Japan to Java
1835	Tea plant (seeds)	China to India
1861	Cinchona plants	S. America – Kew – to Asia
1876	Rubber plants	S. America – Kew – to Asia

H.M.S. *Bounty*, under the command of Lieutenant William Bligh, left Spithead, England, in 1787 and finally, like Cook, anchored in Matavai Bay, Tahiti, in 1788. Having taken on board 1000 breadfruit plants and numerous other seedlings for Kew, *Bounty* left the island in April 1789. Then came the infamous mutiny.

The drawing depicts Bligh and his loyal officers and men being cast adrift by the mutineers. Fletcher Christian and his fellow mutineers returned to Tahiti, thence to Pitcairn Island where they settled.

Bligh and his men were to survive 46 days in the open boat, covering a distance of 3694 nautical miles (4254 statute miles) across the Pacific to safety in Timor. Finally they approached the Kupang roadstead and with colours flying and under sail they rowed in – many near to death. Bligh's second mission, in 1791, to transport the breadfruit to the West Indies was successful.

When cast adrift Bligh's Provisions (for 18 men) were:
    150 pounds of Ships biscuits
    32 pounds of salt pork
    1½ gallons of rum
    6 bottles of wine
    28 gallons of water

For navigation Bligh had only a sextant and no charts.

Bounty was a small ship, carried a crew of 45 and included a gardener from Kew, David Nelson, who, like Bligh, had also been on Cook's last voyage when the great explorer was killed on Hawaii. Nelson was one of those cast adrift with Bligh and he died shortly after reaching Timor.

Bounty's sails filled and she stood away with shouts from those on board of 'Hurrah for Tahiti', colour print by Robert Dodd c1791. (*Courtesy National Maritime Museum, London.*)

Captain Bligh by John Russell, engraved by John Conde, 1792.
(*Courtesy National Maritime Museum, London.*)

A branch of the breadfruit tree with the fruit.

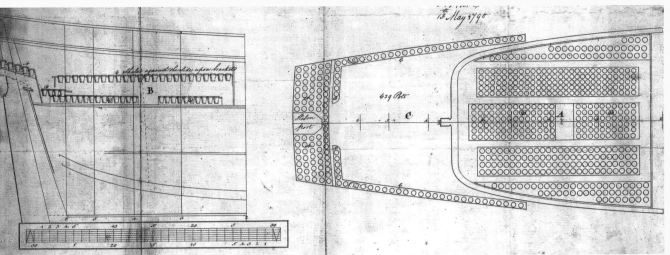

Plan for the stowage of pots on H.M.S. *Bounty*. (*Drawing by A. Ware, 1790, courtesy National Maritime Museum, London.*)

The East India Company's stud at Chatterpore. (*Watercolour by S. Howlett, published London, 1813, by permission of tne British Library.*)

They are a wild race who eat dogs and anything else that breathes however long it may have been dead, which first of all kept me in constant terror of a raid.

To maintain law and order British troops were stationed at several garrisons in Assam, including Gauhati, the provincial capital, and at Sadiya from where two Royal Naval gunboats operated. Later, during the 1840s, upper Assam had three stockaded military camps from which troops of the Assam Sebundy Regiment marched out to counter the turbulent Arbors; these camps were at Dibrugarh, Runagora, on the Dibooroo river, and Jaipur, adjacent to the Dehing river.

There were important aims behind Lord William Bentinck's initiative, both political and commercial, for the peaceful settlement of Assam through trade and commerce, namely tea. This led to Government offering generous terms to private enterprise to take up land and cultivate this hitherto wild region.

▶ this particular part of the country that the Government's first experiments in the cultivation of tea were to be conducted with both the China tea plant and, owing to its recent discovery, the Assam indigenous tea plant.

After the Burmese Wars, the province of Assam was ceded to Britain. The whole region was still in a very turbulent state some ten years later, for although the Burmese had been driven out of the province, there were still numerous incursions by fierce head-hunting tribesmen from the surrounding hills that border the plains of Assam. Oscar Lindgren, a planter in upper Assam from the late 1870s, said of the Naga hill tribesmen:

Transport, or the lack of it, was to play a significant part in the opening of Assam to tea. The *Lord William Bentinck* was the first steamer in service on the Ganges, in 1834. By the late 1830s there were still no regular sailings up the Brahmaputra by any of the four Government steamers in service; only the occasional one went up as far as Gauhati.

The tea operation in Assam was being conducted in an area almost a thousand miles by river from Calcutta, always bearing in mind the many circuitous deep water channels along the entire length of the main river course that the boats would have to negotiate during the dry weather season. Twenty thousand tea plants had to be transported – somehow.

One can form a better idea of the difficulties involved in getting a convoy of country boats up river to an area near Sadiya by looking at the map inside the back cover.

The native country boat could proceed at all times of the year from Calcutta, northwards, by way of the Hooghly and Bhagarthi rivers into the Ganges, after which the route lay south-eastwards to what is today known as Goalundo, thence into the Brahmaputra and on to Assam. Transport by steamer during the dry weather season would, necessarily, have been by the longer all-weather

Garden Reach, from *Views of Calcutta*, by Charles D'Oyly (*Aquatint 1848, by permission of the British Library.*)

route through the Sunderbans.

The Tea Committee were of the opinion that transport of the young tea seedlings should be by steamer, of which there were then only two, and there followed an exchange of letters:

Copy of a Letter from Dr. N. Wallich to Captain Johnston dated 9th July 1835, Calcutta Botanical Gardens.

Town and Port of Calcutta, from *Views of Calcutta* by Charles D'Oyly (*Aquatint 1848, by permission of the British Library.*)

> We have a large number of tea plants here, raised from genuine Chinese seeds which it is very desirable to send to Suddya in upper Assam so as to arrive there before the rains. The Tea Committee are aware of the great difficulty of sending growing plants up the Brahmaputra, as it is a matter of much importance that the seedlings should safely arrive it is intended to make an application to the Government for the use of one of the Iron steamers.

There was a small window of opportunity open for the transport of the seedlings which *had* to be effected during the dry season, as it would have been quite impossible to have attempted the journey at any other time of the year. As time grew near there followed this letter:

Copy of a letter from J. W. Grant, member of the Tea Committee, to N. H. Macnaughton, Secretary to the Government of India, Calcutta, 28th September 1835;

> No steamer being available for the conveyance of the twenty thousand Tea seedlings now ready for dispatch to the Nurseries in Upper Assam, I am directed by the Tea Committee to request that you will procure an order from the Honourable the Governor of Bengal for their being forwarded under the care of a sergeant.

> (Signed) J. W. Grant

A River Journey of 1000 Miles

The sergeant was Sergeant Moore and the form of transport was to be by country boats.

What excuse does one need to tell the story about this truly remarkable river journey? It is all too easy for us today to pass lightly over the problems encountered in those far off days. Here is an incredible tale of adventure, courage and physical hardship undreamed of in our modern world. Things could have been easier had the journey been not 1000 miles but 50, or perhaps even 500, and had the tea operation not been in fever-infested jungle teeming with wild animals and hostile hill tribesmen.

It appeared to many of those involved in the planning of the voyage that thoughts of such insurmountable obstacles as mere distance could be cast aside; the breadfruit plant had, after all, been transported a prodigious distance across the Pacific Ocean to the West Indies, so what more natural than to carry – in a roundabout way – China tea seedlings up a great river to the North-East Frontier region of Assam?

The East India Company was the ideal merchant venturer to set up an operation on the waters of a great river. Yet, no mighty, heavily armed ships would make this journey, just eight small native country craft, each hardly greater in length than, say, two cars put nose to tail. These craft would be sailed, poled and tracked from the river bank when there was insufficient wind for the sails. This then, is the background to an amazing voyage.

Our illustration of the Botanical Garden House depicts the surroundings from which the epic voyage began. Built in the year 1795 its lofty rooms are the happy hunting grounds of botanists who sit perched on their high chairs studying and classifying all manner of plants – including, less than a year earlier, the seeds and leaves of camellia sent down by Lieutenant Andrew Charlton. It is not hard to imagine the eight frail country boats lying along the river bank in readiness

Early one morning in November 1835, not far distant from the elegant buildings of Calcutta, there was great activity at the Botanical Gardens. The gardens, sloping down to the Hooghly river, were extensive, being laid out in broad grass walks. On that day the 20,000 young tea seedlings – the tallest scarcely six inches high – that have been assigned to the Government's trial nurseries in upper Assam are well watered and are then with great care carried down to the waiting boats. Some are packed in teak wood boxes others in earthenware pots.

As the men carefully stow away the plants, others place bamboo matting over the precious cargo to protect it from the hot sun. Then, when all is ready, the ▶

The First Historical Consignment of China Tea Seeds reach India in 1835

A consignment of 80,000 seeds arrive at Calcutta. These seeds are germinated in the Botanical Gardens under the direction of the notable botanist, Dr. N. Wallich.

A River Journey of 1000 miles up the Brahmaputra

Upon germination the 20,000 young tea seedlings that have been allocated to the trial region in northeast Assam leave the Botanical Gardens in November 1835 on board eight country boats on a journey that would take almost four months.

The Botanical Garden House, Calcutta, showing Indian country craft in the foreground. (*Aquatint by J. B. Fraser c1825, by permission of the British Library.*)

Dr. Nathaniel Wallich, botanist and member of the 'Tea Committee', was Superintendent of the Botanical Gardens, Calcutta. (*Drawing reproduced with kind permission of the Director and the Board of Trustees of the Royal Botanic Gardens, Kew.*)

A view of Calcutta, from a point opposite Kidderpore. (*Aquatint by J. B. Fraser c1825, by permission of the British Library.*)

A typical Indian river scene before the steamers came. The Ganges busy with country boats near Sakrigali, Bihar, with the Rajmahal hills in the distance. This lovely scene shows well the laborious method of tracking the boats against the current. The artist, William Prinsep, (1794–1874) was a director of the Premier Tea Company, the Assam Company, and later chairman of the Calcutta Board. (*Watercolour by William Prinsep c1830s, by permission of the British Library.*)

▶ convoy of motley looking craft move slowly out into the main channel on a voyage that will end in the shadows of the Himalayan foothills. For this small band of men it is to be a journey into the unknown.

Besides the boatmen, the trackers and two Malis from the Botanical Gardens, who are to tend and water the plants, there is, of course, Sergeant Moore, who will be accompanying the convoy in a fast paddle canoe.

The journey is being made during the cold weather season which lasts from 1st November until the middle of March when rain is minimal, the river is at its lowest and the current at its most sluggish. It is therefore of the utmost importance that the convoy reaches Sadiya by April, for by then the river will have become swollen, to some extent, by the Chota Barsat, or Small Rains - which come before the full monsoon - making it more difficult to drag the boats against the current.

Averaging between seven and nine miles a day, the convoy makes its way slowly up the 'great river', as the Brahmaputra is known to all who live along its banks. Apart from a few sacks of rice that are carried, fish will augment the meagre rations.

Anchoring each nightfall on the numerous sand-bars in the vast river bed, upwards of eighty men light fires, eat and sleep. The young tea plants, though protected from the fierce rays of the sun, are watered at dusk each evening and this routine is supervised by the two Malis from the Botanical Gardens - a task made no easier by the fleet being often strung out for a good half mile or so of river.

The many fires that have been lit by the trackers and boats' crew make a peaceful and pretty sight as dark descends upon the wide river bed. Before turning in for the night many of the small 'cooking fires' are built up with logs and kept burning fiercely against the wild animals, including tiger and elephant; for the slumbering men the spit and crackle coming from the burning timber is comforting.

During the cold weather season in Assam there rises at night a thick ground mist that clothes the huge river bed, often until mid-morning. At daylight - the coolest part of the day - the trackers, ten or twelve to each boat, commence their arduous task. For each boat and its tracking gang there is a *serang*, or foreman in charge. As the men pull and heave on their stout hemp ropes the sound of their measured chant is at first muffled, but as the sun gets up and the mist clears it carries a quite considerable distance over the still water and sand-bars.

To assist the trackers, the boatmen, each with a pole, endeavour to fend the boats away from continually running aground on sand and shore line. Later, perhaps, in a broad expanse of river and with a favourable breeze, the sails will be run up, but progress is tediously slow whether by sail or rope.

Small groups of huts, squatting like beetles along the jungle-fringed river bank, are the only sign of human habitation. These, infrequent though they are, consist of no more than four or five dwellings all of which have dug-outs lined up on the banks below. Each family cultivates a small slash-and-burn clearing, some of which can be seen from the boats.

After a long two months passage the convoy has reached the important river station and trading town of Gauhati, a small oasis in the middle of nowhere. In the bazaar anything can be bought from snakes to chickens and goats. However, there is little enough time to be spent in the metropolis, for with a further 300 miles still to go, including the rapids at Saikowa, and the time of the Rains approaching, there is no time to be lost.

On leaving Singri it is noticed that many young plants have lost their leaves and are looking sickly, and in spite of the of the efforts of the two Malis in replacing some of the bamboo matting that is cracking and breaking up under the heat, the sergeant is concerned that a greater number may yet perish.

At Bisnath one of the boats has been discharged owing to the fact that thirty-four small boxes, two large ones and thirty-one pots of plants have perished, so that now only seven boats remain in the convoy.

In the dry season the upper reaches of the river are a maze of sandbanks – which vary in colour from light green, where grass has sprouted, to blinding white – mile after dreary mile of them, and it is always difficult for the leading boatman to know which of the deep water channels to take. It is in such places that tigers swim across the channels between islands and sandbanks in pursuit of wild buffalo that frequent the river's huge flood-bed during the dry season.

From our low perspective, standing on the south bank looking across the entire width of the river bed, the unending sandbanks appear not unlike a vast desert, and yet, when the Rains come all will be submerged under a solid mass of turbulent brown water on which huge islands of vegetation sit precariously and hundred-foot trees are swept along like so many matchsticks.

Day after day there is the teeming wildlife on the river: giant fish-eating gharial alligators, the largest a full twenty feet long, laze on the mud banks in the blistering sun, while in the maze of channels Brahminy ducks, ever alert, get up ahead of the leading boat and circle overhead honking loudly, like geese. Families of small turtles, sunning themselves on the trunks of driftwood, drop with a noisy 'plop' into the water, their siesta disturbed by man. Dolphins rise with a swirl close to the boats, showing their long snouts and grey-green bodies before plunging below the surface. The giant hornbill, with its huge wings, swishes through the air to alight on some branch with a raucous kok-kok-kok.

Here also the osprey plies its trade, while numerous flights of duck, wild geese, teal, pochard and the fast flying pintails are always present along the river and in the sky above. So too is the heron and fish eagle, with its long piercing scream. Most spectacular are the great comical looking pelicans, their heavy flapping wings ungainly in flight but always keeping faultless station across the sky.

Picture the scene at the end of the day. The boats are drawn up for the night along shelves of gravelly sand that in places slope down from the tree-fringed bank to the water's edge. Some of the boats lie on sand-bars further out, for it is prudent to keep one's distance from the dark and forbidding jungle whenever possible. There are the now accustomed noises of the night: the gentle murmur of the river, the hoot of an owl and the

Sunset over the Brahmaputra from Bisnath Ghat. "At Bisnath one of the boats has been discharged owing to the fact that thirty-four small boxes, two large ones and thirty-one pots of tea seedlings have perished, so that now only seven boats remain in the convoy".
(*Photo 2000, courtesy Williamson Magor.*)

squeak of an otter.

Not far from the river bank the land holds wild buffalo, tiger, elephant, leopard, black bear, langurs, pig and the occasional rhino which provide a rich if dangerous hunting ground. Such is the country the convoy passes through; a never ending jungle-clad shoreline, hot simmering sandbanks and a vast wilderness, with foothills becoming ever less distant.

At first light there is a deafening silence along the river. As the convoy moves slowly off on yet another long, hard haul, the heavy dew on the pale-green grasses on many of the sand-bars is most evident. Upon each blade of grass dew drops are shaking and as the mist slowly clears and the sun penetrates the slumbering river bed, the grasses shed their nightly load and, no longer weighted, spring back in their thousands until the very ground seems to be alive with their upward movement.

Leaving Dibooroo Mukh the going has become harder, necessitating the continual and laborious tracking of the boats against a quickening current, with the first rapids only a few miles ahead.

It is known that Dr. Wallich, together with other members of the Scientific Deputation, are somewhere in the vicinity and that he has reported in a letter dated 12th February (1836), written on the Brahmaputra above the Dibooroo river, that he had on that day met the convoy:

> I regret to say that a great number of seedlings have died on the way thus far owing partly to the protracted duration and difficulties of the journey, the long confinement under bamboo matting and the numerous rats which infest the boats.
>
> The sergeant has had the whole collection counted over since leaving Bisnath, and it appears that out of 20,000 plants which left Calcutta only 8000 are surviving; considering all the circumstances connected with so large a consignment of young and tender seedlings, the tallest of them scarcely 6″ in height and supported by the experience of many years, I am of the opinion that the loss of three-fifths is not greater than might have reasonably been expected. The remainder still offering an ample and valuable stock for the formation of a future tea plantation.
>
> It is proper to remark that I have every reason to be satisfied with the Sergeant in charge and the two Maullees who are with him have performed their duties with great diligence and attention.

By this time progress in getting the remaining heavy country boats further up the Brahmaputra has become almost impossible. To complicate matters we understand Sergeant Moore's canoe has taken a different channel in the river to that taken by the fleet – at this time of year the deeper navigable channels are maze-like in their wanderings.

To the north, east and west of the convoy, barely ten miles distant in places, are the surrounding foothills. Seen through the heat haze of the plains the nearer jungle-clad foothills rise in a deep blue-green; beyond, the outline of each range of hills becomes progressively lighter in colour, through soft blue-grey to the palest lavender that eventually merges with the silvery white of the snow-capped mountains of the Great Himalaya. Unbelievably high, they look not unlike a giant cloud formation hanging in the sky. It is to the north of these mountains that the Brahmaputra, or Tsangpo, flows from its source for almost a thousand miles of its Tibetan course at over two miles high, before its waters enter tremendous gorges and drop down to the plains – only to continue for a further thousand miles down to the sea.

Unknown to any in the convoy, nor to those of us who are following their progress, it is in these dense jungle foothills that many of the different hill tribes live; Miris, Dafflas, Arbors and Nagas; they cannot be seen but they are assuredly there. It has long been the custom of these fierce and fearless tribesmen, particularly the Arbors, to make periodic incursions into the country along the Brahmaputra.

Lost in the vast and empty landscape, the small convoy of boats have finally reached Kundil Mukh, the vicinity of Sadiya. A handful of locals are watching as the surviving

Naga Hill tribesmen from the Naga Hills. (*Watercolour drawing c1880 by an anonymous artist, by permission of the British Library, O.I.O.C.*)

Journey's end – March 1836, Kundal Mukh, in the vicinity of Sadiya. Undoubtedly a scene similar to this took place almost 170 years ago in a far-flung part of Empire. This depiction shows the type of nursery that Charles Alexander Bruce would have prepared for the reception of the 20,000 young China tea plants. He and Sergeant Moore, I.C. boats, stand by as the young seedlings are transported between the fleet and the nursery, where Malis from the Calcutta Botanical Gardens superintend their planting out on specially prepared beds which would, in fact, have extended over a much wider area of generally sandy land. The low angle perspective of the river cannot fully show the mass of sandbanks and water channels that are typical of the upper reaches of the Brahmaputra in the dry weather period in Assam.
(Pen and ink and watercolour, 1999, by John Weatherstone.)

plants of this strange cargo are brought ashore. After examination by the two Malis, the healthy tea seedlings are carried inland to a small nursery that Mr. Bruce has prepared.

At the very moment the China tea seedlings are being carried ashore and planted out in the nursery, attention back in Calcutta is being switched to the newly found indigenous tea plants that are growing wild in the jungles of Muttack country. We understand that Mr. Bruce, with his knowledge of the surrounding country and the tea tracts that he has found, is to act as guide to members of the Scientific Deputation.

What were the rewards of that epic journey? As things were to turn out the case for the China-type tea plant was not a strong one, for when compared to the lately discovered Assam indigenous tea plant it was not so well suited to the heat of the plains. However, and most importantly, the China plant was later to prove a great success when grown at higher cooler elevations in the hill districts of Darjeeling, North and South India – for which large amounts of China seed was later made available from Assam.

From the surviving China plants the stock of seed became abundant, enabling Bruce and his European Assistant and native helpers to plant up many widely separated nurseries and trial blocks of cleared jungle –

as at Chubwa and Jaipur, where his original plantings can still be seen today.

*   *   *

Chinese artisans, skilled in the cultivation of tea and its manufacture, were brought in as indented labour and sent up river to the jungles of Assam, and it was Bruce who, as Superintendent of Tea Culture, gleaned vital knowledge from them. One can imagine the difficulties involved in both communicating with the Chinese, even with the help of an interpreter, and surviving under almost impossible conditions. BUT, a dangerous competitor to China's world monopoly of the tea trade was about to take the field.

Once established, the China tea plant was a prolific seed bearer throughout Assam during the early years, and among those in the industry it was soon to be labelled 'the curse of Assam'. However, Gordon's visit to China had not been without reward, for no-one in British India had the slightest knowledge of how tea was grown and manufactured until explained by the Chinamen he returned with.

Skilled Chinese tea artisans continued to arrive in the province bringing seeds for some years after Government sanctioned Gordon's second visit to China in 1836. Later, Robert Fortune went on a mission ▶

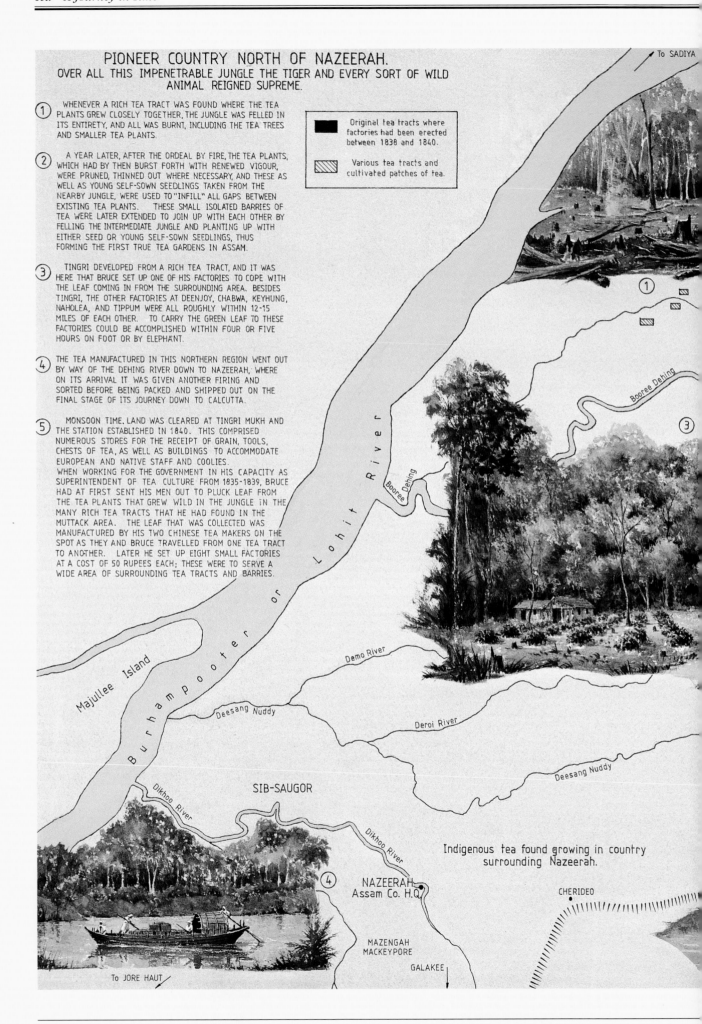

PIONEER COUNTRY NORTH OF NAZEERAH.
OVER ALL THIS IMPENETRABLE JUNGLE THE TIGER AND EVERY SORT OF WILD ANIMAL REIGNED SUPREME.

(1) WHENEVER A RICH TEA TRACT WAS FOUND WHERE THE TEA PLANTS GREW CLOSELY TOGETHER, THE JUNGLE WAS FELLED IN ITS ENTIRETY, AND ALL WAS BURNT, INCLUDING THE TEA TREES AND SMALLER TEA PLANTS.

(2) A YEAR LATER, AFTER THE ORDEAL BY FIRE, THE TEA PLANTS, WHICH HAD BY THEN BURST FORTH WITH RENEWED VIGOUR, WERE PRUNED, THINNED OUT WHERE NECESSARY, AND THESE AS WELL AS YOUNG SELF-SOWN SEEDLINGS TAKEN FROM THE NEARBY JUNGLE, WERE USED TO "INFILL" ALL GAPS BETWEEN EXISTING TEA PLANTS. THESE SMALL ISOLATED BARRIES OF TEA WERE LATER EXTENDED TO JOIN UP WITH EACH OTHER BY FELLING THE INTERMEDIATE JUNGLE AND PLANTING UP WITH EITHER SEED OR YOUNG SELF-SOWN SEEDLINGS, THUS FORMING THE FIRST TRUE TEA GARDENS IN ASSAM.

(3) TINGRI DEVELOPED FROM A RICH TEA TRACT, AND IT WAS HERE THAT BRUCE SET UP ONE OF HIS FACTORIES TO COPE WITH THE LEAF COMING IN FROM THE SURROUNDING AREA. BESIDES TINGRI, THE OTHER FACTORIES AT DEENJOY, CHABWA, KEYHUNG, NAHOLEA, AND TIPPUM WERE ALL ROUGHLY WITHIN 12-15 MILES OF EACH OTHER. TO CARRY THE GREEN LEAF TO THESE FACTORIES COULD BE ACCOMPLISHED WITHIN FOUR OR FIVE HOURS ON FOOT OR BY ELEPHANT.

(4) THE TEA MANUFACTURED IN THIS NORTHERN REGION WENT OUT BY WAY OF THE DEHING RIVER DOWN TO NAZEERAH, WHERE ON ITS ARRIVAL IT WAS GIVEN ANOTHER FIRING AND SORTED BEFORE BEING PACKED AND SHIPPED OUT ON THE FINAL STAGE OF ITS JOURNEY DOWN TO CALCUTTA.

(5) MONSOON TIME. LAND WAS CLEARED AT TINGRI MUKH AND THE STATION ESTABLISHED IN 1840. THIS COMPRISED NUMEROUS STORES FOR THE RECEIPT OF GRAIN, TOOLS, CHESTS OF TEA, AS WELL AS BUILDINGS TO ACCOMMODATE EUROPEAN AND NATIVE STAFF AND COOLIES.
WHEN WORKING FOR THE GOVERNMENT IN HIS CAPACITY AS SUPERINTENDENT OF TEA CULTURE FROM 1835-1839, BRUCE HAD AT FIRST SENT HIS MEN OUT TO PLUCK LEAF FROM THE TEA PLANTS THAT GREW WILD IN THE JUNGLE IN THE MANY RICH TEA TRACTS THAT HE HAD FOUND IN THE MUTTACK AREA. THE LEAF THAT WAS COLLECTED WAS MANUFACTURED BY HIS TWO CHINESE TEA MAKERS ON THE SPOT AS THEY AND BRUCE TRAVELLED FROM ONE TEA TRACT TO ANOTHER. LATER HE SET UP EIGHT SMALL FACTORIES AT A COST OF 50 RUPEES EACH; THESE WERE TO SERVE A WIDE AREA OF SURROUNDING TEA TRACTS AND BARRIES.

■	Original tea tracts where factories had been erected between 1838 and 1840.
▨	Various tea tracts and cultivated patches of tea.

To SADIYA

Booree Dehing

Lohit River

Booree Dehing

Demo River

Deroi River

Deesang Nuddy

Majullee Island

Burhampooter or Lohit River

Deesang Nuddy

Dikhoo River

SIB-SAUGOR

Dikhoo River

Indigenous tea found growing in country surrounding Nazeerah.

(4)

NAZEERAH
Assam Co. H.Q.

CHERIDEO

MAZENGAH
MACKEYPORE

GALAKEE

To JORE HAUT

This map relates to the pioneering area between
the Dikhoo and Dibooroo rivers.
The watercolour vignettes are not placed in any
relation to the map.
(*Watercolour by S.R. Fever, 1984.*)

The Early Stages of the Assam Company's Headquarters at Nazira

THE PLAN

'Inset' relates to the painting, and shows a part of the Nazira station buildings. From the small part shown here of the land and station buildings of the Assam Company's headquarters at Nazira, one can gain an impression of the early working and living conditions of the small community made up of different races whose place of work was the fever infested jungle almost 1000 miles from Calcutta. The making of tea boxes at Nazira was not actually started until 1852*, when a large saw mill (a saw bench with steam engine and boiler as driving power) was brought up from Calcutta. This merely made the job of sawing planks easier and

quicker, with the rest of the operation remaining the same. The tea box factory is, however, included in the picture because it gives an indication of the work that was involved when, some three years earlier, C.A. Bruce set up his first tea making houses and supporting tea box making huts in and around the tea tracts at Tingri, Chabwa, Keyhung, and Deenjoy. The area that was given over to crops and to the nursery would, in fact, have occupied far more ground than is shown in this illustration. The scene depicted is of the 1841 period.
*Prior to this date tea box shooks were brought up from Calcutta.

Pioneering and Trials in the Jungle

DIKHOO RIVER.

1. *Elephants with howdahs strapped to their backs brought in green leaf in sacks, or partially manufactured tea in chests, from the Assam Company's scattered tea barries and tea clearings.*

2. *In addition to the two factory buildings shown (the main tea making house, as it was called, and the smaller withering shed), the verandah or even the interior rooms of the adjacent planter's bungalow might also have been utilised to wither the green leaf that had been brought in from those tea clearings that were reasonably close to Nazira. In good weather, the leaf might also have been placed in shallow wicker baskets and withered outside in the sun. From the more distant tea barries in the northern division where crude tea making houses had been con-*

structed, partially manufactured tea was brought into the station in tea chests, and given another firing or two before it was sorted and packed for shipment. The main factory would contain a line of charcoal-burning ovens, over which the tea was dried or fired, and the intense heat from these would find its way out through the thatched roof – there being no chimneys – with the frequent result that the factory was burned to the ground. During the early years, Nazira was the centre of tea manufacture for the company's holdings, which stretched over a wide area of dense jungle for a hundred miles from its most northerly division to the southernmost. In later years, these scattered tea tracts and barries were developed into tea gardens, with each garden or group

of gardens having its own tea manufacturing factory. During the early years of the industry, the elephant, the dug-out canoe and the country boat were the only means of travel over this considerable area.

3. *Suitable timber for making tea boxes, which had been cut from the surrounding jungle, is seen stacked for seasoning.*

4. *A sawyer's pit is shown to illustrate one of the methods by which timber was sawn into planks for tea boxes, as well as for building purposes. The thickness of the planking made for rough uneven boxes and was also responsible for the great weight of the early tea boxes.*

5. *Tea box making factory. Chinese coolies, jhons, were at first recruited direct from China and Malaya, and from those resident in Calcutta.*

These men were skilled in making the tea boxes, and their lead canister linings; both were very specialised trades unknown outside China. By 1843, after their secrets had been learned, the Chinese were dispensed with and local labour carried on this work. Maintaining a good supply of sheet lead on site was a crucial factor in the early tea box making days.

6. Timber cutting coolies were employed to cut certain trees from the jungle for tea box making; these were then dragged by elephants to the settlement.

7. Country boats carrying chests of tea were poled down the Dikhoo River to the Brahmaputra, and then down to Gauhati, where they were either off-loaded and stored in the company's godowns until the arrival of a government steamer or, failing that,

the country boats would proceed the whole way down to Calcutta. The return voyage would bring staff, coolies, stores, and would take two-and-a-half to three-and-a-half months, with the craft being sailed, poled and tracked up river against the current, and those travelling on board living off the land as they proceeded each day.

8. European staff bungalows of the superintendent and his assistants differed little in construction from those of the surrounding station buildings, which were all made from local materials. The floors were of hard packed earth, and the thatched roof of 'sun grass' was supported by wood or bamboo uprights and rafters, with mud and ekra walls.

9. Crops such as wheat, barley, flax and, of course, rice occupied a good

The early stages of development of the Assam Company's headquarters at Nazira. (Watercolour by S.R. Fever, 1983.)

proportion of land. Nevertheless, great quantities of rice had to be brought up river by country boat for the support of those working not only at Nazira, but also for those working in the more isolated northern and eastern divisions of the company's holdings.

10. Nursery: an experimental area, and a small nursery containing some 5000 young tea seedlings.

11. The labour force was housed in huts made of split bamboo, with thatched roofs. Similar structures were used to store grain and other necessary commodities.

Holborn Tea Establishment (*Drawing 1849, courtesy Guildhall Library, Corporation of London.*)

to China to procure more of the best tea seed and young plants; these were destined for the foothills of the Himalaya in North India, the small-leafed China variety being well suited to higher, colder regions.

Fortune not only learned to speak some Chinese but also shaved his head and dressed as a Chinaman to gain their confidence. He thus managed to travel extensively throughout the tea growing districts of China while at the same time obtaining approximately 13,000 tea seeds. He also recruited a number of Chinese explaining that he wished them to accompany him to India where they were to 'teach the poor Hindoos how to cultivate the tea plant'. Although starting the industry in Assam a decade earlier was of crucial importance, the Chinese had been found to be intractable and more than a nuisance in one way and another. Those that Fortune returned with were no doubt sent packing just as their countrymen had been in Assam – but only after their secrets had been learned!

As already mentioned, in later years and with the expansion of the tea industry in Assam, the small-leafed China variety proved ideal for growing at higher, cooler elevations in other parts of India, around Darjeeling and in the Nilgiri Hills in the South. By then the amount of China seed in Assam was plentiful and this was to prove a most valuable asset for these hill regions, supplying other countries who were later to start their own tea industries such as Ceylon, Russia and Malaya.

Pioneering

A Forward Movement upon the Jungle
The Introduction of the Plantation System

Although he was not an agriculturist, Bruce was a practical man and could see only too plainly the merits of the indigenous tea plant. He had, during the four years that he was in charge of the Government's tea experiments, made many trial plantings with both the China and indigenous plants, Bruce states in his 1839 Report to Government that:

Last year in going over one of the hills behind Jaipore, about 300 feet high, I came upon a Tea tract, which must have been two or three miles in length, in fact I did not see the end of it; the trees were in most parts as thick as they could grow, and the Tea seeds (smaller than what I had seen before) fine and fresh, literally covered the ground; this was in the middle of November, and the trees had abundance of fruit and flower on them. One of the largest trees I found to be two cubits in circumference, and fully forty cubits in height (60 feet or so). At the foot of the hill I found another tract, and had time permitted me to explore those parts, there is no doubt but I should have found many of the Naga Hills covered with Tea.

The Chinese had been endowed with the tea plant (*Camellia sinensis*); so too had the British in India with *its* tea plant (*Camellia assamica*).

As Superintendent of Tea Culture he had charge over a vast region that stretched from the Dibru river, in the north, to the country around Nazira, which was destined to become the Assam Company's HQ, in the south.

Bruce had observed how the local natives cut down to about three feet the tall tea trees that were found growing in the jungle and how, later, they gathered the tender young leaf shoots from which they produced tea. At first his two tea-makers – each with six local native assistants – travelled from one rich tea tract to another collecting the leaf which was then often carried great distances before being manufactured under the supervision of Bruce and his Chinese tea-makers. At the outset of operations and while carrying on this most natural way of collecting the leaf – free, gratis and for nothing – Bruce went further. Fell and burn was the answer.

Whenever a rich tea tract was found the jungle was felled in its entirety, including the larger tea trees and young tea seedlings, and after drying out the felled forest was 'fired'. Drastic treatment for the tea one would think but in Bruce's own words:

It is astonishing with what vigour the tea plants grow up after the fire has been applied, and we

gain from the process; for, from every old stock or stump cut down, ten to twelve more vigorous shoots spring up, so that in place of a single plant you now have a fine bush.

A year later, after the ordeal by fire, the tea plants which had by then burst forth with renewed vigour, could be thinned out where necessary and some of these – as well as seeds and young self-sown seedlings taken from the surrounding jungle – were used to *infill* all gaps between existing tea plants, thus building up small clearings of tea, with bushes spaced roughly 6 feet apart in rows.

The lush new shoots could be harvested after about a year, by which time the whole tea clearing would be 'worked up' as already described. Wild animals ate the fresh succulent tea shoots everywhere at ground level: elephants and buffalo trampled them and the seed was quickly scattered. Yet progress was made.

Whether the tea clearing was formed by the gradual opening out of the jungle, while gathering the tea leaf, or by the easier slash-and-burn method – felling the entire jungle and then setting fire to it all, including the tea – it was nevertheless a formidable undertaking to establish a block of 'cultivated tea'. With the sunlight let in, the tea plants were not the only vegetation to burst forth into growth – the shoots from the jungle tree-stumps required continual cutting back until they eventually died and were overgrown by the tea itself. Furthermore, owing to the difficulties in procuring

The Looshai Expedition: Fort and Tea Gardens, near Cachar. (*Drawing 1872 Illustrated London News, by permission of The British Library*).

suitable labour, many cultivated patches of tea reverted back to jungle. It was a continuing battle.

A good example was Tingri where, in 1837, a tea factory and tea-box-making sheds were erected by Bruce. At first these small isolated tea clearings were no more than a patch of cleared jungle 100 yards square, in which grew irregular lines of a few thousand tea bushes. Over a period of many years these patches of cultivated tea were joined up with each other to form the first true tea gardens in Assam.

During those first tentative years the exploitation of numerous tracts of indigenous tea continued apace, often at great cost. Writing from the jungles of Jaipur in 1839 Bruce was very prophetic:

> In drawing out this report, it gives me much pleasure to say that our information and knowledge respecting Tea and Tea Tracts are far more extensive than when I last wrote on the subject: the number of tracts now known amount to 120, some of them very extensive, both on the hills and in the plains. A sufficiency of seeds and seedlings might be collected from these tracts in the course of a few years to plant off the whole of Assam; and I feel from my different journeys over the country, that but a very small portion of the localities are yet known.

Bruce must have spent all his waking hours travelling over this vast region, through heavy jungle by elephant and by dug-out along the numerous tributary rivers, looking for tea tracts. His beautifully produced maps of the region survive, showing all the tea tracts he discovered, together with copious Reports on the Manufacture of Tea – as practised by his two Chinese tea-makers. He gives no clue as to the exacting conditions under which he must have worked – for instance his only light after dark was a flickering candle stuck in a bottle.

Could Bruce have ever imagined that the tea seeds that he had collected from one of his small experimental nurseries of China tea bushes in the Muttack country, which he had brought and planted at Jaipur, would survive as large healthy bushes almost 150 years later, when photographed by my wife in 1985?

The First Indian Tea

The first samples of tea that were made under Government auspices and came from named tea tracts were dispatched down river and reached Calcutta towards the end of 1837 – and were subsequently received in London the following year. This tea was manufactured by Bruce and his Chinese tea-makers from the leaf of the indigenous plants and was collected from tea tracts at Deenjoy, Chubwa and Tingri. The newly introduced China tea plants, in their trial plots and nurseries, were still too small for plucking.

For the London merchants who had been accus-

A living community in the jungle. Selim Tea Garden, Terai. Planters and Nepalese labour force pose for the photographer.
(*Photo 1868, courtesy Royal Geographical Society.*)

tomed to dealing only with tea that came from the Celestial Empire, the year 1838 dawned on a new era when something other than China tea would cause a buzz of excitement in the trade for, towards the end of May, the sailing ship *Calcutta* left Calcutta carrying to London the first historic consignment of 12 chests of Indian tea. The importance of those twelve rather small and insignificant tea chests, amongst thousands of others from China, could hardly be imagined.

After four of the chests had been presented to East India Company officials, the remaining eight came up for auction at the Commercial Sale Rooms in Mincing Lane, London, in January 1839. The tea was sold for between 16 shillings (80 pence) and 34 shillings (£1.70) a pound which, when compared with an agricultural labourer's yearly wage at the time – about £10 – was phenomenal. The Honourable Company had produced its first tea in British India.

The Formation of the Premier Tea Company

The auction's very high prices attracted the attention of merchants and businessmen, and this resulted in the formation of the first tea company in India, the Assam Company, in 1839. The authorised capital of £500,000 was comprised of 10,000 shares at £50 each.

It had been the avowed intention of the Honourable East India Company to experiment with the cultivation of tea and then to hand over its trial lands to private enterprise for future development. Early in 1840 the Government transferred to the Assam Company two-thirds of its tea lands and forests rent free for a period of ten years. At the same time the Assam Company negotiated with Government for the release of C. A. Bruce, and he joined the company in March 1840.

Charles Bruce was the ideal choice, for having set up the Government's nurseries and opened out numerous rich tracts of tea in the Muttack region, he was the only person with a knowledge of both the cultivation and manufacture of tea. He stood head and shoulders above all others.

Even before the acquisition of these Government lands, the Assam Company had cleared jungle and erected buildings at Nazira, an independent site on the Dikoo river. Following the example of Government, the Assam Company recruited yet more Chinese tea-makers, many from those resident in Calcutta, on the assumption that any Chinaman was a tea expert.

The Assam Company produced its first tea in 1840 – the result of a whole year's production. The 171 chests of tea were put on board the *Helen Mary* in June 1841, arriving at the London docks in mid December.

With the steady conversion that had taken place over the years by 'working up' all the richest tea tracts – by infilling with self-sown tea seedlings and by planting out seed-at-stake – the momentum of felling continued in Assam, but more so, as time went on, in jungle

that contained little or no tea. By then tea seed was plentiful, nurseries were established on all existing gardens, and the resulting plants were used for planting out all future jungle clearances.

In the early 1860s the new industry began to attract men of a different breed: speculators, out for a quick profit on land and shares. Applications for land were enormous and thousands of acres of jungle were felled. This had the effect of producing a 'tea boom' without the tea.

Many of the newcomers, after felling and clearing their patch of jungle, did not bother to work up their properties by planting out seed and seedlings. Few of the new breed even knew what tea plant looked like, nor stayed long enough to find out, but would sell on the land, often containing very small and patchy tracts of tea, as a tea garden.

The ignorance of the speculators was such that, all too soon for many, in the late 1860s the crash came, when the very high prices of the bogus tea gardens plummeted as quickly as they had climbed.

Stability returned in the early 1870s and with it a flourishing industry that would never look back. Indeed the tea industry in India was set to go forward and become the largest in the world. By 1873 approximately 73,000 acres of tea were in cultivation in Assam alone; each and every acre had been carved out of fever-ridden jungle.

The Chinese methods of cultivation on countless small plots of land, where the bushes were numbered in dozens rather than acres, had been replaced by the 'plantation' system. The age old methods of hand manufacture, unchanged for centuries in China, had at first been adopted by the British but then, within a comparatively short span of thirty years, newly invented specialized tea-machinery had been introduced and installed on all but the remotest tea gardens in pukka factories, with brick columns and corrugated iron roofs. The primitive early 'tea making house', with its thatched roof and mud and ekra walls, was relegated to history. This was a giant leap forward in efficiency on an ever growing scale, with which the Chinese could not possibly compete.

The first railway system in Assam was opened in 1884; the 2 ft gauge Jorhat-Provincial and metre gauge Dibru-Sadiya railways were built to connect the tea districts with the Brahmaputra and the paddle steamers, mention of which will be made later.

Thus by the late 1890s the province of Assam, formerly one vast jungle penetrated only by rivers, had been opened up by the steamer, the railway and roads of a kind.

Cachar

Meanwhile, some 200 miles to the south of Assam, further tracts of indigenous tea had been found growing in the state of Manipur, and in particular in the Surma valley in the district of Sylhet and Cachar. Wherever the indigenous tea plant grew, however sparsely, tea could be grown on a commercial scale. Here again the Assam Company was an early participant, the first tea gardens in this region being opened in about 1856. Generally, one referred to 'gardens' in Assam, Darjeeling and North India and 'estates' in South India, Java and Ceylon.

As in Assam, the same method was followed in working up the indigenous tea, in this case the large-leafed Manipuri variety. Assam seed, sent down from Nazira, was also put out extensively and Cachar had the advantage over Assam in that it took only six weeks by paddle steamer to get there from Calcutta and under half that on the return journey sailing down with the current. The first sailings by steamers were made in 1863 and prior to that the journey was made by the slow country boat.

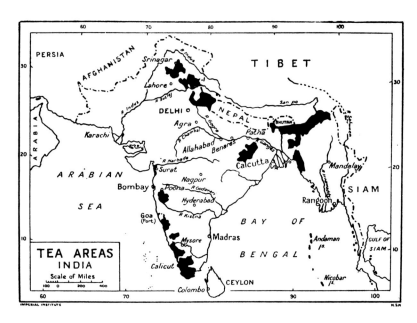

A map showing the tea growing regions in India at the turn of the century.

Unlike the vast province of Assam, comprising the middle and upper valleys of the Brahmaputra, the great tea growing districts along the foothills of the Himalaya were all at elevations of between 1800 (in the valleys) and 6000 feet.

Darjeeling

Land of High Grown Tea

Tea was first planted in this region during the mid 1850s and the labour force which works on the gardens has always been drawn from Nepal. Until the coming of the road and railway, the transport of tea off the gardens was by porters, ponies and bullock carts along rough gravel cart roads down to Silliguri, then on by road and river to the port of Calcutta.

Two marvels of mountain engineering cross each other 132 times on their way up to the town of Darjeeling. The construction of the new hill cart road from Silliguri to Darjeeling was started in 1861 and completed by 1869. The construction of the 2-foot-gauge Darjeeling Himalayan Railway – which is one of the railway wonders of the world and runs for 53 miles – was commenced in 1869, also at Silliguri, and was extended up to the town of Darjeeling by 1881. The railway closely follows the trace of the road.

Consider the difficulties in this hill region 140 years ago. All the tea fields are on impossible slopes and have been carved out of virgin jungle. The pioneers had to fell, burn and clear the land before they could ever think of planting a single tea plant – no mean feat in those far off days when the axe was the only tool available. Nepalese were expert axemen.

The Himalayan bear and the King cobra, both very nasty customers, inhabited the very slopes on which the tea gardens of today stand. There are also many tombstones dotted about the planting districts which tell the sad tale of planters killed by tigers; but what of the legions of garden workers killed by wild animals, taken by fever or bitten by snakes while clearing jungle - *they* had no such monuments! One Darjeeling planter wrote:

> The place was so infested with tigers that their roaring at night often made sleep impossible.

The planters of the day, dressed as they were in boots, gaiters and trousers, stood a much better chance against the bites of poisonous snakes than did their labour force with their bare feet and no such protection.

In spite of the numerous hazards to health and body, there *were* certain things in the jungle that made even the stoutest man's flesh prickle:

> Another sound came borne through the night, a sound that made me catch my breath sharply, a sound that was like a whining groan starting on a low note, rising then falling away in ghastly cadence. Tiger!

The nights were often terrifying for those who sat shivering in a muck sweat inside their frail line rooms, with doors bound shut. They could hear, only too clearly, the low growling of the *shaitan* outside, mere feet away. The attention of the unlucky inmates riveted to a dark and gloomy corner of the hut where, at first, there was no more than a faint rustle, clearly audible above the sound of a thudding heart. Then, a more ominous scratching of powerful paws clawing deep into the flimsy split bamboo walls, and the awful realization that it was after *you*. All that would be heard by the rest of the labour force and planter living close by would be the pitiful screams of the victim as he or she was carried away into the night. Of course humans are not the tiger's natural prey but, a man-eater in the district – that's a different matter, as will be seen in chapter IV.

Words simply cannot describe how grim conditions often were for planters and labour alike during those early pioneering years.

With the establishment of the industry in the Darjeeling region by the early 1860s, tea was next extended down to the Terai, and then eastwards into what is known as the Dooars, where a large and compact area was eventually opened to tea.

Terai

The jungles of the Terai, at an elevation of around 500 feet, were renowned for their steamy heat, malaria and tigers – in that order – and tea pioneers often came and went in quick succession in this dreadful climate. Malaria is always prevalent in hot steamy jungle, although once felled and opened out conditions improve – a little.

In relation to the wildlife encountered when 'opening out' jungle, we have the words of planter Edwin Arnold from the 1870s

Then there was the pantha whose coughing snarl I had sometimes heard close by. One evening a barking-deer shot past my hut. The faintest of movements had come from a patch of long grass out of which the deer had burst. I listened intently; was IT also listening as it crouched there with flattened ears and snarling mouth?

I broke the ensuing silence to summon my coolies, and with drawn knives and yelling voices we all advanced towards the ambush in which the would-be slayer lurked. At the edge of it a strong 'tom-cat' smell assailed our nostrils, a most creepy experience. Then an almost imperceptible wave receded through the grass and we knew the cat was departing.

Makaibari and Selim Tea Gardens were the first to be opened in this region during the early 1860s. Leaping forward in time, it is interesting to know that Makaibari produced some of the world's most expensive tea in 1992 – a particular grade of tea F.T.G.O.P. (Flowery Tippy Golden Orange Pekoe) was sold at £240 a kilo.

North India

By far the most remotely situated tea-growing area in North India was that in the Kangra Valley in the foothills of the Himalaya, some 800 miles west of Darjeeling, in the Kumaon region. Being of high elevation this region was also planted up with the China variety of tea, with the first gardens opened near

North India. *Clockwise from top left:* The bridge over the river Ool, in this remote but beautiful region near Kulu. Early method of hand-rolling the withered leaf. Packing made tea. Transport of tea chests by porters. (*Drawing 1883, The Graphic.*)

In the service of the East India Company

Lord William Cavendish Bentinck, 1774–1839. (*Engraving from the oil painting by Thomas Lawrence R.A., by permission of the British Library.*)

Charles Alexander Bruce 1793–1871. (*Courtesy Jeanette King-Harman.*)

Dr. Nathaniel Wallich, 1787–1854. (*Drawing reproduced with kind permission of the Director and the Board of Trustees of the Royal Botanic Gardens, Kew.*)

Palampur in the late 1850s. It was here that the Government had conducted its early experiments with the China plant in 1835.

Only a comparatively small acreage was opened to tea in the Kangra and Kulu valleys, which were situated some 200 miles to the south-east of Srinagar, as this northernmost region had insufficient rainfall for tea. All this tea, as well as that grown 150 miles to the south-east in Dehra Dun, found its way to the Amritsar market. The region was more suited to growing apples and pears.

South India

Some 1500 miles from the Himalayan foothills is the tea and coffee growing district of South India. Although the first tea estates were opened during the early 1850s, this region had also been the scene of earlier experiments. Two thousand of the China tea seedlings – from Gordon's original importation from China – had been sent to South India for trial planting in 1835.

(In 1985 my wife and I, with the help of a botanist from the United Planters Association, hunted, unsuccessfully, for the original China tea plants that had been put out at the experimental farm at Kaity.)

As in other parts of north and north-east India, small nurseries were set out in the Nilgiri Hills and around Ootacamund, tended by Government officials and others, and the China variety prospered after a discouraging start.

The commercial cultivation of tea in southern India remained in the background until 1853, when the first tea estate was opened. Here, the tea industry grew up alongside that of coffee, which commenced at about the same time. The acreage under tea increased slowly and it was not until the late 1890s that it increased significantly.

And so ended the crucial phase of the tea enterprise in India.

Goodbye Pioneers, we thank you for starting something

It is doubtful whether we who live in the comfort of our homes in the 21st century – with nothing more than a tame cat roaming around the garden, with instant light at the touch of a switch and water at the turn of a tap – can possibly imagine the lonely and often dangerous life of those first planters, whose courage, endurance and fortitude in the face of all adversity made them what they were, the pioneers of the tea industry in India.

Like all pioneers, those who came first suffered most. Primitive shacks were the order of the day while clearing virgin jungle; the whole country was a playground for every kind of wild animal. Many died from malaria, cholera, dysentery and blackwater fever in their lonely neck of the wood – far from home and kith and kin. They came and went as the industry progressed.

Bivouacking out in jungle abounding with wild animals, snakes and leeches, swamped by rain, lying at night on wet ground, shivering with cold and perhaps fever, with only the steady downpour and swirling mists outside for weeks on end – these were conditions of privation that only men of a true pioneering spirit could overcome.

The Indian tea industry became, and still is, the greatest in the world. Once the decision had been taken to go into competition with China as a tea producer, and with the introduction of machinery, the years were numbered before India took over as the world's largest producer. India was fortunate in being endowed with the Assam indigenous tea plant, but then so too was China with its tea camellia.

Lord William Bentinck should receive credit for suggesting a steamer service on the country's rivers – one of the decisions that led to the great advancement of the country.

Major Robert Bruce was the first European to have a knowledge of the Assam indigenous tea plant, in 1823; this he imparted to his brother, C. A. Bruce, who dispatched specimens of the tea plant to Calcutta in 1824. He and Dr. Wallich had a great influence on the development of the industry.

Dr. Nathaniel Wolff Wallich was Superintendent of the Government's Botanical Gardens in Calcutta for thirty years from 1817 until 1847. He was appointed a member of the Tea Committee by Lord William Bentinck in 1834 and superintended the germination of the tea seeds brought to Calcutta by G. J. Gordon in 1835. As botanist he led a scientific deputation to Assam to investigate and confirm the discovery of the tea plant, but it was Lieutenant C. A. Bruce, R.N., who acted as guide to the party during their travels through the wild tea tracts in Muttack Country and it was he who, on Dr. Wallich's recommendation, was appointed Superintendent of Tea Culture. Dr. Wallich died in 1854 at the age of 68.

Charles Alexander Bruce was 40 when he was appointed director of Government nurseries and experimental tea lands in the North-East Frontier Region in 1835. He had previously been in command of a flotilla of HM gunboats at Sadiya, which included the steam gunboat *Diana*. He was unfortunate in failing to gain official recognition for the discovery of tea and the specimens that he had dispatched from Sadiya as early as 1824. It was to be another ten years before similar specimens, sent by Lieutenant Andrew Charlton, were pronounced to be those of the tea plant. Yet the honour of finding the tea plant went to Lieutenant Charlton, who received the gold medal in recognition of this. It is doubtful whether a better or more trustworthy man than Bruce could have been found for the arduous job that lay ahead. Bruce was *the* pioneer of the Tea Industry in India; it was he who first found out how to grow and manufacture tea. He went on to become the first Superintendent of the Assam Company's Northern Division, remaining in tea until his death at Tezpur on the North Bank of the Brahmaputra, in 1871, at the age of 78. His grave was, for many years, at Tezpur Cemetery but recently the tea company Williamson Magor moved it to the company's cemetery at their Pertabghur Tea Estate.

They laid the foundations of two great commercial enterprises which benefited India enormously: river transport, which opened up the vast sub-continent, and a truly great tea industry, the latter still contributing much to the economy of the country.

CHAPTER III

TEA TRANSPORT AND THE PADDLE STEAMER

Inland water transport in India

Top: An iron-hulled paddle-steamer on the Brahmaputra with towing barge. (*Photo c1860, courtesy Royal Geographical Society.*)

Bottom: After a long passage down the Brahmaputra a paddle steamer discharges its cargo of tea. A human conveyor belt carries the chests from ship to shore. The tea warehouses at the Kidderpore Docks in Calcutta were known as the world's tea caddy. For the next stage of its long journey the tea will be loaded on to ocean-going steamers to the markets of the world. (*Photo c1890, by permission of the British Library.*)

Tea Transport and the Paddle Steamer

The fact that the paddle steamer came upon the scene at about the same time as the tea industry started in upper Assam was more than a little fortunate.

In fact it is difficult to say how the new tea industry could have progressed without the steamer, especially when the river was the only means of communication. But first a small digression.

These days the paddle steamer is a rare sight and one is indeed fortunate to have had the experience of taking passage on one. Having been based on the Isle of Wight these past 50 years, when not abroad, I have had the opportunity to travel on our very own Island paddle steamers before they were withdrawn from service during the late 1960s, to be replaced by the motor vessel and now by the catamaran.

Going home to the Island was quite something in those days. On most occasions after boarding at Portsmouth, I would make my way down to the engine deck where one had a wonderful view of all the working machinery, thumping away; the brass all gleaming, the engineer dressed in white overalls, with oil can and oily rag, always tending his beloved engine.

There will assuredly be some old tea planters who spent their working lives in Assam who will likewise remember, with nostalgia, the voyages they made up

and down the Brahmaputra river on the quaint paddle-wheelers of the day. In later years planters flew when travelling from their estates down to Calcutta – a matter of hours instead of weeks, but something lost!

The Introduction of Inland Water Transport in India

But what of those first paddle steamers that were built over 160 years ago for service on the great rivers of India?

By this time the East India Company had considerable experience of transport by water on the world's oceans. From its early years the Honourable Company had maintained its own fleet of ocean-going ships and its own dockyards.

When Lord William Bentinck became Governor-General of India in 1833, immediate consideration was given to the construction of wood- and iron-hulled steamers, to operate on inland rivers.

The idea of establishing a river steamer service had by then taken on a more definite shape with the arrival of the S.S. *Lord William Bentinck* at Calcutta. This vessel was built at Lambeth, London, and steamed out to Calcutta in 1834 to ply the waters of the Ganges between Allahabad and Calcutta – the first inland river passenger steamer in India. By 1836 four steamers were operating on this route.

Some of the first paddle steamers were built in England and steamed out, but others were sent out in sections to Calcutta, where they were assembled completely or were built in Calcutta or Bombay. Two famous names in shipbuilding, the Kyd brothers, who were born in India, owned the Kidderpore Dockyard in Calcutta. In 1836 the Honourable Company bought the dockyard from the brothers and James Kyd

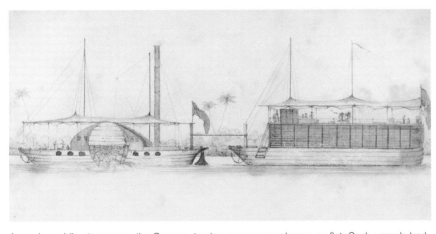

An early paddle steamer on the Ganges, towing a passenger barge, or flat. Such vessels had tall thin funnels and clumsy paddle boxes. (*Brown wash, painted in 1837 by Sir Henry Fane, courtesy National Maritime Museum, London.*)

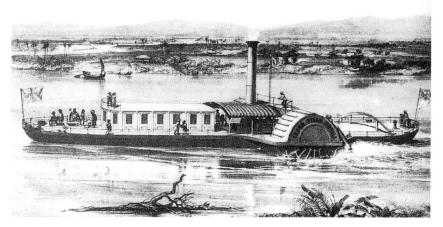

The paddle steamer *Frere*, built *c*1835. (*Drawing courtesy Inchcape plc.*)

became master ship-builder to the Company.

The early paddle steamers were approximately 100 feet in length and 22 feet broad amidships, excluding the paddle boxes. They were rigged for sail and each vessel had two 25 NHP engines.

The steamer provided quarters for officers while a barge, known as a flat, towed behind, had a large saloon with ten or twelve single cabins for the passengers. Cargo was carried on the afterdeck and in the holds of the flat. During the mutiny of 1857 these flats were used extensively for carrying troops. But in the early days the flat was connected by a fixed wood gangway enabling those with cabins on the flat to walk across to the steamer; all passengers messed at the Captain's table.

The early paddle steamers had exceptionally tall thin funnels, clumsy paddle boxes, awnings against the sun and employed 'boys', with wet swabs and buckets of water, to extinguish sparks that fell on the wood-planked decks when the vessel was burning wood or certain types of coal.

During the early years of river transport it was the custom to anchor each nightfall and this almost doubled the time taken on any passage. During the hours of daylight progress was further slowed by the inevitable delays caused by pilots not being at the right stations along the river. Running at night with the aid of a searchlight at the bow and the occasional lamps fixed to poles on shore or to mark bends in the river had not then been thought of. Later, the engines of the more modern steamers provided that extra pulling power essential for navigating the often narrow deeper channels when 'SLOW AHEAD' used instantly to become 'STOP' as groundings were frequent.

There were many problems for the Captains to overcome in the monsoon when the rivers were in flood, and then in the dry season when there were more sand bars than navigable river channels.

One can form a better idea of the difficulties involved in river navigation during the early part of the 19th century if one looks at the map inside the back cover of this book. According to the season there were two possible routes out of Calcutta for the river steamer bound for inland stations.

The 1600 mile journey up to Allahabad on the Ganges was a very circuitous one during the dry or cold weather season, when waters were low. On leaving the port of Calcutta the steamer did not proceed northwards up the Hughli, but downstream in a southerly direction towards the sea to a point north of Saugor Island, in the Hughli estuary, then turning eastwards to take the all-weather route through the Sunderbans to Khulna, thence into the Padma, on to Goalundo and then onwards, either along the Ganges or Brahmaputra rivers.

The huge Ganges-Brahmaputra delta known as the Sunderbans was, and still is, one vast region of mangrove jungle and swamps, inhabited by tiger and alligator and containing thousands of miles of interconnecting waterways through which the direct route was a little under 200 miles. The steamer route was not clearly defined nor was it marked by buoys or poles; the Captains navigated from one known landmark to another by the simple art of reading the water, its current flow and its colour. It was a hazardous business to get through without sailing up some creek only to end up blocked on a mud bank.

During the rainy season, however, the journey was considerably shortened as the steamer could proceed from Calcutta directly northwards up the Hooghly, into the Bhagarthi and then into the Ganges, and on. The native country boat, drawing less water, could proceed along this route at all times of the year without difficulty – and before the coming of the steamship, river travel was by country craft, dug-out and on land by elephant.

The hierarchy within the East India Company was well defined, just as it was in Indian society. The Company's high officials travelled in a splendid looking boat known as a budgerow which was, in style, an ornately decorated state barge, with two or more luxurious cabins. These fine craft were tracked up river by gangs of coolies from the river banks. Company officials of the second rank had to put up with boats called bholias, while for subordinates there was always the dug-out, ideal for penetrating the small streams and rivers. It was often decidedly tough at the low end of the hierarchy, but always comfortable at the top. In moving from one station to another, District officials often made use of two canoes lashed together with platform atop to form a raft for their luggage. But on balance the steamship, when it came, was a very great improvement.

The East India Company set a great network in place. Steamer landing places, known as ghats, sprouted up along thousands of miles of waterways and at these places villages became towns and industry developed apace. Coaling stations had to be maintained with coal for the steamers and this was transported all the way from east Bengal – accounting for almost 40% of running costs.

The opening of Assam to tea owed much to the dispatch steamers of the Government and to the river navigation companies which first experimented in this form of transport.

Tea Transport on the Brahmaputra

During the first years of the tea industry the Government steamer was largely unavailable for Assam so, as only the occasional one went up the Brahmaputra as far as Gauhati, the problem of transporting stores, tools and the like the best part of a thousand miles up a great river to the tea lands was very real. As already shown, this was first achieved by native country boats being sailed and laboriously dragged and poled against the current, and this took in the region of three-and-a-half months from Calcutta up to Sadiya.

Following the lead given by the Honourable Company, the premier tea company, the Assam Company, was next to build, in 1841, its own steamer, the *Assam*. Sections of this iron-hulled steamer, together with its two 50 h.p. engines, arrived from England on board the sailing ship *Gemini* at Calcutta. At 450 tons and 140 feet in length she was a large vessel and the first commercially owned steamer to attempt the navigation of the Brahmaputra, in 1842 up to Gauhati. The venture was not a success owing to defective steering and repeated breakdowns, and after being employed on the Ganges the *Assam* was finally sold to the India General Steam Navigation Company, in 1847.

The very first voyage up the Brahmaputra had been made almost two decades earlier, in 1824, by the Royal Navy's 100 ton steam propelled, sail-assisted paddlewheeler *Diana*, commanded by Lieutenant C. A. Bruce, R.N. It was manned by the Royal Naval Brigade and was built at the Kidderpore Dockyard in Calcutta in 1823.

The Assam Company's stores were obtained, in part, from Calcutta and included such things as cutlery, agricultural equipment, carpentry tools for making tea boxes, as well as coloured beads and pieces of looking-glass for the local native chiefs, who had not previously had the opportunity of seeing their reflection. The Company was fully aware of the value of mirror-glass as a negotiating counter when obtaining labour and elephants from these chiefs.

Elephants were a necessity, especially during the early years of the tea industry, and they, with the country boat and dug-out, were the only means of getting from one place to another. In a country stiff with tigers, it was far safer out on the river or on the back of an ele- ▶

This depiction, produced on 1st November 1810, by William Daniell, shows a point near Gangwaugh Colly, West Bengal, on the Hooghly river. (*Aquatint, 1810, courtesy National Maritime Museum, London.*)

With upwards of 10,000 miles of navigable river in 1ndia, vast areas of the interior could be opened to British manufacture and transport by paddle steamer down to the sea. In this lovely scene of a bygone age, probably on the Ganges, we see a 'steam train' of the Oriental Inland Steam Company, towing a string of four articulated. barges capable of carrying 1,000 tons of cargo and an accommodation barge for passengers which, during the Mutiny of 1857 would have been used for the transport of troops. For such articulated barges of under 2ft draft, the water resistance was small enabling a good rate of speed. The cornpany's vessels were constructed by Messrs Vernon & Son, Liverpool and the engines by Messrs Rennie & Sons, London. (*Chromo-litho 1858, courtesy Science Museum SSPL.*)

CHROMO-LITHOCRAPHED & PUBLISHED FOR THE COMPANY BY DAY

Steam Trains of the Oriental

train exhibited in this picture consists of a Steam Vessel and five barges
ght draught of water articulated to one another so as to permit deflec
in bends of the river or when the vessels get aground, at the same
that only a single bow is presented to the water for the wholetrain,
ad of a bow for each of the constituent barges. Such a train is
able of carrying 1000 Tons of Cargo on a draught of water of

OFFICES 9 BI

HE QUEEN, GATE STREET, LINCOLN'S INN FIELDS, LONDON, 1853.

ind Steam Company (Limited.)

ST. LONDON.

There are upwards of TEN THOUSAND MILES of Rivers in India
susceptible of beneficial Navigation by trains of this character. Such
Navigation when widely established will enable large quantities of
Cotton, Sugar, Grain and other useful products to be transported at a
moderate cost from the Interior to the Sea, and will afford easy means
of access for British Manufactures. The Steam Vessels being

Steam transport on the Ganges. Such steamers were also used for troop-carrying duties during the mutiny as shown in this scene, where the mutineers' fire is being returned by the steamer. Some of the longest voyages ever undertaken were made by these powered vessels in India – as far as Agra on the Jumna, which was 1640 miles from Calcutta, by river. (*Chromo-litho 1858, courtesy Science Museum/SSPL.*)

▶ phant. With a trusty elephant by one's side there was not much to be feared. This giant with a noble character, except when in 'musth' (see note at end of chapter), was largely employed in opening out jungle and for the transport of chests of tea from the gardens down to the tributary rivers to meet the waiting country boats which, in turn, transported the chests downstream with the current to the Brahmaputra and then on to the company's godown at Gauhati, where the tea would await the uncertain arrival of a steamer. An elephant could carry 6 chests of tea in a specially made howdah, while the average sized country craft could take 150 chests, each weighing approximately 80 pounds. By comparison to plywood tea chests the early tea boxes were small but weighty, owing to the thick-planked timber used in their construction.

After the first pioneering steps had been taken by the East India Company towards establishing the Inland Water Transport Industry, other privately owned river navigation companies were formed to enter what was to become a most profitable trade in cargo and passengers on the great rivers: the Jamuna, Gogra, Indus, Meghna, Brahmaputra and Ganges – which became the highways of the country, for there were no roads or railways.

The first true river dispatch company, the India General Steam Navigation Company, had been formed in 1844. The freight wars that developed between the river dispatch companies during the latter part of the century, together with the rapid expansion of the railway system, sank many of the lesser lights and only two famous companies survived: the India General Steam Navigation Company and the Rivers Steam Navigation Company. These two companies went on to amalgamate and form 'The Joint Steamer Companies', which became one of the largest ventures of its kind in the world, right up to the late 1970s.

It is hard to imagine how the tea industry could have developed as quickly as it did in such a remote region, had it not been for the inland river steamer. And with the introduction, during the 1860s, of the immensely heavy tea machinery, huge factory boilers and engines, they were an ideal form of transport.

In later years, stern-wheelers were built and employed along the many tributary rivers, chiefly in the tea regions of Assam, opening out yet more inaccessible tea gardens. Such services were for shallow water operations and the numerous stern-wheelers were a boon for the industry, plying far up the small rivers to get stores and labour quickly in and tea out.

The whole sub-continent had been opened up, first by the river steamer, then later by the construction of a great railway system and finally by roads, of a kind. From the East India Company's initiative grew a great enterprise with many hundreds of steamers, flats and other craft, operating along all the rivers which extended in all directions for over 5000 miles.

From the beginning of the Tea Industry there was an increasing demand for labour to work the ever increasing acreage. The 'deck passenger' trade formed a quite considerable part of the steamer companies' activities, carrying countless thousands of garden labourers 'tween decks' from Bengal up to the tea gardens. Newly recruited labour travelled in groups under a Sirdar (a sort of recruiting sergeant).

Since those first small consignments of tea during the late 1830s, many millions of tons of tea have been carried down the numerous tributary rivers to the Brahmaputra and then on by paddle steamer to Calcutta.

Hard work without our friend the elephant. Upwards of two hundred men labour to pull a giant tea boiler to the top of the hill on a tea estate somewhere in north-east India. A similar boiler is seen in chapter VI, on its way to an up-country estate in Ceylon. Even heavier large main engines, made by such famous names as Tangye and Ruston Hornby, were imported from the UK to run and power the line shafting and machinery in factories. One wonders how they managed to transport these heavy machines to the estates, once they had been off-loaded from the steamers; sheer elephant power and muscle. How else!
(*Photo 1890s, by permission of the British Library.*)

Some Tales of the River

No one could fail to imagine the sheer adventure of steaming slowly up a vast river, the banks of which were rarely less than two miles apart.

One can conjure up the scene in which the early paddle steamer operated. A small speck on a great river, its paddle wheels purposefully splashing round yet progressing with infinite slowness against the vastness of its grand surroundings. Up by the bows on port and starboard sides are two men, probably Lascars; each has in his hand a long bamboo with which, every quarter of a minute, he takes the depths of water, shouting out in a clear loud voice the results to the helmsman on the bridge – for there were countless groundings to infuriate the passengers.

Though the passenger often had to make do with a camp bed on the deck at night, there was one great advantage for those who travelled by steamer, as opposed to the country boat in earlier days, which was the cooling breeze one always got in the middle of a wide river where few insects would

Gauhati. In the scene depicted which is of the 1840 period, a Government official is seen talking to a planter in the employ of the Assam Company. These officials, or agents resided at small towns along the river route to north-east Assam such as at Goalpara, Tespur, Bisnath, and Gauhati, and were paid a yearly retainer by the Company to look after its interests. At these places the Company erected store-houses in which general provisions were kept, and at Gauhati, tea. Accommodation sheds were also erected for its European assistants and coolies where they could stay while proceeding on the long journey up river. During the year 1840 the Assam Company recruited over a hundred Chinamen, who all passed through Gauhati. (*Watercolour by S.R. Fever, 1983.*)

venture. Under adverse conditions during the monsoon, a steamer running against a twelve-knot current could well struggle for days to proceed only a mile or two when the mosquito, or whatever, had a good chance of catching up! A grim statistic of the time was

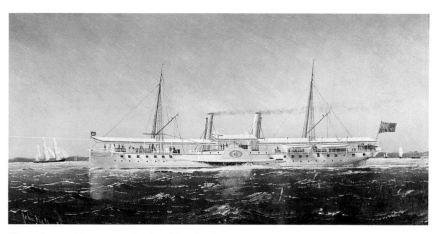

Dispatch vessel *Lawrence*. Steel paddle-wheel steamer, 903 tons, launched 1886. Built by Laird Bros., Birkenhead. (*Painting by John Hall, b. 1837, by permission of the British Library.*)

steamer Captain.

But days spent leaning on the steamer rail with the dark green of the jungle going slowly by and the soothing splash of the paddle wheels going round – this could be the life! The ways of the East would impress themselves upon the passenger.

At the various ghats along the river in later years hordes of workers travelling to and from the tea gardens, would swarm on board, carrying chickens in crates, pigs in bamboo baskets and goats, with legs tied, bleating loudly above the general hullabaloo. They, and their animals, would camp down in the well deck fore and aft packed closely together, eating, sleeping, incessantly talking and not infrequently dying.

Shipboard life, whether on ocean or a great river is, and always was, one of the pleasures for the traveller but not for our planter friend, whose jealous observations of the Captain's daily routine can only lead us to ▶

that approximately a million people died every year in India from malaria, and that did not exclude Europeans.

Pilots were employed on the large rivers to navigate the intricate and often changing deeper channels; moreover, even the main banks could not be relied upon, particularly during the annual floods when they would vanish only to be reformed hundreds of yards away. The Captains could not possibly retain full working knowledge of the ever-changing sandbanks and channels along a river such as the Brahmaputra and so the Pilots took full charge and worked in relays up the river, each having his own length of river where the deeper channels were marked with poles.

The first steamer Captains were European and included in their perquisites the messing of passengers, the sale of liquor and tobacco, as well as the organized business of selling tinned food, cigars, brandy, Holland's gin, cartridges and quinine to anyone who wanted them at every ghat at which the steamer called. Thus the longer a voyage lasted the better it was for the Captain, particularly as it was often necessary for the passengers to supplement their table rations by purchase from the Captain's store. Oscar Lindgren, of whom mention has already been made, took passage from Goalundo on the paddle steamer *Patna*, as late as 1877, and gives us a good insight into shipboard life on the Brahmaputra at that time:

> The Captain would always welcome a day or two of delay caused by the vessel hitting a sandbank in the bed of the river, and who, if business was bad, would make certain that a convenient sandbank was forthcoming.

As the early steamers anchored each nightfall, the voyages were somewhat prolonged. Pleasant though it was on the river, a young man still had his thoughts as he lounged in a long cane chair on the upper deck sipping a glass of tolerably cool beer. Going out to make his fortune in tea – yes, that was a nice thought, but when he recalled the Calcutta agents mentioning the fact that, once away in the Assam jungles there was no return for five years, he became not a little envious of the life of a

Captain James Hay Williamson (1812–1898) was one of the first European steamer commanders. He was co-founder with Richard Magor, of the Tea Agency House of Williamson & Magor in 1865. Today, 140 years later, the Williamsons have not survived but the Magor Family continue in the tea business, and Philip Magor is Managing Director of George Williamson & Co. Ltd. (*Courtesy Inchcape plc.*)

Early years – until the steamer came to upper Assam in 1856, the country craft was the only means of transport.
(*Watercolour by S.R. Fever*)

The sternwheeler *Spindrift*. For shallow water operations on feeder rivers, these vessels were ideal for the transport of stores and labour up to the estates and chests of tea out. Twenty-two sternwheelers were built by the Joint Steamer Companies during the 1890s. These vessels were 100 ft in length and had a maximum draft of 2 ft 9 ins. (*Photo c 1940 courtesy Inchcape plc.*)

Chests of tea were carried off the estates by bullocks and elephants down to the tributary rivers.
(*Watercolour E. Butler 1900.*)

Each country boat was capable of carrying about 150 chests of tea...

...then down to the Brahmaputra and the steamer, and on 800 miles to Calcutta (*Photos c 1940s, courtesy Inchcape plc.*)

▶ the conclusion that he *had* chosen the wrong profession:

> The Captain was not overworked except perhaps with his own affairs. He ascended the bridge when leaving or arriving at a 'port' and in times of emergency. The only exception was when passing another vessel, when time would be spared for a hand wave to his brother Commander, whom you can be sure had been waked up in ample time to return the customary greeting.

A variety of events would enliven the passenger's voyage. There was always the possibility of the steamer running aground; then, for those who had brought a rifle along, the chance of a shot at a wild buffalo in the early morning, a crocodile or at the numerous duck that flew overhead. The early steamer Captains would always obligingly stop engines and put out a dinghy with a couple of Lascars to retrieve any game that might fall to a successful shot.

The Captains were great characters and could be relied upon to tell a good story:

> After dinner the Captain told us stories which we tried, tolerantly, to believe. Many experiences on the river gave him much to talk about, and had taught him to lie in an interesting manner. 'In one day,' said the Captain, 'the whole population of Goalpara died'. We swallowed this statement with the awe that was due it, but in after years I learned that at the time of the incident there was only one European at Goalpara.

In time and as the planting population increased, whenever a steamer was expected up river, those in need of something 'special' in the way of provisions, would leave their tea gardens and ride in on their ponies to the nearest ghat for a rendezvous with the ship's Captain, who could generally be relied upon to have the necessary in stock. At these places flats were permanently moored by the river bank to take on cargo as well as for the accommodation of travelling planters; a sort of hotel on the river.

As we tied up alongside the larger flat we noticed several

Oscar Lindgren lounging in a cane chair. (*Photo courtesy David C.R. Manners.*)

Europeans waiting to board us. That afternoon we visited the Captain's Storeroom. The contents amazed me. It would have done credit to a modern tinned provision shop in Calcutta. 'And all will be gone,' said the Captain, 'by the time we reach Dibrugarh. Planters all up the river know me and will soon polish off the lot.'

The steamer Agent had been suffering from fever for some time and needed quinine, which the Captain could not supply. Brandy, gin, beer and tinned salmon were to be had in large quantities, but of quinine there was none.

Friendships in such isolated parts of the world are eas-

The Brahmaputra at Gauhati, showing one of the islands in the river. In the foreground are two old barges, or flats, smartly painted and fixed together to form a landing stage, or ghat, for the ferry boat. (*Photo C.A.W. 1985.*)

Dibrugarth street scene. (*Photo C.A.W. 1985.*)

the still night air. Then, there is the continual glucking sound of the river as it pushes between the landing stage and the ship's side, the splash and swirl of water as a large fish surfaces close by, while always, the sound of sandbanks collapsing with a muffled splash.

The steamer Company's agent was a key man in such outposts of Empire, and by the late 1850s – when steamers were going up the Brahmaputra as far as Dibrugarh, albeit on a six weekly service – the necessity arose to maintain a permanent presence there and at other ghats along the river. Our passenger tells of his arrival at this North-east Frontier region:

Dibrugarh struck me as a most unpleasant place. The Agent told me that the shooting was quite good along this length of the river (Dibooroo). The steamer Agent's tiger skins made my mouth water. He had a number which he intended to take down to Calcutta to be finally cured, one of which he prized greatly, as it had charged his elephant and nearly killed the Mahout. It had taken five bullets to kill the tiger and the Agent was naturally very proud of it.

ily made between men, and what more natural than to find our passenger and his newly found friends settling down for a pleasant evening on board, long before the last rays of a blood-red sunset had dropped behind the forbidding jungle-fringed shoreline.

Imagine the scene. The steamer, made fast against the creaking sides of the flat, her night lamps casting a warm glow along the dim outline of the vessel. A small group, including the Captain, sit around a table on the upper deck. On the table there are numerous glasses, a few bottles and an open box of Burmah cheroots. The haze of pungent smoke coming from those smoking the planters 'joy' assures the party of a mosquito-free night of drinking. From under the table comes a continual happy chattering noise where the Captain's pet monkey sits; it must be the most travelled monkey on the river. The occasional sound of laughter carries on

Because of the all important communication that the steamer provided with the outside world, the town of Dibrugarh, like many others along the Brahmaputra, developed, though the garb of civilization was thin at first. It soon became a port with a line of landing flats moored along the river; native huts, in various forms of construction, the steamer agent's 'house', which was not much better, a small bazaar and a hotel, though the reader should in no way be confused by the use of the word hotel.

Our passenger has travelled up the 'great river' for 600 miles since leaving Goalundo and it has taken 33 days finally to reach Dibrugarh. He has come a long way, in fact, from England – some 5000 miles. With a feeling of excitement and thrill of the unknown ahead of him, our friend finally redeems himself with regard to his previous thoughts about the Captain.

We sat down to our last lunch on board, pledged the health of the Captain in a bottle of French wine, and ultimately bade each other

INDIAN TEA.
THE PLANTER'S
POST OFFICE.

The Christmas mail arrives by elephant – why not?

farewell, hoping to meet again before we were much older. I had learnt to like the Captain and departed with regret which I believe was mutual.

I mounted my pony and proudly took my way to the Dibrugarh Hotel, where, according to instructions contained in a letter I had received, I was to stay a couple of days to lay in stores that I was to take on to the Tea Garden.

Many came with hopes of making a fortune in tea, others for the sheer challenge and adventure of it all; only those who had actually arrived in the jungle knew better – that the life of a planter had its drawbacks.

'There is one person he writes to every second day, heedless of the fact that his letters will arrive in England in batches of three and four a mail.'
(*Original, pen and ink and watercolour Christmas card 1875.*)

It is never easy to know when to interrupt the story, but let me tell you of an experience that has some bearing upon hotels in this part of the world:

Some 110 years after Oscar Lindgren departed from the Dibrugarh Hotel, my wife and I – having looked askance at that very same hotel while passing through the town – were anxiously looking for somewhere to bed down for the night.

Arriving at Tinsukia a little after sunset we made our way to the hotel which was situated in the main street in what must have been a lately cleared area, with native boutiques either side.

The fourth in our party, the Tea Research Association's entomologist, Bipul Gope, left us for the night to go to his family who lived somewhere in Tinsukia, promising to return at 7 am the following day. After we had given our driver a few rupees for his necessities, he opted to sleep the night in the car, which seemed sensible in the circumstances. The Director at Tocklai, Dr. Banerjee, had, the previous day, tried to telephone the Managers of Chubwa and Jaipur estates in order that we might be put up there, but as was so often the case in Assam the lines were dead.

A slight devil-may-care attitude gripped me as we stepped into the 'hotel' which was, frankly, rather low, discounting the fact that it appeared to be a one-storey building. From the outside it had appeared almost identical to the long line of boutiques on either side of it, from where dim shapes could be seen squatting around oil lamps. My wife looked long and hard at me and I managed a rueful grin.

One couldn't call it a run down hotel as it had obviously only just been 'run up', as the walls of our bedroom were finished in cement plaster which was still drying out. I use the term 'bedroom' simply because that is what it must have been. It had two beds in it

though not the sort one is familiar with in the western world. These beds were more like charpoys, but without the string; they were merely plank boards.

Not daring to try dinner but dying of thirst, our liquid intake never being equal to the hot day conditions, I asked for two cups of tea, without cream, because that is the way we like it. Some ten minutes later the Inn keeper, who spoke good English, returned to say 'Sorry Sar we have no cream, can it be without milk?' We each had three cups which filled us up to some extent. Other luxuries included a very small two-bar electric fire which crackled and flashed dangerously until the power was turned off at about 9 o'clock, leaving us shivering for the rest of the night, it being the cold weather season.

Undaunted by the breakfast that was put before us we attacked it as though it was caviar. (It was time to go. This part of our stay is continued in the next chapter under 'In Search of the Original China Tea'.)

This shows, does it not, how soft we western city dwellers are today, compared to those early tea men; it is all a matter of what you get used to really. Some years later when lunching with an ex-Assam planter and his wife, we learnt that the main street in Tinsukia was considered by British planters 'to be the longest urinal in the world'. I can say from our experience of this unusually long main street, that our planter friend did not exaggerate in the least.

To return to the story. Whether he was a 'first timer', as many of the early proprietary planters were, or going out to open an outgarden to an established estate, as Oscar Lindgren was, this was a defining moment when he remembered those Calcutta agents – so far removed now – sitting in their comfy offices, telling him that once away in the jungles there was no ▶

The Mahratta Nightjar. As its name suggests this bird operates during the hours of darkness. This fine drawing, by John Gould, comes from one of his seven volumes of *The Birds of Asia*. Each volume contains 50–70 exquisite lithographs. These pictures and hundreds of others portraying the birds of different countries of the world were executed between 1850 and 1883.
(*Hand-coloured plate by John Gould, by permission of the British Library*.)

The Assam Peacock-pheasant. (*Hand-coloured plate by John Gould, from his* Birds of Asia, *1850–1883, permission of the British Library.*)

▶ return for five years; that sort of thought could concentrate the mind, but the die was cast and he was happy with it.

Having received a note from the Manager of the estate he was going to and together with a few of the estate's workers, to act as bearers, it was time to start the journey inland – seated on his pony.

The Indescribable Jungle, but watch out for fire-flies

This is when the newcomer got his first true impression of the jungle; seeing it at a fair distance along the river banks from the safety of the steamer was simply not the same. To the town-dweller his introduction might well have been a little frightening. Growing up the massive trunks of trees are great thick gnarled lianas which to his inexperienced eye look not unlike giant snakes lying in wait for him. A chill runs down his spine every time a twig snaps in the undergrowth, like a pistol shot, but if only he has eyes to see it, a small pig scuttles away deeper into the thicket. Eventually, our Lindgren pulled up in front of the Manager's large wooden bungalow – the pony rather too quickly sending him A over T into the mud, after which it went off, unaccompanied, to its stable at the back of the bungalow.

Lindgren was to live in comfort for three months as a paying guest in his Manager's bungalow while he

learnt the ropes, in field and factory, in the days (1877) when the newly invented tea machinery had not been installed on all the estates. Before leaving the 'big bungalow' and during the many evenings they spent together, he came to realise that his Manager talked 'Tea' in an informative way and that he was one from whom he could learn quickly. However, this turned out to be unjustified as Tea was his only subject, just as the bottle – now and then – was his only object.

Finally it was time to move on: his task was to open out 300 acres of jungle as an 'outgarden' to the estate, where he would be left to his own devices with an invitation from the Manager to take care and visit him at least once a month. The thoughtful Manager had previously sent a couple of estate workers to erect a hut in which Lindgren was to live while felling and planting up the new outgarden.

His first night spent in a crude basha surrounded by jungle was another new and uncomfortable experience. After an early meal, cooked by his chokra (house boy) and before turning in to his little crib for the night, he busies himself stuffing a candle into a bottle and checking his supply of matches. The night feeding animals are out, there is one hell of a din going on in the darkness of the surrounding jungle and his ears are filled with this new and unaccustomed orchestra of the night. He gets a real fright when he sees what he takes to be the glinting eyes of a tiger, looking at him from the jungle perimeter, but then, the eyes move – in different directions? He quickly learns that two fire-flies, when seen hovering at approximately six inches apart on a level plane at three feet high, look almost identical to the eyes of a tiger; it is when the eyes move 'in unison' that he should worry!

Try to imagine the scene. Bright moonlight shafts down through the overhanging trees – there are shadows everywhere. A breeze, more faint than he can detect, stirs the leaves of a small sapling close by and in so doing plays strange tricks with the shadows that jump and dart not six feet from where he stands. This sudden movement startles him as, rooted to the ground, he instinctively feels it to have been made by a wild animal. It is only then that he detects the breeze, accompanied by fluttering leaves and the slight swaying of branches. The shadows leap and dance again, but this time he knows the cause.

By day there is the 'whoo whoo' of the Gibbons as they crash through the branches and swing high in the canopy above, feeding as they go; the startled flight of a Peacock pheasant as it is flushed out by some travelling denizen of the forest; the alarm call of the all-seeing langur, from the safety of the trees above as it looks down upon a prowling tiger, and this, in turn, sends every animal running for its life.

By night the trumpeting and bellowing of a herd of elephants; the alarm call of a Sambur as it gets wind of a leopard, and then a rarer more eerie sound that once heard is never forgotten, the high-pitched melancholy wail of a lone jackal. Then at dusk, or just after dark, there were other less worrying noises of the night, such as a monotonous 'Tk-churr' of the nightjars, almost like the purring sound of a sewing machine working, sometimes continuing without pause for a minute or two. Of course there was the ever-present cacophony of millions of frogs and crickets, croaking and clicking away in the close vicinity of his hut. One pioneer had this to say about this little beauty:

> There is a creature of the grasshopper tribe which makes day and night hideous with its noise, and for this insect I entertained the most cordial hatred. The sound it makes is quite indescribable, but seems most like a couple of metal saws going through a plate of sheet iron. For hour after hour I sat and stewed, listening to the maddening shrill of the cicadas perched in millions in the trees and bushes around.

This then, at the age of twenty, was Oscar Lindgren's introduction to life in the wilder parts of upper Assam and a long planting career. After 45 years in tea he retired in 1922 to Kalimpong, near Darjeeling, where he married, had a large family and cultivated pineapples, pears and sugar cane. He died aged 88, in 1946, and his grave is in the cemetery at the MacFarlane Church, Kalimpong.

The majority did not make their fortunes and many never came out of the country alive, their tombstones, many now overgrown, stand as a monument to these intrepid tea pioneers. Lest we forget, they are all part of the TEA STORY.

Note: * The term 'musth' describes a condition that occurs during the rutting season, when tame elephants are subject to fits of temporary fury. This condition is called 'mudda' in Sri Lanka, a paroxysm which speedily passes away, but during its height it is dangerous for even the animal's mahout to approach.

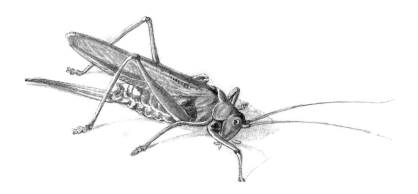

One of the grasshopper tribe – call it what you will. A few thousand of these in the immediate vicinity of your bedroom makes for a noisy night!
(*Watercolour by G. Cunningham.*)

CHOTA AND BURRA SAHIBS INTO THE 20TH CENTURY

and a visit to Tea Country

Assamese pluckers. (*Photo 2000, courtesy Williamson Magor & Co. Ltd.*)

Chota and Burra Sahibs

The Men Themselves at Work and Play

As we go forward in time it is all too easy for us today to forget what the early planters achieved, against all the odds, when starting a completely new industry in the wilds of distant Assam. Who in Britain, Europe, or for that matter anywhere, knew the whereabouts of Assam, or cared, so long as he could get his cup of tea? Certainly he did not give a thought to the men who planted and cultivated the tea plant. But what of these men, their living conditions and their way of life?

Before we get into the nitty gritty about some of the trials and tribulations of living in a hot country under conditions that might be called sparse, the reader may just wonder how, in days of old, one became a planter, in some far removed country, albeit somewhere in the glorious Empire. Well, from experience, it helps a lot if you can tell the London directors of that tea or rubber company – in whose comfortable offices you are sitting being interviewed for the job – that your father and grandparents have been tramping these far-distant lands planting this and that, and that you therefore know the 'form'. Add to this the fact that you are brilliant with bat and ball, like a sporting adventurous life and don't mind mosquitoes, snakes, etc., and you're in! Furthermore, you may wonder how the earlier generations of these men came to know about the lucrative profession of planting; well, let's just say they were Scottish and liked to travel! The under-mentioned poem rather sums up the situation:

I looked up and saw an advert for tea,
And I said to myself 'that's the job just for me',
Kaisa Hai, Kaisa Hai, Kaisa Hai,
There's no blooming future for him, you or I.
I packed up my bags and to London did go,
The directors they quizzed me as to what I did
    know,
I said I knew nothing, they said that's just grand,
There are plenty like you in that far distant land.

– and another, in the same vein:

Distant Lands Enchantment
I've failed for the navy and army,
    the church and the law, so you see
The only profession left me ...

my last hope ... an assistant in tea.
You may not believe me, but I'm chockfull of
    brains
The one thing I can't do is think hard.
But I'm sure I'll love tennis and polo and golf.
I can work hard and play hard and drink hard.
And this, it appears, at least, so one hears,
Is what's wanted. It sounds just like jam
So I'll pack up my box and make tracks for the
    docks
And that heavenly place called Assam.
I'm told the commissions run into a lac;
That the life is well ... sporting and healthy.
It's your own blinking fault, if you're handed the
    sack;
But with luck you'll retire, hale and wealthy.
There's my first cousin Charlie, he's just home
    on leave;
He had never a bean to his name.
He's as full of rupees as a monkey of fleas;
All the men in Cachar are the same
I may be a fool, I was one at school;
But I'm making my mind up instanter
To clear out and go, by the first P & O
And hurrah for the life of a planter.

Can we possibly imagine today what it must have been like? The temporary huts they erected while opening out jungle on a new tea garden were dingy and damp, and often leaked like sieves from the thatched or leaf-sewn roof and sides whenever it rained hard. The mists that hung around the jungle during the monsoon drifted right through them.

Sickness was a life-threatening problem for planters and their labour force, who lived as a small community often miles from the next embryo tea garden. If one disregards such minor things as leech bites which turn septic, hook-worm, which affected most of the labour force, the bites of poisonous snakes when cutting down and clearing forests, tigers and the periodic attacks by hill tribesmen, perhaps the most deadly of them all was the anopheles mosquito that plagued everyone during the rainy season. Amoebic dysentery was yet another scourge.

Planters generally suffered from a low fever, a form of malaria which was only kept under by swallowing 5 grains of quinine every day during the rains – unpleasant though it was to take. Attacks could last a few hours daily, or a whole week. Coming forward a bit in time, my parents had frequent attacks of malaria and while returning home on leave from Malaya during the early 1920s, my mother was carried down the companionway at the side of the ship on a stretcher when it called at Aden. She languished in hospital there for a week and nearly died before they were able to take the next liner on.

Teak wallah Reginald Campbell, when working the teak forests adjoining the Naga Hills in Burma during the 1920s, commented upon the 'night life' he enjoyed inside his temporary basha:

> There were two chief kinds of mosquito. The commonest were large fellows with striped legs who could give you dengue fever but not malaria. Then there were little, brown, harmless-looking chaps who came out only in the evenings and who stood on their heads when biting you: these were the dreaded anopheles, the females of which could give you malaria but not dengue.

It was exactly the same for the planters just across the border in Assam, as this little menace knew no boundaries – it was everywhere, fully capable of making life sheer hell, sending even the strongest man home with a fever-ridden body within a few short years.

At the outset of the fever the patient suffers a high temperature and ague, his legs ache, his eyes sting, his skin is hot and dry and he has bouts of shivering. He turns in, puts on all the pullovers he can find and tells his house boy to bring the 'medicine chest', which in fact is a tin box containing the rarest of essentials: he swallows 15 grains of quinine, 10 of aspirin and then lies there, more or less stupefied, to sweat it out under as many blankets as can be found. We should remember that the early planters did not, however, possess or have the luxury of quinine.

Travelling for the sick must have been torture during those early pioneering years. The first part of a long journey from the tea garden was spent swaying in the howdah on an elephant while passing through jungle down to a river to transfer to the comparative comfort of the country boat.

In the more restricted stretches along the smaller tributary rivers, two wooden dug-out canoes, lashed together, would form a *mar*, with a platform placed across, on which a make-shift hut is erected to shelter the traveller or sick man. Such craft, drifting down with the current, would go on to Tezpur or even down to the flesh spots of Gauhati which was quite a considerable distance. In the pre-steamer days this form of transport was the only alternative to the country boat, apart from the paddle canoe itself. One can imagine the dangers that beset the traveller during the rainy season, when the rivers were high and swollen and the traveller was swept along on a strong, swirling fast current. To return back up river was often quite impossible.

The seriously ill might be sent all the way down to Calcutta, which, during the early years of the industry, took up to two months, with the current, and this was sufficient to kill an already sick man.

We know from the written accounts of some of these intrepid tea men how they lived and spent their days – and nights – under the most Spartan conditions. Fitted carpets had not been thought of, even back in the old country, and a gunny sack or two thrown down on the hard mud-packed floor of his basha (hut) was comforting in that it did, at least, keep the damp from his feet – for a while. To be woken at night by an elephant breaking into and smashing up the store in which the rice for the labour force, and himself, was kept, was a little more worrying than being bitten by mere insects.

Oscar Lindgren, who was still planting in Assam during the early 1920s, said of his nightly tormentors:

> Besides mosquitoes, Assam is endowed with a marvellous selection of things that fly; some so heavy that their impact would shake my refuge appreciably – or so it seemed. I thought it necessary always to keep a light burning and, in the rainy season, the light attracted many thousands of insects each night. Many of these died and fell to the ground, only to afford succulent food for my few fowls. After a good night there was seldom any need for the fowls to be fed.

Planting tea, coffee or rubber were professions that whole families followed, from the days of being in the service of the East India Company, with each successive generation going into the Indian Civil Service, or embarking upon a career in planting.

During the 1920s the Charleston may have been the rage in a certain part of the world, but out in the more remote parts of Empire the Chota and Burra Sahibs (Assistants and Superintendents) struggled on as only they knew how. With the passing of each decade conditions improved for planter and labour force alike – but very slowly.

There was still an awful lot of jungle being felled and opened to tea during the early part of the 20th century, but slowly life on the estates was becoming more congenial, and in the years to come the planter would be the envy of many back in Britain, though it still might have been an illusion to some!

Hard at Work – Felling and Clearing

Felling and clearing has always been a favourite field work for the planter, as the bustle and hive of activity that takes place in a new clearing is undeniably exciting. The sound of axes falling sharp and quick goes on all day accompanied by the shouts of the axe men as one by one the forest monarchs crash to the ground amidst a shower of leaves and broken branches. The ▶

The Evolution of the Bungalow

With quotes by planters of the day

'My hut had only just been finished before I arrived and the furniture consisted of boxes. A box served as a table, another as a chair, and a third as a sideboard, and so on. The hut was small, its walls consisted of sun dried thatching grass fastened to a bamboo frame.'

(Courtesy Royal Geographical Society)

'The rats simply swarmed and at nights they came forth from their hiding places and ate up everything within their reach. One woke me up by actually sitting on my forehead. There was no mistake about this for I seized him there, and threw him to the other end of the room.'

(Drawing – G. Cunningham)

'The place hummed with anopheles mosquitoes which were lighted to our persons by thousands of willing fireflys. On a busy night in the rains those mosquitoes that could not settle awaited their turns in the shadow of the patient thrown on the walls'

(Courtesy Inchcape plc.)

Chota Sahibs of sorts

'First, foremost and funniest of all is the 'Chota Sahib' who is in his first year in tea – who counts his time in the country by months as others do by years, and who longs for the day when he can say, like Faither, "I haven't been twenty five years in the country for nothing, I can tell you" – nice phrase that, but common, beastly common.'

One of these Chota Sahibs might think, wistfully:

The Assistant

'I wish I were a manager
With umpteen quid a year,
What a glorious life with a
　　handsome wife
And never a boss to fear.

With unlimited powers and no
　　fixed hours
And never a care about muster
(To go out at night and come
　　back when it's light
Is an old managerial dastur).

With a bungalow like an old
　　chateau
And a most expensive car,
A blooming toff with all day off
For that is what managers are.'

The estate bungalow of the 1980s. The Manager's bungalow on Shumshernugger Tea Estate, Sylhet, Bangladesh.

Dappled sunlight filters through the foreground trees onto a well cut lawn in this attractive garden, bounded by tea bushes. Beyond, lush tea fields carpet the estate. M. A. Azim, with his wife Nadira on Shumshernugger. (*Photos courtesy Duncan Brothers (Bangladesh) Ltd.*)

Assam – 'Opening out'

Extending the estate acreage

Felling and clearing. The extraction of timber by trolley for building purposes and for factory firewood showing planter with labour grouped around a trolley which runs on a miniature railroad.

The heavier timber is dealt with by elephants. (*Photo c1900, by permission of the British Library.*)

Weeding young tea seedlings in the nursery; transplanting to fields, and pluckers in mature tea under shade trees.

All photos 1920s, courtesy Tony Andrew.

This quick sketch was to have been the prototype for a further two or three paintings, each progressively more detailed. It is included as a tribute to artist Sidney Fever, whose splendid paintings illustrated my last book, and who died after completing this sketch. It depicts the period during, the 1830s when Charles Bruce discovered rich tracts of indigenous tea growing in the Muttack jungles of Upper Assam.
(*Watercolour S.R. Fever.*)

Old-style thatched bungalow (*Photo c.1905 by permission of the British Library.*)

Deer and other animals delighted in trampling newly prepared nursery beds. The culprit brought to book, or something for the table? (*Photo showing Oscar Lindgren, courtesy David C.R. Manners.*)

Interior and exterior views of the 'Ooty Club'. Built by Sir William Rumbold in 1832, it was first a hotel, then a convalescent home for the Army, before being converted into a club by a group of army officers in 1842. The rules for the game of snooker were invented here and the club has been used by planters and their wives until this day. (*Photos C.A.W. 1985.*)

▶ fallen forest is now a scene of the wildest confusion, ten feet deep with withering foliage, massive tree trunks at all angles and broken, splintered branches lie as they fall. The pleasant smell of resin coming from ten thousand cuts pervades the whole clearing and is something one is unable to forget. The topmost branches of the felled trees are lopped to pile and burn, fires are lit, a pall of smoke hangs over the clearing – all are a part of the operation. The smaller timber is trollied away to be used for the erection of sheds or as fuel in the factory, while the more massive trunks are pulled out by elephants and dragged to a sawyer's pit to be sawn into planks for the construction of buildings and factory extensions.

Whether working the teak forests of Burma and Siam, or on the tea estates in India and Ceylon, the trained elephant is a capital asset and is also man's best friend in the jungle. The price of an elephant during the early pioneering years of tea was Rs. 300 (then about £25 sterling). It is a known fact that all elephants dislike dogs, and though this story comes from the teak forests of Northern Siam, it illustrates the point. Reginald Campbell describes an unusual incident that concerned one of his dogs:

I was approaching a camp one evening, when I came upon a hobbled tusker of ours right in my path. I stopped dead, but the red pup, now almost fully grown, disregarded my warning and instead of staying at my heels as Sclave was doing, went gaily on ahead. The tusker bubbled and swayed ominously as he watched the pup advancing (I have mentioned before how elephants instinctively dislike dogs), and then, quick as lightening, the great beast snatched up with his trunk a huge branch near him and hurled it straight at the pup. It missed him by matter of inches – it was a mercy he wasn't killed – and the throwing of it provides a remarkable instance of an animal, other than a human being or a monkey, realizing the use of a missile. For the benefit of the sceptical I should explain that by no stretch of the imagination could the incident be regarded in any other light; that tusker definitely took up and aimed that branch at that dog; I saw him do it at close quarters and I saw the expression in his tiny pig eyes.

During the early years when game was abundant and man was daily encroaching upon its habitat with the axe, the labour force was at great risk from a variety of accidents and mishaps, not to mention illness. Leopards would often lie up during the heat of the day in the dense cover of the tea. Pluckers move across a tea field more or less in a straight line, each taking a row of tea bushes. In most cases when pluckers unknowingly approached a leopard it would sneak off, but when it found itself between two lines of converging pluckers it would bolt through the line, severely mauling some of the pluckers as it went.

Perhaps this is the right place to tell a planting story, vouched for by a tea planter who had the reputation of being one of the biggest liars in Assam:

Coolies were felling trees in a forest, making a clearance for a tea garden. A monstrous python made its appearance, and the workers rushed from the place. One of the men reported to the planter who came along with his gun; the coolies, recovering from their fright, accompanying him. He was shown where the snake had been discovered but, unable to distinguish it amongst the timber, looked for the largest felled tree. Mounting the trunk to secure a better view, he asked that the location of the snake be pointed out, 'You are standing on the python, Master,' came the reply.

Many of the planting tales undoubtedly have more than a glimmer of truth in them and I can tell you, from personal experience in this work, that piles of fallen stacked timber, such as that shown on page 68, do attract and provide hiding places for snakes of all kinds, including, in India, the king cobra, which is a very nasty customer; it is the only snake that will attack without provocation.

However much conditions had improved one should not get the impression that from the turn of the century it was an easy life for those who lived and worked on the tea gardens, which were still very isolated and Assam is a big place. It should be remembered too that head-hunting Naga Hill tribesmen continued to make periodic raids into the tea districts during the late 1920s and early 1930s.

Though only a small proportion of estates were attacked, those situated in close vicinity of Nagaland and the Lushai Hills were very much in the firing line. During the early years in Assam, most of the half dozen hill tribes treated large tracts of the Assam valley as their very own. As law and order was established, together with an ever-expanding planting community, less was seen of them – as raiders. In 1869 Lushai tribesmen attacked seven Cachar tea gardens and the Manager of Alexander Tea Estate, Dr. Winchester, was killed and his six-year-old daughter, Mary, carried off with other captives to their tribal villages in the hills. A punitive expedition was later mounted and all the captives rescued. The early pioneering days had their dangerous moments – tribesmen and wild animals, and most feared were the turbulent Abors, another hill tribe.

All tribesmen were proud, independent characters who would never think of working on an estate. The labour force had to be drawn from afar. The indigenous labour, both Assamese and Singphos, were lazy and because of their addiction to opium and their generally demoralized condition, had no difficulty in overcoming the natural impulse to work.

Drug taking was common among tea garden workers and ganga, the dried leaves and small stem of hemp, as well as betel, from the Areca nut palm, were in everyday use. The continual chewing of betel and the blood-red juice that is spat from the mouth at frequent intervals, is said to cause goitre, and in some cases cancer of the throat.

The sprawling thatched-roofed bungalow (on page 72) tells its own story of the continuing improvement in the life-style of the planter in Assam; with a palatial bungalow and an army of servants he was now the envy of many. There were those among the new breed of planters who had already forgotten the men who had made their life possible, hardly a generation ago, through guts, determination and sheer hard work.

Clubs and Sport

Before the arrival of the car and the Club, a hospitable planter's bungalow acted as a sort of meeting place; in effect a Club House.

At weekends, dressed in their best clothes, they would start out early on their ponies passing along well-worn jungle paths for some centrally situated planter's bungalow where they would meet for drinks, a meal and some gossip. Upon departing, where we in England say 'Have one for the road', planters in India would say 'Have a tiger frightener'.

▶

(Photo 1906, by permission of the British Library.)

This little ditty just about sums up the planter's life. To the uninitiated 'goebur' means 'farmyard manure', which was used in the past for establishing young tea.

The Manager

I wish they would say 'You can be the V.A.
And keep the whole gang up to scratch',
I've been so long in tea, they couldn't do me,
But would find I was more than their match.

I'd make them obey and grow tea my way,
Especially old so-and-so;
He can't argue the toss if I am the boss,
Which is one thing I'd soon let him know.

To come out in October and talk about 'goeber'
And compost and pruning and such
And find out their dodgings (such with free board and lodgings)
Would suit this tired soul very much.

The Visiting Agent

If I could afford to get on the Board
And smoke my cigar at the table;
With a nice dividend at every year's end
And get forty per cent, if I'm able.

I'm tired of Sylhet, but I'm not too old yet,
And I want a nice house by the sea.
But I must have the cash, for the wife cuts a dash
To make up for the years spent in tea.

If I'm made a director (a profits collector)
I'll see they're kept short in Assam,
I'll live in good style and I'll die worth a pile –
That's the kind of man that I am.

(Photo 1860s, courtesy Royal Geographical Society.)

The Director

I wish I could be an assistant in tea
And start my life over again,
You've only two-fifty but needn't be thrifty,
For that's not the way with young men.

The ladies adore you, your life is before you,
You've the nerve and the legs for a horse,
And dance till the dawn and set to with a yawn
And take life as a matter of course.

But I spend my life playing bridge with my wife
And discussing the past with old cronies:
I've got money and gout; and I long to come out
And be young with my debts and my ponies.

Planter Oscar Lindgren (in jodhpurs) with great friend Colonel Hurst, 1913, Darjeeling Planters Club.
(Photo courtesy David Manners.)

75

A Shooting Anecdote, India. The scene depicted with huntsman and dog is typical of Samuel Howlett's *Sporting Prints of the English Countryside*. His English sporting scenes always included huntsmen, dogs, pheasants and rabbits, set in a rural landscape abounding with oak trees and hedgerows. Here, he has drawn his more exotic subject, the tiger, against a piece of suitable Indian jungle while the rest of the picture, including the huntsman, is more true to his English scenes.
(*Watercolour by S. Howlett, published London, 1813, by permission of the British Library.*)

'The most sought-after tiger from 1920 until 1930 was known in the United Provinces as 'The Bachelor of Powalgarth'. Here he is after being stalked on foot and shot by Jim Corbett who stands above him. This magnificent animal was l0' 7" when measured over curves.
(*Photo 1930, by permission of Oxford University Press.*)

This depiction of the attack by the 'monkey-like wildman' on the gold prospector and his boatmen, comes from Oscar Lindgren's book. It shows the three men in their cave with the Subansiri, to the right, flowing alongside.

▶ Only planters can talk shop all day; there must have been other attractions but none that they could think of apart from that all important topic, planting; whether the rains would continue for a month longer than they should, for their new plantings, or perhaps a new seed nursery that had been trampled and ruined a few nights ago by a large Sambhur; a close shave with a cobra and so on. Oscar Lindgren said of this nursery problem:

> These nurseries were a constant source of worry as they were nice and soft, and so were attractive to deer. These delighted in actually dancing on the bed at night. This night duty was added to my other work, resulting in the death of a number of Sambur deer, which were devoured by the coolies, being too coarse for my taste.

With the building of the first pukka club houses in the planting districts, came tennis courts, while someone at the Ooty Club in the hills of South India thought up the game of snooker, and before long many of the clubs had snooker tables. The cooler airs of Ootacamund and Darjeeling, both at over 6000 feet, were a temporary haven for the fever-stricken British, jaded by the heat of the plains – if they could get there, but most could not. A more sociable life was developing; the hard working, hard playing planter had arrived on the scene – for prior to that it was just pioneering – with an occasional game of polo and plenty of hunting and shooting.

The Club provided an opportunity for the planter to meet his fellow countrymen, and some relief from the daily grind of supervising jungle clearance together with the many tiresome tasks one would hardly imagine: forever holding court and sitting in judgement over the squabbles of his labour force; a chicken stolen, someone knifed or murdered in the lines, all had to be resolved, sometimes with the help of the police – if there were any, and during the early years there were not. I remember my father telling me of some strange happenings on, or adjacent to, my great uncle's rubber estate in Malaya during the 1880s, and that included murder for which no one was punished. The identity of the murderer (a European) was known to the local planters though he was never actually committed for trial in Singapore. Being out in the wilds had its dangers and its compensations – for some!

Talking of Clubs reminds me of the uses that a strong billiard table can be put to. Ex-Assam planter Kim Dodwell told me of a case of rabies, when a planter was bitten by a rabid dog. It was while this particular planter was at a club in Cachar, during the 1920s, that he had such a bad attack of uncontrollable convulsions that his fellow planters had to strap him down on a billiard table.

Whether in the mist-laden hills of Darjeeling, the Nilgiri Hills or the plains of Assam, the life was the same – all in the name of the tea camellia and 'two leaves and a bud'. During the 19th and 20th centuries the hard working Scotsman was everywhere in the East. Many came from a poor background and left Scotland for the wide world as engineers, railroad builders and planters.

Though most bachelors and married planters would not miss a Saturday at the Club, there were those who preferred to go out with gun and fishing rod while some took up entomology. The most famous naturalist planter was E. P. Gee, who made a study of the flora and fauna of the region. In 1953 he discovered a hitherto unknown species of monkey – the Golden Langur, *Presbitis geei*, in the foothills bordering Bhutan, 250 miles W-S-W of Pathalipam.

Nestling below the foothills in the churchyard at North Lakhimpur are the graves of three planters who had been drowned all together in the same capsized dug-out canoe. The small cemetery also contains the grave of Lycett Burd, who died from septicaemia after being mauled by a wounded tiger he had followed up in thick khagri at Pathalipam.

It was in this very region of North Lakhimpur - or rather in the foothills above Pathalipam - that a most singular happening took place a little over 120 years ago which I think you will agree is worth including, especially as it comes by way of an Assam planter.

An Historical Relation

Gold, Adventure and the Yeti on the Subansiri

The story concerns none other than our planter friend

Oscar Lindgren, in fact it is HIS story that I shall now relate. The story concerns a white gold prospector and a 'monkey-like wildman' on the Subansiri river. In the Sanskrit language the name Subansiri means Gold River.

Having planted tea in the employ of the Upper Assam Company since his arrival in the country in 1877 and completed his agreement with the company, Lindgren decided to forsake tea in order to take part in the railway 'boom' – for a while.

The year 1883 found Lindgren working as a sleeper-contractor for the new Dibru-Sadiya Railway. At first he employed his men felling jungle, cutting sleepers along the Dibooroo river and then floating them down to Dibrugarh, where the Chief Engineer, together with a few Europeans and a large labour force, were installed. The river front at Dibrugarh soon became a hive of activity with as many as four or five paddle-steamers, all with their flats laden with coolies, rails and heavy machinery, which were being discharged daily.

During later construction of the railroad and while working in the vicinity of Makum, near Tinsukia, Lindgren had in his charge eighteen elephants belonging to the railroad company which were used to extract timber from the jungle before sawing into sleepers. It is from this point that I relay this unusual account by Lindgren:

In 1883, whilst engaged in sleeper-cutting at Makum, a European, barefoot, came one day to my tent and politely asked if I could oblige him with a cup of tea. It was sufficiently startling to find a European in India with no shoes or socks, but the rest of his appearance was equally unexpected. His clothes were of thick material and unpleasantly heavy for a hot moist climate: they were worn so badly that portions of the man's skin were visible here and there, for of underclothes he seemed to have none. He wore no hat and his hair was long, shaggy and uncombed, which with a beard of outlandish dimensions gave him the appearance of one who had not seen civilization for many months.

Sitting inside my comfortable tent, and fortified by a meal washed down with draught beer, he told me his story, which I put down here as nearly as possible in his own words.

Story of the gold prospector.

I came to India about 18 months ago to work as a miner in the Assam Railway's coal mines at Margherita. I worked there for a

year, but disliked mining in such a climate, and resigned. The Company was prepared to send me back to England, but having heard that there was gold in the bed of the Subansiri river I prepared to go prospecting, having already had experience of such work in Australia. It is perhaps nine months since I started exploring Subansiri with two natives who have been with me until quite recently.

I went to Sadiya from Margherita and stayed there with the Postmaster taking care to remain hidden during the daytime, in case the authorities interfered with my plans. The Postmaster arranged for me two natives and a dug-out canoe, and one night we quietly dropped down the Brahmaputra and entered the Subansiri river.

We took things easy when going up river and stayed at villages on the banks, where we were always fed and entertained hospitably. We have slept under rocks, up trees and in caves, in fact anywhere safety seemed possible. In time we passed beyond the range of villages and reached rapids which prevented further use of the boat. We hid the boat in the jungle and proceeded on foot as best we could.

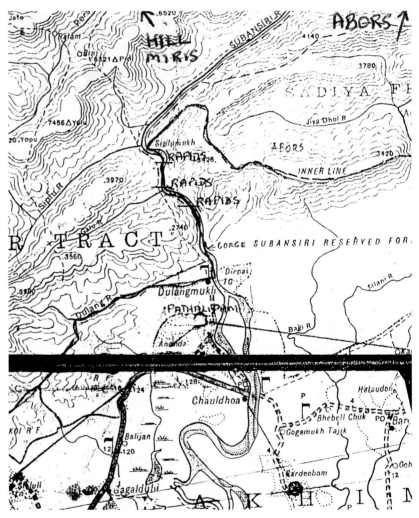

This map shows the route taken by the gold prospector in 1883 when, having left Dulungmukh on the plains, he and his men started to follow the fast flowing river on foot up through dense and steep forest, first circuiting the impassable gorge and then onwards to the first of the three rapids. (*Map courtesy J.L.C. Strang.*)

After a journey of some 70 miles across the plains the party would have entered the foothills above Pathalipam, where a succession of frightening and tremendous gorges – with vertical rock cliffs hundreds of feet high falling sheer into deep water – would have made for frequent detours away from the river course. Fresh-water dolphins and 'gharial' alligators fish the waters between the three lower rapids; herds of elephant move up incredibly steep slopes. Tiger, Ghoral and Methan too; all these and more were present 120 years ago. From such a place of natural beauty and wildness we continue Oscar Lindgren's narrative of the gold prospector's exploits:

> It was not for some time that we reached a place well inside the hills above a wide rapid where the sands were very rich indeed, and where there were occasional nuggets embedded in the quartz. We stayed there for several months collecting gold. So far there had been much hardship, but nothing had occurred to make me suppose that my trip would end anyhow but successfully.
>
> It is true that one of the natives had said for some time that we were being followed and watched by a monkey-like wild man, but I had taken little notice of this, not believing such a thing possible. But as a precaution and to reassure my companions, we had fortified the entrance of the cave in which we lodged, and a fire of driftwood which was very plentiful was kept burning at night by the stone barricade.
>
> One morning, very early, the wild man, or whatever he was, attacked the cave. I happened to be awake and had time to seize my rifle and fire whilst he was on top of the barricade. The invader dropped, wounded, and was hacked to pieces by the two natives. To this day I do not know if he was man or beast. Perhaps he was a bit of both. My companions made such a mess of him in their anxiety to make certain of killing him that it would have taken a scientist to decide exactly what this monster and terrifying invader really was.
>
> The wild man was cut into pieces, which were thrown into the river and so carried away.
>
> After this startling encounter my companions refused to remain longer where we were, and I was prevailed upon to push higher up the river.
>
> Proceeding up river and washing as we went, a fair quantity of gold was recovered, and we were not molested further for some weeks.
>
> We had all regained full confidence when it was disturbed one morning by the appearance of savage looking men on the opposite bank of the river. Their intentions were obvious from the fact that their arrows were falling thickly in our encampment.

Having escaped down river to the plains and then on to the confluence of the Subansiri, Brahmaputra rivers, the prospector and his two boatmen eventually reached Dibrugarh, where we will return to the story:

> I lost my way in the forests, and after wandering about and steering roughly for Margherita by the sun, by chance I came upon your clearing and at once sought you out.

Lindgren concludes this somewhat shortened story by saying:

> Such was the story of this extraordinary man. After some persuasion he produced two gold nuggets each about the size of a pigeon's egg. And these satisfied me that his story was at least satisfactorily correct.
>
> After thanking me, and being shown how to reach Margherita by following the railway trace, the man passed on and I never saw him again.

It is hoped the reader will forgive my going on a bit, but now comes the important part – the explanation, the theory, call it what you will, regarding the monkey-like wild man; was it, just possibly, a Yeti?

It is interesting to know that in 1946 an expedition was made, from England, to investigate this very region through which the Subansiri flows. The area chosen was a five or six acre swamp in a river valley some six miles into the foothills and about four miles west of the Subansiri, near the Siplu river. Reports had been received of some unusual tracks in the reeds that could not possibly have been made by elephant, Mithan or Gaur. Expedition members found no evidence of any such animal.

In this part of the foothills Miri tribesmen live higher up, to the west of the Subansiri, while the Abors live in the interior forests to the east of the river. It was undoubtedly one or other of these hill tribes that attacked the gold prospector of long ago.

It is said that another hill tribe, the Daflas, used to sacrifice virgin girls to the creature in order to please their gods. Their descriptions of this custom are very variable, handed down over many years. Such a creature might well live in a cave, indeed the cave in which the gold prospector stayed might have been its lair.

It is also a fact that the national emblem of Bhutan is the Migoi (Yeti), which has been depicted on that country's postage stamps in the past. Furthermore, it is known that the Everest mountaineers Eric Shipton and Lord Hunt photographed some extremely large and odd-shaped footprints which they came upon in snow when climbing in Nepal. These footprints can only have been made by a large biped, the scale of which is clearly seen in the photographs, when one can compare them with the ice-pick which had been placed beside them for comparison.

India investigates Bigfoot sightings

Authorities in India are to investigate claims by terrified villagers that "bigfoot" hairy giants are roaming the jungles of the remote northeast.

The creatures have been spoken of, and occasionally spotted, for years, but a rise in the number of sightings over the past month has prompted authorities to look into the matter further in the Garo hills area of Medhalaya state.

Daily Telegraph 2007.

The man-eater of Garhwal

HUMAN BEINGS KILLED
BY THE CHOWGARH MAN-EATER

Village	Number
THALI	1
DEBGURA	1
BARHON	2
CHAMOLI	6
KAHOR	1
AM	2
DALKANIA	7
LOHAR	8
AGHAURA	2
PAHARPANI	1
PADAMPURI	2
TANDA	1
NESORIYA	1
JHANGAON	1
KABRAGAON	1
KALA AGAR	8
RIKHAKOT	1
MATELA	3
KUNDAL	3
BABYAR	1
KHANSIUN	1
GARGARI	1
HAIRAKHAN	2
UKHALDHUNGA	1
PAKHARI	1
DUNGARI	2
GALNI	3
TOTAL	**64**

ANNUAL TOTALS

1926	15 KILLED
1927	9 KILLED
1928	14 KILLED
1929	17 KILLED
1930	9 KILLED
TOTAL	**64**

Human beings killed by the Chowgarh man-eater

The Chowgarh man-eater held sway over hundreds of square miles of mountain and valley for a period of five years before it was finally brought to book by Jim Corbett, on 11th April 1930. He said, after examination: 'The tigress's claws were broken, and bushed out, and one of her canine teeth was broken, and her front teeth were worn down to the bone. It was these defects that had made her a man-eater'.

(Photo of the Bachelor of Powalgarth and details on this page are from The Man-Eaters of Kumaon by Jim Corbett, published by Oxford University Press, London, 1944.)

'Another sound came through the night, a sound that made me catch my breath sharply, a sound that was like a whining groan starting on a low note, rising then falling away in ghastly cadence.

Tiger!'

Discounting the evidence of the footprints for a moment, it would seem obvious that such a creature does NOT live in the snow regions, where it has supposedly been seen by mountaineers and others, but was MIGRATING over the high snows from one FOREST REGION to another. What could possibly sustain a large and presumably slow moving bi-pedal creature at high elevations in snow? Far more likely it is a deep forest dweller like a gorilla or an Orang, but not arboreal. 'Orang Utan' comes from the Malay language and means literally 'wild man of forest'.

Lord Hunt, who led the successful British expedition to climb Mount Everest in 1953, believes there is such a creature but that it just has to be found. If indeed it does exist it may well have migrated, many years ago, eastwards to the dense untrodden forests of western China.

The Tiger in India

The vast sub-continent of India was the playground of the tiger; it reigned supreme and was both admired and feared by all. Deaths in India over the years, by tiger alone, were numberless, yet the human is not sought as prey, or food, but the occasional tiger becomes a man-eater because it is old, wounded or finds – sometimes by sheer accident – that humans are easy prey and develops a taste for human flesh; it is then a very dangerous animal.

To go with the delightfully mischievous drawing by the renowned 19th-century watercolour artist, Samuel Howlett (p.76), here are some interesting facts relating to the tiger in days of yore, for alas we all know the fate of this beautiful animal today. If you should wonder what tigers have to do with tea, ask any old planter from India – if you can find one – or indeed any villager who is of a certain age, and he will probably tell you that the tiger was a most natural phenomenon.

During the early years of the Tea industry in north, south and north-east India, when the order of the day was fell, burn and clear the jungle, the wild animals came in direct contact with those working on the plantations. The local natives paid due respect to the tiger but the newcomers and many Government officials did not; they shot them whenever they could, for sport. Naturally it took revenge on many of these sportsmen, but the dice were loaded against it when huge tiger hunts took place with hundreds of beaters driving the tigers towards the guns of sportsmen perched in the relative safety of a howdah on the backs of trusty elephants. Jim Corbett was no such man.

Of course Assam had its share of tigers but if any part of India could be termed famous for this splendid animal then the Kumaon might spring to mind, simply because of the exploits of that great shikari, Jim Corbett. He, with his faithful old dog, Robin – always at his side no matter what danger – hunted down, on foot, many man-eaters. Major Jim Corbett's courage is not doubted in his campaign to rid dozens of small hill villages of the scourge of man-eating tigers during those now distant years; his name lives on with the village folk of the United Provinces. The Corbett National Park perpetuates his name – a sanctuary for tiger and wildlife.

The East India Company had considered the Kumaon and neighbouring hill districts, at elevations of between 4000 and 6000 feet, suitable to establish its stock of China tea plants, which had been germinated from the original importation of seed brought from China to Calcutta by G. J. Gordon, in 1835. Though 20,000 of the young China plants were dispatched from Calcutta to various places in the Kumaon, in 1836, the region proved to be too far north in latitude, with insufficient rainfall, and these importations had only limited success in the years that followed. The tiger had no such problems in this part of the world, where none other than the Champawat man-eater held sway at a somewhat later date.

This particular tiger had killed 200 human beings in Nepal before being driven out by armed Nepalese; moving just across the border into the Kumaon district in north-west India, it continued to kill a further 234 villagers in this beautiful part of the world where tea gardens are interspersed with fruit orchards in clear sight of snow-capped mountains. A well-known Shikari in the district had been deputed by Government to shoot the man-eater, but without success. So it was that the Deputy Commissioner of Naini Tal enlisted the help of Jim Corbett to take over.

The tigress, as it later turned out to be, held the hill people in constant terror and fear of this roaming Shaitan (Devil). The villages vary in size and population from a hundred souls to a small family of two. Footpaths over hills and through thick forest connect the villages. The fact that the tigress's domain extended over a hundred square miles of hills, that it never killed twice in the same locality and hardly ever returned to her kill, undoubtedly led to her long life and escape from those who sought her skin.

Having received a report of the killing of a young girl outside the village of Pali, Corbett decided to base himself at Champawat village, some fifteen miles distant; this was to prove fatal for the tigress.

One more villager would die before Jim Corbett followed up and shot the Champawat man-eater, whose infamous tally of 436 victims is included in the *Guinness Book of Records*.

Tigers are good swimmers and (changing countries) are known to have swum from the mainland in Malaya across to the island of Penang, to hunt for pigs. My father told me that he once rowed across from the mainland to the island in a dinghy and saw quite a few sharks, but no tigers! A tiger that is a man-eater, will kill by night or day when the opportunity arises, lying up in the jungle fringe close to a paddy field where villagers are working, collecting water or firewood – a slow stalk, the merest rustle of a leaf, a quick dash that ends in a choking scream. A few bones, threads of clothing and trinkets are all that the victim's family may find. Such pitiful remains, such as a few fragments of bone, are collected up by relatives of the family and carried to the banks of a nearby stream for cremation, so that the ashes may be carried down to the sacred waters of Mother Ganges.

J. Fayrer, writing in his book *The Royal Bengal Tiger*, gives some astonishing figures compiled from Chief Commissioner's Reports of the Central Provinces of India during the 1860s which provide very accurate sources of information.

> In one instance, in the Central Provinces, a single tigress caused the desertion of thirteen villages, and two hundred and fifty square miles of country were thrown out of cultivation. This state of things would undoubtedly have continued, but for the timely arrival of a gentleman who happily was fortunate enough, with the aid of his gun, to put an end to her eventful career.

From another Government Report it is interesting to know that as many people were killed by wolves, as tigers:

> In Lower Bengal alone Government Reports show that in the six years ending 1866, 13,400 human beings were killed by wild animals: 4218 persons were killed by tigers, 1407 by leopards,

4287 by wolves and the remainder by other animals.

The remainder probably being those killed by bear, elephant, buffalo and snakes.

From another Report – almost a hundred years later in 1949 – 7396 deaths were due to snake bite alone in India. So it will be seen that during the pioneering years of the Tea industry in India, when hundreds of plantations were being opened, the jungle was a dangerous place to be for all those concerned, quite apart from the hill villagers throughout the country; who amongst us today could say that this was not so?

Returning to north-east India, one of the biggest clubs in the Assam tea district was the Jorhat Club, which is situated within a stone's throw of the Tea Research Association's Tocklai Experimental Station. During World War II, the T.R.A.'s Guest House and some of the bungalows on the station were occupied by units of the British and American armies, in those dark days when Japanese forces came so close.

Planters' wives would organize club activities including tea and tennis matches, as well as dances, with often a live band playing into the small hours. This sounds wonderful until one realizes that in many parts of Assam planters and their wives were often marooned on their gardens for months on end during the Rains. The consequence of this was that when they

The Victoria Memorial, Calcutta. (*Photo C.A.W. 1985.*)

did meet up a lively evening was had by all.

On occasion the need arose to find a new cook. Many a planter's wife will have received a note or letter written by another planter or his wife, often many years earlier – brought and presented to her on a silver salver saying:'The bearer of this note has served me for two years to his complete satisfaction. If you are thinking of giving him a berth, be sure to make it a wide one'. Sometimes such notes were handed around for years by the proud owners and travelled many miles with the said cook doing his best to earn an honest living in his chosen profession – while never, somehow, finding a billet!

By the 1930s, and after almost a hundred years of hard pioneering in the field and in the factory, during which time the Indian Tea industry had become a goliath in the world production of tea, life on the tea gardens throughout India was the envy of all. This would seem to be a good place to slip in a poem:

Planter's Poems – The Search

There was a Burra Sahib of Assam
Who said, 'What a fine fellow I am
By ingenious devices
I get wonderful prices
Tea planting is money for jam'.
Hearing this they tried hard in Cachar,
And you know what fine fellows they are,
They dried and fermented,
Withered to percentage,
But the 'char' is the catch in Cachar.
They had a go at it, too, in Sylhet
Who the stalwarts were there I forget,
They had peculiar names,
Such as Havering Hames,
And MacDougall, McQuackle, McBeth.
There came a loud cry from the Dooars,
'Their teas are inferior to ours'
By the middle of August
This cry was less raucous,
Owing, they said, to continual showers.
There was a young man from Terai
Who joined in the hue and cry,
His wonderful experiment
Created much merriment
As his average went down by a pie.
So they approached a big wig in Darjeeling
Who was looking on with superior feeling
'Tell us', they hissed
'before we're dismissed
How to raise our price by a shilling'.
He said 'Ha-ha' and 'He-he'
'and why do you come bothering me
I advise you to try
The blokes at Tocklai
They are the fellows to see'.
The Pundits there said 'It is a matter of toil,
Constant watch less the bacteria spoil
The whole kibosh'
(voice from the back) 'what bosh'
You've surely forgotten the soil.
This led to a great argument
One Pundit was heard to lament
There's no use denying
One valley's not trying'
So receiving no answer they went.
Now Brokers and Planters should find
Some help in this solution of mine.
When you were created and me
Were created the Districts of Tea
Good, after their *own particular* kind.

(Burra Sahib = Big Master)
The Assam Review 1931

The Aeroplane

From Keyhung Estate to Calcutta in 6 hours!

The arrival of the motor car, the aeroplane and with it the construction of a number of small airstrips, did much to open out the vast tea growing region in Assam, which is almost the size of Czechoslovakia. These modes of transport suddenly brought the remotest gardens within 7 or 8 hours flying time from Calcutta. The early pioneers had their dreams of reaching the 'big city' in a record breaking six weeks, but those dreams only included the elephant, over the first few miles, and then the native country boat, going down with the current – the sky was strictly for birds.

A young man out from Britain would first become an Assistant, and after a period of between five and ten years, depending upon vacancies and retirement of senior staff within the company, would then become a Manager or Superintendent. Then, for some of the more senior staff, the next stage in their career would be to become a Visiting Agent who, as the title implies, visited and reported upon the condition and state of other tea gardens.

Continuity was good for both the smooth running of the garden and for the labour force, whose children grew up with someone they all knew, and in most cases liked and respected. The modern practice is for Indian Managers and Assistants to move from one garden to another every few years, which is unsettling for everyone concerned.

After a lifetime in tea – for most it was 35 years – came that final voyage back to the old country and retirement, where he had little else to do but talk about the good old days. This was when, having passed through the many stages in life, he would consider himself the happiest of mortals to become a Director and get on the Board of his old Tea Company; and yet, his real dreams were of the days when he was a young Chota Sahib, with his ponies. Ah, well!

After the war, tea companies took on hundreds of British Assistants to replace those who did not return, also to replace the many retiring older men who had stayed on past retirement age to run the estates during hostilities. Labour trouble also increased on estates in Assam, compared to previous years, while in Darjeeling and the Dooars tea districts the troubles were severe, ▶

Dry season. The Brahmaputra from the Belle Vue Hotel, Gauhati,
Assam. Brahminy Kites, with buffaloes on a sand bar.
(*Photo C.A.W. 1985.*)

Our Assamese driver – Krishna Temple. (*Photo C.A.W. 1985.*)

with many planters beaten up and one, to my knowledge, killed by his labour force. Before Independence most of the tea companies were British owned and the labour force on all the estates regarded the Burra and Chota Sahibs almost like God. However, big changes were to come about.

After Independence

With Independence, on the 15th of August 1947, came a slow but gradual change due to various factors.

Since the last British planters left India, Club life has gone on much the same as it did before and nationals continue to hit the ball hard, play tennis and golf and, of course, watch television which might make an old tea hand turn in his grave; sitting down watching something move on a small box – far better to go out with rod, rifle and hound. Today, the wives of planters are very active and do a great deal for the estate labour, as well as for village welfare.

One of the original 'named tea tracts', KEYHUNG, which was worked by pioneer C.A.Bruce during the late 1830s, was to be the stamping ground of one of the last British planters in the region, Chris Allen, who left in 1982. Now, he and other retired tea men can meet up once a year at the Eastbourne Reunion and talk about the good old days in Assam.

In November 1962 China invaded India, from Tibet, their troops coming down through the mountainous region of Arunachal Pradesh on the North Bank of the Brahmaputra. Planters' wives and many of the planters were evacuated to Calcutta until the Chinese withdrew after a week or so. During this period many planters left Assam to seek employment elsewhere.

In 1966 the Rupee was devalued and between sixty and seventy percent of British planters left the country. Many had been born in India, sent home for education in England, and returned to carry on doing what their fathers and grandfathers had done. For some of those 'returning home' it was often harder as they hardly knew the old country. During these times of changeover, the British planter could still remit money from India to the U.K. but at an unfavourable exchange rate. Then came the Indianisation of Sterling Tea Companies when they were allowed to retain 74% of the Rupee share holding, and this took until 1977 to finalise.

During the late 1970s the United Liberation Front of Assam (ULFA) started its activities. ULFA wanted tea companies to transfer their headquarters to Assam so that their profits might be invested in the State. These troubles continued spasmodically and in 1990 and 1991 intimidation and threats of violence towards staff and labourers on estates were frequent; some were assaulted and others kidnapped for ransom.

In 1989 Assam had yet more troubles, this time coming from Bodoland. Here, in the tea-growing region on the North Bank of the Brahmaputra, the tribal Bodos had been active, cutting rail links and closing down government offices and killing over a hundred local people. From their past experience in poaching in the Manas Tiger Reserve, they had become expert in the use of firearms and guerrilla tactics. To meet this threat the Indian Government greatly increased the number of soldiers in this region where the many tribal people want to create Bodoland as a separate State. In November 1990 Assam was placed under direct Indian government rule in an attempt to end the escalation of terrorism which was destroying the State's tea industry.

However, the situation in this vast region in the State of Assam is continually changing and sometimes there are better years, but in others more serious flare-ups occur.

A journey through other Indian tea estates, tea research and other travels

The family of the man who helped us locate the old China tea trees, grouped in front of their dwelling house with walls of mud and ekra. (*Photo C.A.W. 1985.*)

Tocklai

Tocklai was established at Jorhat Assam in 1911 and is the oldest and largest tea research station in the world.

Photos courtesy Tocklai

The station's guest house where visiting planters stay while on refresher courses. (*Photo C.A.W. 1985.*)

100-year-old sturdy tea bushes after pruning.
(*Photographed by C.A.W. in 1985.*)

A trial area with mature tea seed bearers. (*Photo by C.A.W. 1985.*)

Tea pests and diseases

The entomology department contains beautifully made wooden display cabinets with sliding drawers containing lepidoptera mounted and labelled for future reference. Specimens, in insect or larvae form, are predators of the tea plant, its leaf, roots and stems, as well as the various trees that are grown to shade the tea. A dedicated band of scientists live within the attractive complex.

Entomology Department. (*Photo courtesy Tocklai.*)

The laboratory, research in progress.
(*Photo courtesy Tocklai.*)

A large library contains countless reference books on tea.
(*Photo courtesy Tocklai.*)

Chubwa Tea Estate

Was originally worked and developed by pioneer Charles Alexander Bruce, in 1837, from rich tracts of indigenous tea plants that he found growing in the dense jungles of upper Assam.

Once planted, the tea camellia does not readily give up its tenacious hold on mother earth.

Names of Tea tracts fully worked in 1838.	Length and breadth of Tea tracts.	Number of plants in each Tea tract.	Average produce of single Tea plants.	Produce in 1838.	Remarks.
No. 1 Tringri,	267 by 90	5,000	4 Sa. Weight,	260 Seers	
No. 2 Tringri,	155 by 70	2,340	3-12 Sa. Wt.,	160 ,,	
No. 1 Kahung,	480 by 210	1,36,000	1 Sa. Weight,	680 ,,	
No. 1 Chubwa,	200 by 160	8,200	1 Sa. Weight,	410 ,,	The plants are
Deenjoy,......	223 by 171	8,400	2 Sa. Weight,	210 ,,	small in this tract including China plants.
				1,720	
From Shady Tracts, ..	..	..	..	390	
				2,110	
The probable increase of the above Tracts for 1839. .. 527					
Probable produce of 1839. .... 2,637 Seers				5,274 lbs.	

The number of indigenous tea plants referred to above found growing in their wild state were, as found, cut down to 3ft to form bushes and that constituted a tea tract. The size of the tea tract is in yards. The table is from Bruce's Report on the Extent & Produce of Tea Plantations in Assam, 1839. *(By permission of the British Library.)*

A part of the original planting of China jat tea, the plants having been taken from the Government's nursery at Sadiya, near Kundilmukh and then put out 6ft x 6ft by Bruce on Chubwa in 1837. After being plucked for 100 years the tea bushes were abandoned in 1935 and have, over the intervening years, grown up (arrowed) and been cut down regularly by the villagers for firewood. The man with the bow and arrows proved his ability by hitting and removing from its branch a berry at about 15 yards – a lucky shot, I think not.
(Photo 1985 by C.A.W.)

The entrance to Chubwa Tea Estate. *(Photo 1985 by C.A.W.)*

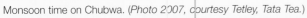
Monsoon time on Chubwa. (*Photo 2007, courtesy Tetley, Tata Tea.*)

Evidence of the hardy tea bush

The entrance to Jaipur tea estate in upper Assam.

When Bruce came this way there was heavy jungle throughout the region, with the attendant dangers of wild animals and hostile hill tribesmen.

Jaipur Tea Estate

The first experimental steps in the tea industry were taken when these China tea plants were put out – as seed – at Jaipur about 1837 by Charles Alexander Bruce, pioneer of the tea industry in India.

The marble slab was erected in 1937 to commemorate the centenary of the plantings by Bruce.
(*Photos 1985 by C.A.W.*)

Jaipur Tea Estate. This field of Assam hybrid tea is directly adjacent to the block of China tea put out by Bruce in 1837. Pluckers carry firewood back to their lines. (*Photos C.A.W. taken in 1985.*)

C.A. Bruce

Bruce states in his 1893 'Report on the manufacture of tea' written while residing in the jungles around Jaipur that:

'The China black tea plants which were brought into Muttock in 1837, amounted in all to 1609 – healthy and sickly. Many of the plants were then in flower, and had small seeds. They are about three feet high, and were loaded with fruit last year.

I collected about twenty-four pounds of the China seeds, and sowed some on the hill of Tipum in my tea garden, and some in the nursery-ground at Jaipur; above three thousand of which have come up, are looking beautiful, and doing very well.'

… and so they still are today, 170 years later!

C. A. Bruce, Etching executed *c*1850.
(*Courtesy Jeanette King-Harman.*)

93

Nalani Tea Garden, upper Assam. Plenty of flat land; a newly planted clearing of tea and shade trees infinitely suitable for employing mechanical tea harvesters.
(*Photo by permission of the British Library.*)

Calcutta – A Visit to Tea Country, 1985

Our intention was to locate and photograph the original China tea plants that had been planted out by the pioneer of India's tea industry, C. A. Bruce, at Chubwa and Jaipur estates in upper Assam in the year 1838. This tea had been photographed last by W. H. Ukers about a hundred years later, during the early 1930s, just after the bushes had been abandoned from plucking and the photograph was shown in his book *All About Tea*, published in 1935. Though various writers have mentioned the existence of these old China tea bushes, by reference to Ukers's writings on the subject, the exact whereabouts of those on Chubwa Estate, whether dead or alive, was not known – even to those in the tea industry in India, as it turned out.

Being quite unaware of the unsettled state of the country in upper Assam in 1985, my wife and I thought it would be a challenge to go and see if we could find these very old tea bushes, a part of India's tea history. It was 50 years since Ukers saw, photographed and left this old abandoned tea to continue his wanderings throughout the tea countries of the world; would we find them? We decided we would – if they were still living.

Calcutta hits you, as it always will. The streets would undoubtedly be a Grand Prix race circuit for everything that moved on wheels were it not for the obstacles. Whereas one does not expect to see cows and dogs wandering across the streets in the western world, here it is a common sight. Apart from a predominance of antiquated transport of all kinds, the slow ubiquitous bullock cart and its apparently unharassed driver – forever twitching his stick and grunting at the unfortunate animal – add greatly to the confusion.

Our taxi pulled up with a screech outside the hotel, which looked decidedly promising on account of its plush-looking interior foyer and a very smart Sikh doorman, who gave us a decent salute and a beaming smile. Depositing our scanty luggage at the reception desk and, having exchanged a few travellers' cheques for a bundle of Rupee notes, we found a couple of chairs and took the weight off our feet.

There seemed to be many tourists coming and going all the time and the whole place was a bustle of activity. Most interesting of all the travellers to observe are those in large groups who, having staggered off the airport bus, actually manage to walk the intervening twenty yards to the hotel reception desk, where couriers fuss around them like bees around a jar of honey.

Some of the new arrivals lose no time at all in descending heavily into large comfy chairs, where, perspiring profusely, they immediately light up cigarettes and call in loud voices for drinks; not that they have to shout too loudly as the hotel staff are always in very close attendance.

While reclining in one of those very same large and comfortable chairs, fortified after the dust of our filthy taxi journey with two large ice-cool drinks of lemon juice at £2 apiece, our attention is taken by yet another incoming group. There is something very odd about this group of humans; no, *singular* is the word. We watch them closely, about forty in number, as they stand along the entire length of the reception desk. They have a sober appearance, are well dressed – in an old fashioned way – but are quiet, almost dignified, which is an unusual trait in such a crowd. The situation intrigues me and I fall to wondering where on earth I have seen their like before. The truth is, I haven't; they are Russians – Russian tourists!

The next influx of tourists is a smaller group of Americans who proceed, amidst some confusion, to 'clock in' at the reception desk. They move over noisily *en masse* to a smart boutique by the lift, just where we are sitting, where black-haired, brown-eyed assistants expertly sum up their potential customers. The women in the party all appear to be interested in the jewellery, and we hear one of them say 'These rings aren't glass, are they?' Many customers had taught the assistants to lie with consummate ease, and with a condescendingly sly smile one of them says, 'Oh no Madam, these very good quality emerald rings'. Since the lady mentions it, they do look uncommonly like glass – and for 50 Rupees and 50 cents too! Likewise, the gold trinkets look uncommonly like brass, but you would think they were not so in a hotel of this fame; perhaps that is the reason such boutiques do so well!

Up to Assam

At the airport next morning we awaited our flight up to Assam, travelling first to Gauhati, where we would stay the night, and then on, via Tezpur, to Jorhat.

During a long wait for a delayed flight due to fog, and while killing time exploring the vast airport hall, we met a very nice couple with their small children who turned out to be Pranab Barua, the General Manager of Brooke Bond India Ltd. and his wife. They were also bound for Gauhati and then on to visit the Game Reserve at Kazaringa. Imagine our surprise meeting a 'tea man' so early in our travels,

The Baruas were extremely helpful when we eventually landed at Gauhati, calming over-zealous airport officials, who looked upon our Assam entry permits with great suspicion, as our final destination was to the restricted region to the north. Having found a taxi for us, which we were to share with an Indian couple who were also going to stay at the Belle Vue Hotel in Gauhati, we said our goodbyes to the Barua family. We little dreamed that we would meet Pranab Barua when we were returning from Madras three weeks later. Our luggage having been lost, he again came to our rescue, at midnight, at Calcutta airport. This gave me a very good impression of the staff at Brooke Bond, and we decided henceforth to drink their tea. Besides, I do like monkeys, as my parents had had a pet one when planting in Malaya when I was young.

Arriving at the Belle Vue Hotel, the cockroaches that scuttled across the bedroom floor were, as we later learned from Claude and Ginny Godwin, past Chairman of Lipton, all part of the of the accommodation. Perched on the top of a hill the hotel was noted for its views of the Brahmaputra.

The flight onwards was by Fokker Friendship aircraft to Tezpur, on the north bank of the Brahmaputra. Here, Mig Fighters of the Indian Air Force were constantly landing and taking off, as this North East Frontier region had been a troubled zone since the Chinese invaded in 1962. India and China contest their border as the latter rejects the McMahon Line drawn between British India and Tibet in 1914. The Indian State of Arunachal Pradesh, which borders on the south the plains of Assam, is claimed by China.

Jorhat

Tocklai Experimental Station

Arriving at Jorhat airport we were spotted by a couple of policemen and escorted to the police station. The station, a sort of wood Dak-type bungalow with a corrugated iron roof and steps leading up to a verandah, was surrounded by a dusty compound in which several mangy looking dogs lay around under trees. Inside, the Inspector sat at a very impressive desk.

Our permits and letters of introduction to the Tea Research Association in Jorhat being in order, a police car was soon speeding to the Tea Research Association's Tocklai Experimental Station. After meeting the Director, Dr. B. Banerjee, in his office, we made our way across well-cut lawns and past a pond to the Station's Guest House which was to be our headquarters. Here, we arranged for an Assamese driver to take us up to Chubwa and Jaipur estates the next morning. The Director had previously arranged for us to be 'looked after' by the Station entomologist, Bipul Gope, who would accompany us on our travels in upper Assam. This serious young man had an old fashioned way about him and was to prove an excellent companion who, with the older driver, formed a likeable pair of 'keepers'. At that time the region was in a state of unrest, with severe friction between the Central Government and the Assam Government. In fact these troubles were to increase over the years, both on the tea estates and in Bodoland, where Bodo tribesmen would become increasingly hostile to local government rule, blowing up buses and engaging in a spate of killings.

Riding type tea harvester. For greater efficiency could this monster ever replace the traditional plucker in the tea fields of Assam in the 2lst century? With a capacity of 10 bags, each holdir g 20–25 Kgs, the total weight of green leaf collected at one time is 200–250 kgs. (Pf oto 1998, courtesy Matsumoto Kiko Co. Ltd., Japan.)

In Search of the Original China Tea

Knowing we had a full day's drive ahead of us we left the station soon after sunrise. We had decided to go up to Dibrugarh, passing through Sibsager and then turn eastwards to Tinsukia, from where we would be within easy striking distance of Chubwa and Jaipur estates.

Arriving at Tinsukia as it was almost dark we rashly chose to stay the night in the wrong 'hotel' – not that there was any choice. The reader who has come this far will already have learnt, in the previous chapter, of the misfortune that befell us at this dwelling house.

On a cold but beautiful morning we set off for Chubwa Tea Estate which, with Jaipur, which we will visit later, was the scene of C. A. Bruce's early activities at the commencement of the tea industry during the late 1830s; one could say his old stamping ground, but a very different and more dangerous place in those far off days when there were no roads and thick jungle everywhere. It should be remembered that he was almost a thousand miles from Calcutta – in those days over three months travel.

Turning off the road we entered Chubwa Estate and after a drive along a fine avenue of shade trees, flanked by tea, the car pulled up in front of the Manager's bungalow. The chung-type bungalow, built in the early 1900s, was comfy but sparse inside; with bedrooms leading off from an attractive balcony verandah, a generous sitting and dining room – it would have been quite a palace to Bruce. His basha would have been similar to that of the busti wallah's dwelling, that is, if he was lucky – very lucky!

After a cup of tea with the manager and his wife, we left for the factory where he enlisted the help of a couple of old factory workers and then, leaving him in peace, our little party started off on foot in search of the site of the original planting of China tea plants; these tea bushes had last been photographed by W. H. Ukers in 1934, just after this tea area had been abandoned; now, no one knew anything of their whereabouts – would we be able to find them?

On such a morning it soon became hot but pleasant work exploring the estate boundaries, which seemed a likely place to look. After about three hours tramping the boundaries we had quite a following. Local villagers, young and old, came out to see the two white faces and enquire what we were doing, where had we come from and where were we going; what was our occupation and were we very rich. Were we married and if so the number of children, their sex and ages, and if not married, why not. Sometime later, Gope, who had been in earnest discussion with another group of villagers, came over and excitedly said, 'I think we have found them, this old man remembers the old China type tea bushes when they were being plucked when he was a small boy and they were part of Chubwa.'

Ahead of us on a patch of neglected land overgrown with tree saplings were the tea trees, not easily recognizable at first at a distance, but yes it *was* the original tea – a part of India's history. The Tocklai scientist pronounced the tea trees to be of the China jat (type), with its characteristic small leaf.

Abandoned during the 1930s, the tea trees had since been cut down every five years or so for firewood, after the land had been handed over to the villagers under the Land Sealing Act. The stocks of the old trees, as placed, are approximately 6 feet by 6 feet apart. This small block of original China tea should have been preserved, by keeping it in plucking, as had Bruce's other China plantings at Jaipur Estate.

We drove back to Tinsukia that day happy in the thought that, having come 5000 miles, we had found what we were looking for – with the help of the villagers and our ever helpful scientist from the Tea Research Institute at Tocklai.

Before leaving Tinsukia the following morning we visited the beautiful Krishna Temple, or Shiva Dham. The Temple has a central pond in which there is a statue of Lord Shiva and this is surrounded by a fine marble colonnade and murals which give the Temple an exotic appearance.

On the road to Jaipur we passed through famous Keyhung Tea Estate, the scene of some early pioneering by Bruce. This estate was one of the last to have a British Manager, Chris Allen, who, after thirty years in tea, left Assam in 1981. At Jaipur Estate, unlike Chubwa, the original plantings of China tea have been preserved. This small block of tea, now surrounded on all sides by fields of large, broad-leafed Assam hybrids, is still growing strongly and is plucked, on average, 25 rounds a year. Our pictures on pages 92 and 93 tell the story.

Standing in the middle of these very old and sturdy China bushes one feels a sense of history. What would Charles Bruce have thought if he could have known that almost 150 years later (in 1985) his tea would still be yielding its leaf. One also knew that here, at the outset of the East India Company's operations, there was dense heavy tree jungle everywhere and that Assam, in those dark days, was a truly dreadful place for tigers.

It was time to leave. We sped southwards, passing through Nazira and arrived back at the Tocklai Station in the late evening. It is sad to record that when we visited the Nazira cemetery, which contains the graves of many of the Assam Company's staff, most of the tombstones lay unseen under impenetrable undergrowth – so much for some of the pioneers of India's great tea industry.

Return to Tocklai

Tocklai is an experimental station *par excellence*. The tea camellia, like all our garden plants, has its diseases and this danger is multiplied in any form of monoculture. There is a great deal more to the industry than the mere plucking of leaf and its manufacture into tea. The importance of research cannot be overestimated.

For everyone in the industry there is always that nasty business of Pests and Diseases, and to meet this threat the Tocklai Experimental Station was opened in 1911. The early pioneers of the tea industry had little time for such thoughts as other gigantic battles occupied their daily lives. At the Research Station every aspect of tea is studied from its growth, production and manufacture to the propagation of high yielding clonal tea. The station stands on land that once belonged to the Jorehaut Company, which was founded in 1858. Gradually, over the years, buildings have been added to house the various scientific departments and these include a small experimental factory where various types of tea machinery are tried out and developed. Among these was McKercher's invention of the C.T.C. machine which can supplement or replace the orthodox tea roller which has been used in tea factories for well over a hundred years; the C.T.C. machine crushes, tears and curls the leaf.

Machinery! No doubt this subject is a bit of a bore for the reader and tea drinker, but such comparatively new inventions are essential to the continuing progress of a huge worldwide industry. As tea drinkers we should not forget that each one of us will drink approximately 90,000 cups of tea in our lifetime – over the age of ten, that is. Statistics, well, one has to include some in a book, just to keep the boffins happy!

In the main typing pool there is an army of typists, for with over a million acres of tea in India, letters in answer to queries about pests and diseases go out to estates all over the country every working day; the station's filing system is second to none – inherited from the British. The scientific staff includes microbiologists, biochemists, entomologists and plant physiologists, each with an intimate knowledge of his subject.

The Indian Tea Industry has, from its early days, provided enormous quantities of tea seed – both China and Assam jats – to other countries to start their own tea industries, naturally at a price.

At Tocklai Experimental Station, every known pest and disease of tea – and there are scores – is studied and if a remedy is not at hand one is sought with which to wage an ever continuing war against such beauties as the Cockchafer grub, the attacks of Red spider mites or the wind-blown spores of Blister Blight. All very uninteresting to the tea drinker, but to the industry that provides our daily cup of tea it is of the utmost importance.

This labour intensive industry provides employment for in the region of one and a quarter million estate workers, and if all those who work in tea-related jobs are included, approximately one and a half million people depend upon the tea industry for a living in India.

During the monsoon in Assam the leaf growth is so rapid the bushes must be plucked every six days or so. Hand plucking has been the mode from the early years.

P. R. Longley, who was planting in Assam and the Dooars from 1920 until 1950, mentions what must have been an early attempt – in the late 1940s – in the preparation of a field of old tea for mechanical harvesting of the leaf:

> One of my last jobs in the Dooars was to plant tea in a new way in preparation for the machine. This was hedge planting, five feet by two feet apart, to allow for mechanical cultivation and plucking. With the cost of labour so high today, mechanisation of outside work must ultimately be introduced. Leaf will be cut instead of plucked. This will make the period between flushes longer, but the flushes will be heavier. The machine cannot select leaf, like the human being can, and as a result more stalk will reach the factory.

If a change to mechanical harvesting is contemplated this can only be made when old, poor yielding tea is uprooted as only then can the new young tea be planted out in long continuous straight rows, sufficiently wide between rows to accommodate the riding-type diesel tea harvester. This type of planting results in a decrease in the number of bushes from approximately 8000 down to 6000 per acre.

Such a saving in labour costs would have its dark side putting many thousands of estate workers out of work, and in some producing countries governments are opposed to mechanical harvesting for this reason. Though the collection of leaf on estates in Darjeeling and the hills of South India is necessarily a hand plucking operation, because of the steepness of the terrain, there are vast acreages of tea in Assam that might be harvested by mechanical means. But, what of the traditional tea estate and its labour force – and importantly a way of life – should this not be considered above all else? It would be a momentous decision if the Indian Tea Association were to introduce mechanical tea harvesters – but Assam is a very flat and therefore appropriate place for mechanisation.

The last European Director left the Tocklai Experimental Station in the late 1970s. He and his senior staff, who were originally all European, lived in attractive bungalows on the station. Today the Director and his staff are all Indian.

In the entomology department there are many beautifully made wooden display cases containing lepidoptera, all mounted and labelled for future reference. Many of the specimens are, in insect or larvae form, predators of the tea plant and the various trees that are grown to shade the tea. For each of these pests there is, it is hoped, a recognised and proven treatment.

India alone, with a little over a million acres of tea, produces approximately 700,000 metric tons of tea annually. It helps to concentrate the mind if one realizes that this is equal in weight to twelve ocean liners each the size of the *Queen Elizabeth II*. That's an awful lot of tea!

►

Chowrastra, Darjeeling (*Photo C.A.W. 1985.*)

► ## *Onwards to Darjeeling*

Though our stay in Assam had been immensely interesting we were looking forward to the prospect of the cooler airs in the tea fields of Darjeeling. Practically the whole of our last day in Assam was taken up by an exhaustingly hot drive down to Gauhati, where once again we stayed at the Belle Vue Hotel. We were told by Dr. Banerjee that while passing through Kazaringa Game Reserve we might see some white Rhino, but no such luck.

The next morning, while kicking our heels at Gauhati airport, we saw a large crowd of a hundred or so hill tribesmen waiting for a flight to somewhere we knew not. Dressed in their colourful shawls, some in bear-skin cloaks, they presented an unusual sight, their Mongolian faces creased in smiles and excitement as they watched aircraft landing and taking off. Whether they were Miris, Dafflas, Nagas, or Lushais we could not tell, but our experience in seeing them was the richer before we left Assam.

After flying westward to Bagdogra airport we stayed the night and took the 'toy train' up to Darjeeling the next day. Though the train left at 8 o'clock it did not arrive at Darjeeling town until almost 5 o'clock in the evening - just 52 miles! This was due to mist in the higher regions, the journey normally taking seven hours. Our destination was the Windermere Hotel.

There will be many old Darjeeling planters and their wives who will remember the owner of the Windermere, Mrs Tenduf La, who, we understand, was generally known by one and all as Mrs Tender Flower. This hotel has been in her family since 1939, and when we stayed there in 1985 this elegant lady was almost 90 years old.

With its continuing atmosphere of a bygone age, the hotel is grandly sited and was originally built in the early 1860s as a residence for British planters who were then opening the first tea gardens in and around Darjeeling. To take afternoon tea on the terrace, with its stunning views across a deep valley through which the Rangit river flows to the snow covered mountains and Mount Kanchenjunga beyond, is an experience one cannot easily forget.

The Chowrastra, situated in the upper part of Darjeeling town, occupies a rare piece of flat ground. Along the leafy roads that radiate from this point are many lovely and enchanting walks, with seats for those with a mind to sit and stare in wonderment at the view. Today, the native shops that are centred around the Chowrastra are mainly concerned with the tourist

Snow covered mountains and Mount Kanchenjunga. This line of mountains runs from the Mishmi Hills above Assam, in the east, for 1500 miles to the north-west frontier. *(Photo 1985.)*

trade, but hardly forty years ago there were European shops: tailors, booksellers, photographers, chemists and drapers, Whiteaway Laidlaw & Company, who also had branches in Ceylon and Singapore. All catered for the resident European population who lived and worked among these lovely mountains, tea planters prominent among them. Today, the native population of Darjeeling is approximately 100,000, the town extending from its lofty height at the Chowrastra down the hill to the native bazaar on the north side.

Tiger Hill

Having risen from our beds at four o'clock, my wife and I arrive at the summit of Tiger Hill a little after 5.30. This might seem more adventurous than it actually is, for, as tourists, we have taken a Land Rover to within a few hundred yards of the observation area on the summit and walked the rest. We have pyjamas and pullovers underneath our clothes for extra warmth.

Our photograph shows the view looking due north towards the great Himalayan range of mountains that stretch for over fifteen hundred miles from the Mishmi Hills above Assam, in the east, to the Punjab on the North-West Frontier. As the slanting rays of the sun catch Mount Kanchenjunga - distant some 45 miles - we look down into the unseen, mist-filled, forested slopes below, for it is there that the tea gardens lie, around and below the town of Darjeeling.

At certain times of the year tourists flock to one of Darjeeling's tea factories to see how tea is manufactured, happily departing with their purchases of that elusive Muscatel flavoured tea.

Having previously decided to visit the tea fields on the northern slopes below the town, that face the

Kanchenjunga massif, we had already arranged for transport. Our guide for the day was to be a microbiologist from the Tea Research Association in the town.

Paradise – with Two Leaves and a Bud

Just imagine the life of a planter in this lovely part of the world! Every day he goes about his work in the tea fields, up steep slopes and down into the deepest valleys, where the tea bushes edge the very waters of the Rangit river.

The morning air is still sharp as our Nepalese driver, a cheery fellow, Devenath, the microbiologist, my wife and I set off in an open Land Rover down the Tukvar road to Sikkim.

For a few brief moments my thoughts return to Assam, where we had passed a couple of dreadful nights in Tinsukia – now just a bad dream – and here we were, not a week later, starting out on a beautiful morning motoring on impossible slopes through lush green tea fields, with snow-capped mountains ahead. What a contrast to Assam!

I cannot deny that our feelings of anticipation and excitement, tinged at odd moments with doubts and worries – for we were not born yesterday – have affected both me and my wife greatly. The reader, sitting at home in the comfort of an armchair, need have no such qualms or worries. If I were able, in mere words, to wax lyrical about the grandness of the scenery all about us, so lyrical in fact that I might at some future date be put up for some great literary award, you would still not comprehend fully the serene beauty of our surroundings, nor know of the feeling of complete peace as we zig zag steeply down the mountainside with wondrous views of snow and mountains.

Traversing steeply downwards all the while, warm air rushes past us up the mountainside to the cooler air above.

We have now dropped from around 6000 feet to the river bed at approximately 1800 feet in a little over an hour. The heat of the steamy valley is most evident. On the return journey we will visit some tea gardens.

As the road climbs up the spur of the mountainside back to Darjeeling we pass the bungalow on Singla Tea Estate, followed higher up by Barnsbed bungalow.

When the Tea industry was first started in this region during the late 1850s, there was a great demand for tea seed. By then the Assam Company had more than sufficient seed, both Assam and China jat, for its own needs, and was therefore able to supply large quantities of China seed to Darjeeling, which it had obtained from the original importations of China stock. Nurseries were established in various parts of Darjeeling in which many tons of China seed were sown, the resultant seedlings being planted out in the new clearings, or, the seed itself was put out directly in

We had many stoppages. A crowd soon gathers in the middle of a tea field. (*Photo C.A.W. 1985.*)

the clearings as seed-at-stake.

Replanting on the steep slopes in this region is extremely costly and often results in the loss of much valuable soil too. When uprooting between 2500 and 3000 old poor yielding tea bushes to every acre, the valuable top-soil – that has been held up for over a hundred years by the extensive root systems of the bushes – is loosened and is at risk from heavy rainfall, for with no cover, the exposed soil is subject to erosion and is washed down steep mountainsides to the rivers below, before the roots of the newly replanted tea can spread and anchor it. Nowadays soil rehabilitation is carried out with legume cover crops and weeping grass is planted to prepare the soil for the young tea plants. The cutting of silt-pits, or drains, on the contours of the land helps hold up the valuable top-soil which – every six years or so, when the bushes are pruned – is dug out and thrown back around the roots of the bushes above each drain.

Landslides are common in this district. In the great flood of 1968 nearly 2500 acres of tea was lost or buried during massive landslides, when continuous rain fell for just three days; another 2000 acres of land suitable for tea was either totally or partially destroyed. This was a terrible set-back for the industry. Quite apart from the loss of this acreage of tea and land, the damage caused on gardens to factories, roads, bridges, culverts and dwellings of the labour force and staff bungalows amounted to Rupees 98 Lakhs – equivalent to £600,000 Sterling.

While climbing steadily back to the town we stop the Land Rover and look at a field of really old tea bushes and our thoughts go back in time to those long forgotten bearded, pith helmeted pioneers who stood on these very slopes, bivouacked and camped in these valleys, by some small stream or river a hundred and forty years ago.

Every night he would sit alone inside his hut in the flickering yellow light of a candle as hundreds of insects flew around it, many burning themselves, falling in heaps on what passed for a table and upon the hard mud floor beneath, almost concealed in darkness. The noise of the nightlife would be truly deafening to a newcomer, who would assuredly never be able to get to sleep. But to the lonely occupant it was all part of his surroundings – if it were possible to take that now accustomed noise away, it would be he who would be unable to sleep for the lack of it! By far the loudest noise would come from thousands of cicadas clicking away all around, and it is the noise made by the male cicada – the loudest in the insect world – that can be heard over half a mile away. If his hut was sited close to running water there would be added the night chorus of the frogs, their croaking only dominated by the inter-

A cold morning as Tukvar children return with old tea bushes to their lines. Old tea, when uprooted, provides a source of much-needed firewood for the estate labour force. (*Photo C.A.W. 1985.*)

mittent calls of the larger animals.

Such a place of natural grandeur is not lost upon a man who lives in close harmony with nature. Each morning at cock-crow, as he turns out of his little cabin, the air is sharp and fresh, the valley is still lost in a deep mist. Daybreak for all the wild life is a time of change; either they are going to bed after a night's foraging or are coming out for the day. Man is very much the intruder upon the scene. As the mists clear and the first rays of the sun penetrate the floor of the valley, the buzz of insect life is most evident; the call of the jungle fowl as he drops from his night's roosting place high up in a tree, or the flash of yellow as a late returning leopard springs from the now sunlit clearing into the shade of the jungle boundary, to lie up in his favourite lair all day.

Our thoughts of the past disappear as a tea factory comes into view, ahead and above us. As we drive back the sun is setting, it is getting chilly and we are looking forward to a cup of tea after a wonderful day. This evening, after dinner, we will sit in the drawing room and just take it easy. I have no doubt we shall sleep well. The Tea Research Association's field officers, Messrs Dasgupta and Devenath, have accompanied us everywhere and have been more than helpful. In all we have spent six nights at the hotel, two days in the tea fields and looking at cemeteries, the others wandering around Darjeeling, Kalimpong and Sikkim.

From Darjeeling station the train climbs slowly up to the famous loop, 'Agony Point', where you can get off the moving train – if you dare – run across and jump on again, and then on to Ghoom Station, the highest point on the line at almost 6500 feet above sea level. We take a last admiring look at the majestic snow-capped mountains before dropping down to the plains below.

The Toy Train approaching Ghoom Station, Darjeeling-bound. (*Photo 1985 C.A.W.*)
Two marvels of mountain engineering cross each other 132 times on their way up to the town of Darjeeling. The construction of the new hill cart road from Silliguri to Darjeeling was started in 1861 and completed by 1869. The construction of the 2-foot-gauge Darjeeling Himalayan Railway – which is one of the railway wonders of the world and runs for 53 miles – was commenced in 1869, also at Silliguri, and was extended up to the town of Darjeeling by 1881.

CHAPTER V

COFFEE – CINCHONA – TEA

Part of Sri Lanka's Plantation History

Peacock Hill Coffee Estate, Puseellawa, looking down to the village of Gampola. Left, the planter's bungalow and right, coffee stores and pulping house. (*Lithograph 1864, from O'Brien's 'Views in Ceylon'.*)

CHAPTER V

Coffee – Cinchona – Tea

In leaving India we follow the tea story across the narrow stretch of water known as the Palk Strait, to the island of Sri Lanka (formerly Ceylon). Here, tea has been commercially grown for the past 137 years.

Sri Lanka has a little over half a million acres of tea which is mostly situated in the centre of the Island; a green carpet of tea covers every mountainside throughout the Central Hill District. However, it is the history of Ceylon's plantation industry, and particularly how tea supplanted coffee, that concerns us initially.

The first Europeans to claim the Island of Ceylon by force of arms were the Portuguese. Their fleet, carried by wind and current, arrived in the year 1505, at the fine natural harbour of Galle. But it was not until 1517 that they formed a trading settlement – at Colombo.

The Portuguese rule, which had endured only in the maritime districts, ended in 1656, when they were driven from the Island by the Dutch. Both the Portuguese and the Dutch built massive stone-walled forts at the Port of Colombo – parts of which may be seen in our picture on the following page – and at Trincomalee, Negombo, Jaffna, Batticoloa, Matara and Galle. The British appeared on the scene towards the end of the

18th century, capturing Jaffna and Trincomalee in 1795, and Colombo the following year.

Although the cinnamon plant is indigenous in Ceylon and the Portuguese had previously traded in the spice, its cultivation as a plantation crop does not appear to have been undertaken until 1770, by the Dutch. Previous to this the bark was harvested by the Sinhalese from wild or uncultivated trees growing in the moist jungles. In 1770 the Dutch opened a cinnamon plantation on the outskirts of Colombo, on land that today forms an attractive residential part of the town, known as Cinnamon Gardens. The cultivation of cinnamon was carried on by the British into the 20th century, but was never an important revenue earner.

As has already been mentioned, Ceylon's great plantation industry was originally coffee, not tea, and it was one of the Governors of the Island, Sir Edward Barnes, who, in 1825, opened the first coffee estate in the hills close to the Botanical Gardens at Peradeniya, near Kandy. This immediately led to a rush to buy land by coffee speculators in Colombo.

Some of the first Europeans to become coffee planters were drawn from those resident in Colombo.

Point de Galle. This panoramic view shows the old Dutch walled town of Galle, looking across the bay to Closenberg Island.
(*Pencil sketch by A.G. Mason 1840.*)

Some had been bought out of the regimental ranks by the new owners of land in the central hill districts, others were adventurers out from Britain. This odd mixture of men, none with any agricultural experience, were taken on for the specific task of opening out jungle, setting out nurseries and planting the land with coffee. The beginning of the 19th century held tantalizing opportunities for the more adventurous.

For those who arrived out from Britain during the early part of the century, the port of Galle was their destination after a sea voyage of about five months, sailing around the Cape of Good Hope. Sailing ships also put in at Colombo, but until the breakwaters and harbour facilities

View of Colombo, taken from the Roads and showing Adams Peak.
(*Lithograph by Langlume by permission of the British Library.*)

were built in the 1880s, it was always a dangerous procedure to anchor in the open roadstead, especially when winds beat up from the south-west during the monsoon.

The 80 mile journey from Galle up to Colombo lay along a lovely coconut palm fringed road that never strays far from the shoreline. Even if travelling in the luxury of the Royal Mail coach the journey would take almost a week, as there were eight staging posts for the horses along the route.

So it was from the town of Colombo that the first coffee pioneers started out for Kandy and the interior. Picture the scene. At the head of a small motley looking convoy, our pioneer, mounted on his horse, is followed by his small band of men who trudge slowly along a deeply rutted mud road. Progress is governed by the speed of the bullock cart, slow at the best of times, which brings up the rear. Onto this is loaded his provisions and this includes dried fish, a sack of rice to feed his companions and himself, axes, lining rope, cartridges for his gun, candles and sacks of coffee seed.

This is perhaps the right place to narrate an account, given to me by Joan Gottelier, about three such travellers who made their way up to Haputele. The story concerns the three Coombe brothers whose uncle, Sir George Pilkington, owned Poonagalla Estate. The story has been passed down that after landing at Colombo the three brothers proceeded up to Poonagalla, 130 miles distant, with one horse between them, taking it in turns to ride and walk. It is interesting to know that the last of the Coombe family, Gorton Coombe, retired from Poonagalla in 1960.

These then were the conditions under which the coffee men made their way, on foot or by horse, up to Kandy and to the hills beyond. There must have been many such travellers strung out along the route; all going to try their luck in coffee.

Passing through scattered villages, bivouacking each night under the stars or in torrential downpour, when every stream and river became impassable and could not be crossed for days, even weeks, the first coffee pioneers were, in the main, strong young adventurers – they had to be!

At first the route lay north-eastwards through malarial swamps, hot and sticky, until some 52 miles later they reached the hills at Rambukana. The next 13 miles, during which they climbed to 1690 feet at the top of the Kaduganawa Pass, was a testing time for all. Ascending the deep luxuriant gorge, with its dank cool air, broken axles made progress slow until, after some

Chatham Street, Colombo, with, through the trees, the old lighthouse and clock tower.
(*Photo, c1900.*)

The taking of Galle from the Portuguese, by the Dutch. (*Woodcut from a drawing by Baldoeus c1652.*)

12 hours of steady climbing, they reached the summit of the Pass.

The village of Kaduganawa provided a timely resting place for men and animals alike. Major Thomas Skinner, when engaged upon the building of certain sections of the road, said of the local Sinhalese villagers and of the men who took the road up through the Pass:

> At every stage I was received courteously, and provided with what I needed. On the 28th March 1829, I lost my dear friend, and the service of the most valuable officer in Captain W. Dawson, commanding officer Royal Engineers. The poor fellow died in my arms.

From the village of Kaduganawa the road lay at a happier gradient, downwards to the relief of all. Before the construction of the Satinwood Bridge, over the Mahaveli Ganga, at Peradeniya, the crossing was made by native ferry.

For those who made the journey a little later, say during the 1840s, the Queen's Hotel in Kandy must have been a welcome sanctuary and base when journeying on – into the pioneering belt of forest around Gampola. As yet more arrived, each pushed on further into the interior, across the Gampola ferry, into Pusselawa and on to take up their claims of land in the beautiful hills they had glimpsed from afar.

Two of those pioneers were the Worms brothers

who had opened, in 1839, the Rothschild Coffee Estate, which they named after their famous cousins, the Rothschilds. James Emerson Tennent describes a visit

Sinhalese, Kandian and Malabar females. The Kandian, standing, is holding a portion of the talipot palm, used for protection against rain or sun. (*Lithograph c1860.*)

to Rothschild Estate in 1846:

> At Pusselawa our home on many occasions was
> the hospitable bungalow of Mr. Worms and his
> brother, the proprietors of one of the finest plan-
> tations in the island. Their estate, which now
> consists, besides unfelled forest, of upwards of
> one thousand acres of coffee trees in full bear-
> ing, was commenced by themselves in 1841,
> when the new enterprise was still in its infancy.

Fire – Smoke – Toil – and Coffee

The coffee men and their labour force laid low the
primeval jungle at a frightening pace. The steady 'click'
of axes upon the forest giants went on all day, reverberating around the mountainsides. The Sinhalese villagers were adept with the axe, in fact more so than the
Tamils, but there was much work for all.

After the 'burn' scores of small pockets of flame
smouldered over the blackened land amongst the tan-
gled mass of burnt timber, and no mountainside was
without its pall of smoke climbing lazily into the nearby jungle to disappear amongst the lush green leaves
and drive out the sleeping flying foxes. This was the
life for the coffee men; you could tell they loved it by
their unbounding enthusiasm for the job in hand.
Everywhere there was fire and smoke – all in the name
of coffee.

If you asked any planter what his
chief bug-bear was on his property,
he would probably have told you
that, apart from getting his coffee
crop off the estate, it was Pests and
Diseases, and in particular *Golunda
elliotti coffaeus*, the coffee rat; this little charmer could play havoc among
the coffee bushes.

Their first reported appearance on
the coffee estates in the hills around
Kandy was in 1847. Whenever there
was a scarcity of their normal food,
the seeds of the nillu plant, they
would migrate in vast numbers
across the land, and it was a serious
problem for the planter when his
estate was in their path. His bushes
would be stripped of young buds and
flowers, and such were their numbers that as many as a thousand were
reported to have been killed in one
day on a single estate. On the plus
side, however, the rats, some eight or
nine inches in length, were much
prized by the coolies, who ate them
roasted, fried in coconut oil or made
them into curry, thus adding meat
protein to their normal diet of rice. In
fact, the Tamils had a marked prefer-

ence for working on estates in districts which were
subject to the rodents' periodic incursions.

By the year 1868, 176,000 acres of virgin forest had
been felled and coffee planted in its place; the way
ahead looked bright for the coffee industry which, at
one time, was the largest in the world – but its days
were numbered.

A field of coffee in flower or with berries is a beautiful sight. Mrs. R. K. Clark, one of a large family who
planted coffee and tea in Ceylon and South India from
the early years, recalls a visit to Hangran Oya Estate,
Ambagamawa in 1881:

> When the coffee was in blossom, the whole
> estate was covered with the little jessamine-like
> flowers and the air filled with sweet scent. The
> blossom would ripen all at once and I remember
> my little dog being so astonished one morning at
> seeing the whole place all white he put his tail
> between his legs and bolted for the bungalow.
> When the coffee was in fruit every bush was a
> mass of red berries.

What of the coffee planter and his accommodation?
The evolution of what was to become, in later years,
the grand bungalow, was all too slow for the tough
characters of the coffee days. The luxury of a pukka
bungalow built of stone – with chairs and furniture on
wood-planked or cement floors – was quite unknown ▶

The coffee pioneers travelled on foot, by horse and in bullock carts into the beautiful hills
of the interior. (*Lithograph 1864, from O'Brien's 'Views in Ceylon'.*)

Kadienlena Bazaar, Nawalapitiya, Kadienlena and Fettercairn coffee estates were opened prior to 1857. (*Drawing 1874, by permission of the British Library.*)

A newly built Lindula church on Lindula Estate, a division of Waltrim Group. (*Photo Skeen, 1883*)

Part of Ceylon's plantation history

Coffee - mid 1870s and 1880s

Craigie Lea Estate, Kotagalla. (*Photo Skeen c.1883.*)

Logie Estate, Talawakelle. (*Drawing 1875, by permission of the British Library.*)

ABOVE
In 1815 the British army for the second time fought its way up to and captured Kandy, and thereafter the town was garrisoned by the Ceylon Rifle Regiment. The view is from the hill, a little below the garrison cemetery, looking down on the lake and the Malagawa Temple. A carriage road runs around the margin of the lake. On the opposite side from the town are the monasteries of the priests and, above them, the residence of principal civilians and merchants. After the

opening of the first coffee estates, planters would ride into Kandy every month to obtain provisions and to collect money from the 'Chettes' – Moormen traders – to pay their estate labour force. For those who came from afar and stayed the night at any of the small boarding houses or at the Queen's Hotel, built in 1841 – seen right of centre facing the green – a pleasant stroll around the lake was a welcome change from their lonely estates. (Lithograph 1864, from O'Brian's 'Views in Ceylon'.)

FAR RIGHT
Kaduganawa Pass – looking up. The ascent into the Kandian hills begins at Rambukana, at 290 feet and, from there on, the road winds its tortuous way over the next 13 miles through dense forest and along steep precipices until it reaches the village of Kaduganawa at the top of the Pass. The tall monument was erected in 1832 to commemorate Captain Dawson, who planned and superintended the construction of the road. (Engraving c1860.)

The fulfilment of a prophesy; the rock was pierced and the road taken through

LEFT
*Kaduganawa Pass –
looking down. There
was an ancient prophecy
amongst the Sinhalese
in the Kingdom of
Kandy that, whoever
should pierce the rock
and make a road from
the plains, would receive
the kingdom as his
reward. The Portuguese
and the Dutch failed,
and the prophecy was at
last fulfilled by the
British, who pierced the
rock and built the road.
(Photo c1890.)*

▶ to them. Many lived in glorified hen-coops, with a thatched roof or under nothing more than an umbrella or the broad leaves of the Talipot palm.

Coffee planter John Capper gives us an interesting insight into the life of one of his brother coffee planters when he visited an embryo coffee plantation in 1840:

> On learning that we had reached the 'bungalow', I looked about me to discover its locality, but in vain; there was no building to be seen; but presently my host pointed out to me what I had not noticed before – a small low-roofed thatched place, close under a projecting rock, and half hidden by thorny creepers. I imagined this to be his fowl house, or perhaps a receptacle for tools, but was not a little astonished when I saw my friend beckon me on, and enter at the low dark door. This miserable little cabin could not have been more than twelve feet long by about six feet wide, and as high at the walls. My friend told me that when he had finished putting up this little crib, had moved in his one table and chair and was seated, cigar in mouth, he thought

himself the happiest of mortals.

Coffee had reigned supreme for over forty years when, in 1869, a leaf disease (coffee rust, *Hemileia vastatrix*) appeared. With each successive year the disease spread throughout the coffee plantations, slowly at first, weakening the bushes until they died, stunted and leafless.

The Superintendent of the Royal Botanical Gardens at Peradeniya, Dr. G. H. K. Thwaites, was involved from the outset in the battle to find a preventative, but none was found.

Such was the boom in coffee prices, the momentum of jungle felling continued after the appearance of the leaf disease, and over the following ten years a further 100,000 acres of coffee was rashly planted, a lot of which was smitten too. The coffee men hoped the disease would go away but it did not.

During the period from the 1870s until the late 1890s, when a few were still planting coffee and others pulling it out, upwards of 250,000 acres of dead and dying coffee bushes were uprooted – mainly using elephants – and burnt in the fields.

A superior dwelling house! All that one could expect when opening out jungle for a coffee plantation during the pioneering years. No shops, no doctors but with a rifle there was no need for the former. The date of the photo is not known but it was probably taken during the 1860s.
(*Photo courtesy John Benest, planter, who found this and other photographs in Torrington Tea Estate bungalow, Agra Patanas, in 1939.*)

Tea Seeds – A Present from Calcutta

Back in 1839 the first tea seeds had been received in Ceylon at the Botanical Gardens. Dispatched by Dr. Wallich, Superintendent of the Calcutta Botanical Gardens, this seed had been collected at the East India Company's trial tea lands and forests in upper Assam, from the indigenous tea plants that had been found there (*Camellia assamica*).

The seeds were germinated at Peradeniya and the resultant seedlings were given to a handful of enterprising coffee planters, who established them on small trial plots of land on their estates. These experimental plantings of tea were forgotten by the main body of coffee men during the following thirty years – but tea did grow.

A field of coffee interplanted with cinchona, foreground, and beyond in rows – showing Tamils shaving the bark of cinchona trees. Reproduced from a photograph found in Torrington Tea Estate bungalow by tea planter John Benest and given to the author by Chris Greenhow. (*Photo 1880–5.*)

The coffee planting Worms brothers were quick to switch to experimenting with tea, having put out china tea seedlings on Rothschild and Condegalla coffee estates which Maurice B. Worms had brought from China in about 1841. Emerson Tennent writes of Rothschild in 1846:

> On this fine estate an attempt has been made to grow tea; the plants thrive surprisingly, and when I saw them they were covered with bloom. But the experiment has hitherto been defeated by the impossibility of finding skilled labour to dry and manipulate the leaves. Should it ever be thought expedient to cultivate tea in addition to coffee in Ceylon, the adaption of the soil and climate has thus been established, and it only remains to introduce artisans from China to conduct the subsequent processes.

Cinchona – 'Medicine Plant'

Anyone who has had anything to do with malaria will know the importance of the cinchona plant, as quinine is made from the bark of the mature tree. In the past this foul-tasting mixture was a life-saver for so many in the tropics, including planters.

It is estimated that approximately 40 million people world-wide are infected with malaria all the time, of which between one and one and a half million die annually.

It is the female anopheles mosquito that carries the malarial parasite and feeds on the blood; unlike the male it has mouth parts specially adapted for doing this. The desire of the anopheles for the blood of ani-

mals and humans is insatiable, the usual time for feeding being at dusk or dawn and to a lesser degree during the night. The insect rarely takes more than a minute to engorge blood and transmit malaria, if it is infective. With all mosquitoes there is an egg stage, a larval stage and a pupal stage from which the adult winged form emerges.

Long ago scientists thought they could eradicate the disease. A British doctor, Ronald Ross (later Sir Ronald) was working in India treating soldiers when he came upon a paper suggesting mosquitoes might spread the malarial parasite. He collected the most common anopheles mosquitoes and fed them with the blood of people infected with malaria and proved that it was the female mosquito that carries and injects the malarial parasite into the human bloodstream. Ross reasoned that if the breeding grounds of the mosquito were targeted – marshes, lakes and swamps – and oil spread on the surface, breeding would be curtailed. A mammoth task world-wide.

With disease research during World War II, DDT was to reduce malaria dramatically, but the mosquito fought back and soon became largely resistant to DDT spraying. The drug quinine kills the malarial parasite but has to be taken daily over a long period of time, to keep the disease at bay. I remember my father, who, like myself, was born in Malaya, telling me he often swallowed 5 or 10 grains of quinine a day during the 1920s and 1930s when planting. In 1940 scientists took molecules of quinine to adapt and make a drug called Cloriquina, but within a decade resistance to the drug had, once again, developed in the mosquito. The immune system of the mosquito is ever active and adaptive.

During the 1970s Chinese scientists discovered a ▶

Peacock Hill Coffee Estate, Pusselawa, with manager's bungalow at left, pulping-house, drying grounds and stores to right. Gampola, the early pioneering region, in the background. (*Lithograph 1864, from O'Brien's Views in Ceylon.*)

19th-century coffee picker and sack

1869 coffee leaf disease strikes

Coffee

Original plantings – 1200 bushes per acre

276,000 acres of dead and dying bushes uprooted and burnt = 331 million bushes

19th-century tea plucker
and basket.
(*Photo 1870s, courtesy
Royal Geographical Society.*)

Tea

Replanting of 276,000 acres

Put out as seedlings (or seed-at-stake) at 2850
plants per acre = 700 million tea seedlings

Allowance has been made for planting vacancies
caused by cutting paths, roads, drains

Sir Thomas J. Lipton

Mr. James Whittall
FOUNDER AND
LATE PARTNER OF
WHITTALL & CO.

Mr. G B Leechman
Founder, 1866
FORMER HEADS OF
LEECHMAN & CO.

Mr. Kirkman Finlay

Sir John Muir, Bart.
EARLY PARTNERS OF JAMES FINLAY & CO. LTD.,

Mr. Wilton Bartleet
Senior partner
Bartleet & Co.

Mr. Patrick Gow
The late founder of Gow,
Wilson & Stantion

Mr. James Forbes
One of the founders of
Forbes & Walker

TWO WELL-KNOWN BROKERAGE HOUSE FOUNDERS

Mr. George Payne
founder

Sir Josehp Lyons
FOUNDER OF J. LYONS & CO. LTD.

Thomas Twining
1675 - 1741

Richard Twining
1749 - 1821

TWO FAMOUS TWININGS

Mr. Joseph Tetley,
Chairman

Mr. William Tetley Jones
Managing Director

OFFICERS OF JOSEPH TETLEY & CO. LTD.,

Arthur Brooke

Mr. W. J. Thompson
1778 - 1852

Mr. W. J. Thompson
1844 - 1931

TWO NOTABLE THOMPSONS

Daniel Harrison

Joseph Crosfield

Smith Harrison

Great names in tea.

new plant-derived drug, Chin Hw Su, to combat malaria. Some fifteen years later the drug was still not available to the western world, owing to the Chinese Government's wish to maintain secrecy over its startling discovery. Then, during the 1990s, China and the United States co-operated and the drug became available world-wide.

To-day, DDT is still heavily used in many ways and the United Nations and the World Wide Fund for Nature is hoping to ban the pesticide entirely, as it is known to build up in mammals, birds and wild-life. However, as mentioned, nearly 2 million people will die of malaria this year. No wonder it was a scourge greater than all the other dangers of the jungle.

In Ceylon the first trials were made with cinchona – *C. officinalis* and *C. succirubra* – in 1861, at the Hakgalla Gardens in Nuwara Eliya. The valuable curative effects of quinine in malarial fever were known in 1639, when a preparation of cinchona bark cured the Countess of Cinchon, wife of the Viceroy of Peru, the plant being afterwards named in her honour. This medicinal plant is native to the forests of the Peruvian Andes and is sometimes called Peruvian bark.

The first plantings of cinchona in Ceylon were made by James Taylor and this was followed by other coffee planters during the early 1860s, when coffee was still booming. By 1867 the cinchona trees had come to maturity enabling stem shaving, and the first cinchona bark reached London in 1868. By 1872, 500 acres were in cultivation and this had risen to 6000 by 1877. Two completely new plantation industries had therefore been started, cinchona and tea, but only one was to last – TEA.

The cinchona industry rose rapidly and by 1883 64,000 acres had been planted and the export of bark was at its height in 1887, with 16,000,000 lbs. Over production, both in Ceylon, India and especially Java, led to a drop in prices of the drug, from 15 shillings (75 pence) to 1 shilling and 3d (about 7 pence) per ounce in 1890.

As the industry suffered, an ever increasing acreage of cinchona trees were cut down to ground level, thus obtaining many times the quantity of bark than by the traditional methods of branch lopping and barking, or shaving the trunks by means of a poke-shave, great care being taken not to cut into the cambium. Cutting the trees to ground level provided a final bumper crop, albeit at very low prices. The roots of the trees still had to be uprooted leaving the surrounding coffee. Much of the cinchona had been interplanted with the coffee, as may be seen in the photograph of Tamils stripping bark.

An interior scene in Ceylon, by L.B. Clarence, described as a 'tea auction' shed or club house.
(*Pen and wash c 1874, by permission of the British Library.*)

James Taylor

James Taylor

1835–1892

Pioneer of the tea and cinchona industries in Ceylon

Born in Scotland 1835
Arrived in Ceylon 1852
Naranghena/Loolecondera Estate from 1852–1892

The legend of James Taylor lives on in Sri Lanka today. His birthplace was at Moss Park in Kincardineshire, Scotland. The living quarters of the Taylor family was to the left of the main building.

James Taylor (second from left). Apart from 'temporary accommodation', pukka bungalows of the period were constructed with local materials: timber from the forest, granite stone from the numerous slab rocks.
The photograph was taken in 1867, the year Taylor planted that now famous No. 7 field with 19 acres of tea on Loolecondera estate.
(*The above three pictures, courtesy Bartleet and Co., Colombo.*)

Part of Ceylon's tea history

Put out by James Taylor in 1867, this 19-acre field of tea was the first to be planted on a commercial scale. There had been earlier experimental plantings by the coffee planters when the bushes were numbered in dozens rather than acres.
(Photos CAW, 1982)

More about James Taylor

The first tea seeds were received at the Peradeniya Gardens in 1839 and were sent by Dr. N. Wallich, Superintendent of the Calcutta Gardens. These Assam indigenous tea seeds had been collected from the East India Company's tea forests in upper Assam.

James Taylor and his friends experimented in the manufacture of tea in his bungalow: the green leaf that was brought in from the fields was first withered and then hand-rolled on the verandah, while drying was done in chulas, or clay ovens over charcoal fires, on which wire trays were placed to hold the leaf, or dhool.

He never married, his only love was tea.

Sir Thomas Lipton's showpiece Dambatenne Tea Estate

Lipton owned some 5500 acres of tea in Ceylon

The Superintendent of Dambatenne takes a photo call, with tea carts leaving the factory.

The Lipton planter.

Dambatenne factory – weighing up the leaf from the fields.

Leaf coming down a wire chute from the
fields to Laymastotte factory.
(*Hand tinted photographs c.1900.*)

Another set-piece photo with chests of tea leaving Eadella Tea Estate.

▶ ## *Fire - Smoke - Toil - and Tea, The New Industry*

Most of the early pioneers who had laid low over a quarter of a million acres of virgin forest and planted coffee in its place had gone, and now their sons were burning that coffee. A fine Coffee Industry, the country's heritage, was slowly on its way out.

Once more fire and smoke could be seen on every mountainside, but this time the coffee planters' hearts were heavy – the fire and smoke came from their own dead coffee bushes. The coffee picker, with her sack, would disappear from the landscape. Out of the ashes of the coffee bushes arose, like a phoenix, an entirely new industry, tea, and with it the plucker, with her basket.

By the time Ceylon planters had embarked upon the country's new tea industry, some solid pioneering had been done by their compatriots in India. The tea expertise that had been so hard gained in India, first from the Chinese, by C. A. Bruce, and then by the Assam Company, and others, was freely given to the coffee planters. Nevertheless, the coffee men were up against the wall. Many of the fine coffee estates went bankrupt, their owners returning to Britain ruined men; others hung on.

Just two years before the coffee leaf disease was first noticed, coffee planter James Taylor had cleared a small block of jungle on a steep hillside and planted, in 1867, 19 acres of tea. This was the first commercial planting of tea in Ceylon, as opposed to the many small trial plantings that had been made during the previous years. The estate was Loolecondera.

During the years of change from coffee to tea, the late 1870s to the late 1890s, old coffee stores were utilized by converting them into make-shift tea factories. It was a costly operation for the planter to pull out and burn the hefty coffee bushes, only to be left with nothing but bare soil for which he had no tea seeds – unless he could pay for them. Although large importations of Assam tea seed were shipped into the island from Calcutta, the situation was grave.

Hundreds of coffee estates lay abandoned during those hard times and with no income to pay the labour force thousands of Tamils left to return to their villages in southern India. Many proprietary planters stayed on, their labour force working, short of food and often without pay, standing loyally by their employers.

The year 1890 was, for Thomas Lipton and others, the ideal time to buy estates, which in many cases were being snapped up at knock-down prices. By the late 1890s only a comparatively small acreage remained under coffee, and it too would soon be uprooted and the land replanted with tea. Thomas Lipton bought his first tea estates in the Haputele district in 1890: Dambatenne, Laymastotte and Monarakanda, were later followed by the purchase of Pooprassie, Bunyan and others, amounting in all to some 5000 acres.

Gradually, as the new tea industry took shape and income returned, the first pukka tea factories were built in which the new-fangled tea machinery was installed. The tea industry was on the move.

To avoid the need to purchase tea seed, each estate would reserve a small piece of land on which to plant its own tea seed bearers. This all took time to come to fruition, as seed trees only come into useful bearing after about ten years.

In addition to well over a quarter of a million acres of coffee that had been uprooted, burnt and replanted with tea, a quite considerable acreage of virgin jungle and patna land was being planted up first time with tea.

By the turn of the century and after a tremendous battle by the planters, 380,000 acres of tea was growing beautifully. Land on which the elephant, leopard, elk, bear and wild boar had roamed was now orderly, well established tea estates.

CHAPTER VI

INTO THE 20TH CENTURY

With 'two leaves and a bud'

No mechanical devices to crop the flush, just two hands plucking 'Two Leaves and a Bud'.

A new clearing of young seedling rubber trees. It takes seven years before the rubber tree reaches a girth of 21 inches at three feet from the ground and is ready to be tapped for its latex. Early in 1876, a young botanist, Henry Wickham, collected seeds of *Hevea brasiliensis* from the jungles of the Amazon which were then dispatched to Kew Gardens. Later, after germination, several thousand young rubber plants were shipped out to Ceylon in Wardian cases. (*Photo c 1900,*)

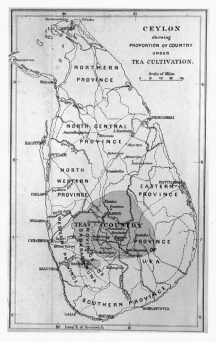

The main tea growing area in the Central Hill Districts. (*Map c.1900.*)

Into the 20th Century with 'Two Leaves and a Bud'

The V.A. Comes to Stay

An institution that brought greater organisation and efficiency, and took the tea industry into the 20th century, was the Agency system. The many managing agencies of estates, of which the earliest to be founded was Mackwoods & Co. in 1841, and George Steuart & Co. in 1843, were responsible for the management and smooth running of the estates. Agency wallahs, who all wore collars, ties and coats, and sat on their back-sides in their comfy Colombo offices with fans going round, sent out rude letters to the hard-working manager squatting on his estate in rain and sunshine in the devil of a bad mood as he is in the middle of some nasty labour troubles and, furthermore, has received a communication to say his Visiting Agent will be arriving on the morrow to inspect his property.

The visit of the 'V.A.' was something special in any manager's calendar. Some of these generally unloved characters, who were all senior planters, used to 'lord it' over their lesser brethren.

Famous among V.A.s were the Retties, who reigned on Spring Valley Estate for sixty-six years from 1865 until 1931. Wilfred Rettie was one of those who used to send their dressing boy ahead to prepare things, and some even sent a menu – to keep the great soul happy while slumming it in someone else's bungalow. The superintendent, or manager, while putting up with such indignities, still had his own dreams:

The Manager
I wish they would say 'you can be the V.A.
And keep the whole gang up to scratch',
I've been so long in tea, they couldn't do me,
But would find I was more than their match.
I'd make them obey and grow tea my way,
Especially old so-and-so;
He can't argue the toss if I am the boss,
Which is one thing I'd soon let him know.

This V.A. phenomenon is, as we have already seen, common to both India and Ceylon. The Colombo agents were European, ran mercantile firms and acted as middlemen between boards of directors, either in London or Ceylon. Though they were experienced on the financial side of running estates, Agency Houses have always had on their staff ex-planters with a personal

knowledge of practical planting. The bond between the Colombo agent and the planter has always been strong and goes back to the coffee days; they also appointed Visiting Agents.

An insight into the varied daily working life of an Agency man is provided by ex-planter W. B. (Bill) Atkinson, when working for Whittall & Co., Colombo, who were, among many things, agents for the Orient Steam Navigation Company:

> The regular Orient Liner had left Aden outward bound, and, as usual, cabled on to the next port of call, Colombo, its requirements of stores, fresh fruit, oil and water. A curt ultimate sentence read 'Have homicidal maniac on board in straight jacket. Kindly remove at Colombo.' Well, Colombo did boast a lunatic asylum, but hardly for European accommodation. However I reserved a single quarter. The patient proved to be an Australian man and he was carried down the gangway in a jacket to my launch, where I had two hospital attendants waiting. During the trip ashore the patient was staring at me with such a concentrated look that I felt distinctly uneasy; I had a vague feeling I had met him in the past.
> The Captain told me his name. It turned out that we travelled together on the S.S. *Barrapool* to Australia in 1931, and he had taken me to his father's house. He later became a member of the New South Wales Legislative Assembly.

Visiting Agents were very busy, responsible men, running their own estates which, in turn, were visited and inspected by others, when they would receive some of their own medicine, though no doubt somewhat diluted – as V.A. to V. A.! During the changeover from coffee to tea, when estates changed hands frequently, there was a great demand for independent professional valuations of plantation properties: the condition of factories, expected crop, bungalows, coffee and tea acreages etc.

Conditions on the now orderly, well run estates had improved greatly and it was no longer the up-hill battle to survive that it had been for the early coffee men, but, like all happenings coming from the past, as things ▶

Tea carts at Bandarawella. Before the railway was opened to Kandy, a pair of Indian humped bulls would pull a cart loaded with coffee from the hill regions down to the port of Colombo, averaging 20 miles a day. (*Watercolour drawing, 1895.*)

Tea carts - Trains - Motor transport

Tea carts leaving an estate. (*Photo c.1895.*)

The opening of the railway, in 1867, was to Matale and then to Bandarawella, thus enabling the quick transport of coffee and later tea to the coast.
(*Photo c.1895, by permission of The British Library.*)

The opening of the 'new' road up to Balangoda Group bungalow, showing the estate lorry, cars and motor-cycle with side car. Lt. Col. W. E.E. Megget is standing in the foreground. (*Photo c.1918, courtesy Mrs. Joan Turnbull.*)

improved they became less exciting – that certain feeling of doing something for the first time is missing. Life was more enjoyable, though many would tell you that it was not – at least until the 1920s and 1930s. It should be remembered that their compatriots in Assam were still subject to occasional attacks by hill tribesmen as late as the early 1930s – but conditions in Ceylon were more civilized.

The hard working, hard playing planter had arrived on the scene. A good number of proprietary holdings had been taken over by large companies. John Fergusson, writing in 1883, sums up the situation:

> Ceylon, in fact, is a sort of 'incubator' to which capitalists send their eggs to be hatched, and whence they received from time to time an abundant brood. Money has been sent here to fell our forests and plant them with coffee, and it has been returned in the shape of copious harvests to the home capitalist.

Though many proprietary coffee planters had returned to Britain, broken men, and others had found their last resting place in the many cemeteries that dotted the mountainsides, young men intent on taking up a career in planting were arriving with every ship at Colombo. The ships of Bibby Line, Clan Line and P & O, all had their quota of would-be planters on board, a large proportion of which still came from north of the English border.

While the coffee and cinchona industries were in their death throes, yet another great plantation industry was starting up – rubber.

Rubber (*Hevea brasiliensis*) was first introduced into Ceylon in 1876, seedlings being dispatched in Wardian cases from the Royal Botanic Gardens at Kew. The plants were put out at experimental plots in the Henaratgoda Gardens, and the first commercial planting was made at Kalutara, in 1883. By the year 1900 some 1750 acres of rubber had been planted and this had been increased to a colossal 534,000 acres during the years up to 1929. Like tea, rubber was to go on and today forms a considerable acreage in the country, equal to that of tea.

Transport

During the early coffee days the crop was carried for miles in two bushel sacks on coolies' heads, along steep mountainsides, over patana land and through jungle down to the nearest cart track. Besides the tea and coffee carts that trundled slowly down to the coast in pre-railway days, much use was made of pack-bullocks to carry the coffee crop off estates down to the waiting cars. Moorman traders as carriers, owned their own bullocks and carts and were employed by the estates to carry their crops and essential stores.

River crossings had to be made and there were a number of ferries over the Mahaveli Ganga which slowed the carts down even more, with many a horse, bullock, cart and driver lost when capsizing in mid stream. This is what pioneering was all about; trail driving into the hitherto untouched jungles.

The first mechanised transport was that of the railway steam locomotive which did wonders to speed the coffee, and later tea crop, down to Colombo. From the opening of the Ceylon Government Railway, in 1867, the plantation industry was particularly well served by the broad-gauged railroad.

Though the tea cart was still very active in the transport of chests of tea to the railway stations, the coming of the motor vehicle brought with it the arrival of the 'estate lorry', which further speeded things up. We have to thank a past resident of Rothschild Tea Estate, Joan Turnbull, for the photograph of one of these wonderful looking estate lorries, from Balangoda Group (previous page). Although such lorries were in common use by the late 1920s, only a few proprietary

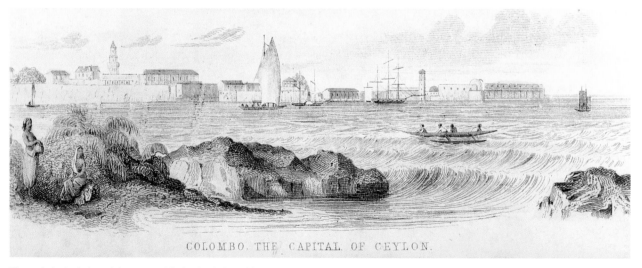

COLOMBO, THE CAPITAL OF CEYLON.

The artist's depiction of the town of Colombo is from Mutwall, in the days when sailing ships had to lay off in the open roadstead. The lighthouse, with its fine clock, is plainly visible as are the old stone walls of the fort, parts of which were built by the Portuguese and Dutch (*Lithograph c.1850.*)

planters and managers possessed a car, while an assistant could not afford to run one for another decade or more, and anyway a motor bike was ideal for getting around on steep and twisting roads. There were many accidents.

Until the arrival of the above-mentioned contraptions, the horse was the planter's only means of getting around on the estate, for visiting neighbours and to ride into Kandy or to the Club at week-ends. Tea was an all year round business whereas during the coffee days, when no crop was coming in for eight months, planters would ride into Kandy or down to Colombo where they would purchase provisions and idle away the time with their brother planters.

Shipping Tea

Sri Lanka has three good ports: Colombo, Galle and Trincomalee, the old Royal Navy base until 1957 and known as Trinco. The transport of coffee and tea has always been down to Colombo, with a small amount going to Galle.

By 1958 racial troubles had started, Sinhalese and Tamils were at loggerheads and in that same year strikes occurred at the Colombo shippers' stores, leading to a complete halt in the movement of tea through the port, and this in turn led to the suspension of tea auction sales there. Not only were there mountains of tea piling up in the Colombo go-

Coffee store. (*Sketch Illustrated London News 1872, courtesy British Library.*)

downs but on the estates too, for although crop was coming in and being manufactured daily, chests of tea could not be dispatched and space was becoming limited in the factories throughout the Island.

Tea was building up everywhere. With no movement from wharfside to ship, lighter men, who ferried the tea out to the waiting cargo ships, were idle, steel-helmeted police and soldiers patrolled the docks – what could be done?

The switch was made quickly and efficiently to Trincomalee, on the north-east coast, with estates dispatching their tea by lorry down to the old Naval base. This rather wild and generally uninhabited region of the island was the haunt of elephants, and the stretch of road between Habarana and Trincomalee was known to the lorry drivers as 'Elephant Run', as there were many hold-ups.

For six successive years after the strike began, ship-

ments of tea from Colombo dwindled, while those from Trinco mounted. Then in 1964, a cyclone devastated lighters and the harbour facilities at Trinco and once again the tea trade returned to Colombo, which immediately responded with emergency arrangements to handle the extra tonnage, as will be seen from the statistics.

	Colombo	Trinco	Galle
1958	177,430	40,659	50,464
1959	151,242	109,407	64,295
1960	141,695	123,147	63,715
1961	95,003	163,794	66,943
1962	63,405	192,692	71,226
1963	72,755	214,079	56,338
1964	136,127	180,898	41,361
1965	234,714	172,044	–
1966	287,702	121,515	–

▶

Planters Fowle and A. P. Craib playing chess in the old Bopette Division bungalow.

Lellopitiya Estate, Ratnapura District

Alexander David Callander arrived in Ceylon from Scotland in 1899. In the early 1900s Lellopitiya Estate was opened, and formed into LLP Estates Ltd. In 1920 A. D. Callander was a major shareholder and the property remained in the family until the Government nationalized the estates in the Island in 1975. In the 1930s, when these photographs were taken, the acreage of the estate was 1830 acres, comprising 600 acres of tea, 900 acres rubber and 15 acres with buildings etc. The tea factory (top right) burned down in January of 1945 and a new factory was in operation on 19th July 1946.

Planters J. G. Allan and C. J. Strachan look down on the old tea factory from the Udadaluwa Division bungalow.

The 'Transport Team' gets a wash-down behind the Big Bungalow. These bulls, with their carts, were used to transport produce to and from the estate. (*Photos 1930s, courtesy Ralph Callander.*)

The clipper ship *Tweed*, Colombo Harbour, 1888, seen from the old Customs sheds. (*Oil painting. Depicted by S. R. Fever in 1974.*)

The construction of the harbour was begun in 1875, prior to that sailing ships and the early screw-steamers would take on and discharge their cargoes in the open roadstead, often with a high surf running when winds beat up from the south-west during the monsoon. In those days tea chests were ferried from wharf to ship in lighters, a slow and labour intensive practice, and this was carried on until the late 1950s., when vessels were able to dock alongside the new facilities, part of which are seen under construction in the photo, left, taken in 1956.

The Container vessel. Tea transport from the Celestial Empire to the Western world was at first made by the grand but cumbersome merchantmen of the Dutch and English East India Companies, then by sleek and elegant tea clippers which were, in turn, superseded by the steamers; nowadays our tea is brought in the container ship – an incongruous sight at sea, if ever there was one.

Containerisation

It was the palletization of chests of tea during the 1970s that led to containerisation. Today, a large modern container ship can carry approximately 8000 huge containers; the product, if tea, can be loaded from shore to ship in 20 ft containers by massive cranes onto these fast vessels and transported to ports around the world – then loaded on to special freight trains straight to the major tea packers, thence to our supermarkets.

The evolution of the Estate Bungalow

In the pioneering days white women were as rare as white elephants, but there were exceptions. (*Photo c. 1881.*)

Log cabin life 1881 – a hunting morning

'Now then, just look alive!
The coffee bring, the butter and the bread:
With eggs and pie, and pudding too
the table quickly spread!
Hi, Carpen-boots and gaiters quick:
And see they're all well oiled,
My breeches too, of cannomore
Are those eggs nearly boiled?' ...

The umbrella, the tent and the leaves of the talipot palm were all used by the first timers for their only shelter in the jungle by the side of the small clearing that they were endeavouring to open out. The order of the day was work, from dawn till dusk.

The pioneer's first shelter, the leaves of the talipot palm. (*Water-colour by S.R. Fever 1984.*)

Log cabin life – a working day. (*From 'Scenes in Ceylon' 1881 by Hamilton and Fasson.*)

Planters get together at the week-end for drinks and a curry lunch. (*Photo c. 1880s, courtesy Hutchinson, London.*)

A modern bungalow. Hellbodde Tea Estate bungalow. Colourful beds of flame red, yellow and orange cannas contrast vividly against a well-cut lawn of blue grass. (*Photo 1998, courtesy Vernon Tissera, Superintendent.*)

Craigie Lea Tea Estate. 'The Car' – Frank and Maud Waring, with offspring Eileen and Archie Waring, with German governess and horse-keeper. During the General Strike, F.E. Waring and his son Archie drove a train in Colombo.
(*Photo c.1913, courtesy Mrs Joan Turnbull.*)

▶ By the late 1960s the Port of Colombo had seen the last of the tediously slow, labour-intensive practice of ferrying cargo on lighters between ship and shore. In 1958 the new harbour facilities were being built which, when completed, enabled cargo vessels to tie up alongside a concrete wharf. At about the same time a new monster, quite unlike a ship, appeared on the scene – the Container vessel. Top-heavy and looking for all the world like a block of flats, the container vessel is very efficient but very ugly.

By the time the new Queen Elizabeth Quay project was commenced, in 1999, some 250,000 containers a year were being handled by the port, which, with the completion of the QEQ, is expected to rise to a million. Today the tea is carried in huge containers on these leviathans with a negligible quantity air freighted.

Bungalows - Clubs - Sport

The British Colonist, unlike the Dutch in Ceylon, made the country their temporary home and did not intend to die there, though many did. For them it was a place of work or business, after which they would retire to Britain – God willing. Though this was generally the case there were those who fell under the spell of The Pearl of the East, retired and stayed on, just as a small minority of the British in India did.

It is true that the life of the early British planters in Ceylon did not equal, in hardship, that suffered by his compatriots in India who, instead of being the odd 100 miles from the sanctuary of Kandy, or Colombo, were getting on for 1000 miles from the equivalent, in Calcutta – with a tediously slow boat journey down the Brahmaputra to match. Nevertheless both started with pretty crude living conditions.

Life on the estates at the turn of the century was difficult for women, as there were no doctors, no nursing homes and nurses had to be privately engaged in Colombo. Women, in particular, had to go through a great deal in those days in maternity cases. Planter R. K. Clark's wife recalls conditions in this respect:

Late one night I had a message from a man living 3 miles off, saying his wife was threatened with a miscarriage (her first child) and was very ill. He had sent 3 coolies off in different directions to find a doctor, but no one had come. The doctor might be at the other end of the district and in any case had to ride the whole distance consequently they were often not in time.

R.K. and I walked down together and found the poor husband nearly distracted. I went in and did what I could and soon after my arrival the baby arrived too, but was not living. The doctor fortunately arrived while I was wondering what to do. I stayed on and nursed my friend for three days until she could get a nurse from Colombo.

Before club houses, a hospitable planter's bungalow would be the venue for a dance, and his garden for tennis. The following story, again told by Mrs. R. K., occurred on Coldstream Estate; the Superintendent was Harry Carry:

Harry Carry spoke Tamil fluently and could make himself up to look like a Ceylonese, and on this occasion we were all sitting out on the tennis court in the dusk, when two coolies came rushing on to the court, shouting in Tamil and apparently very drunk.

The men hustled all the women away, and then discovered that the 'coolies' were Harry Carry and Mr. McCausland. We had all met on that occasion to go to Darrawella Races where we went in a bullock cart with chairs inside. I've gone to many a dance in that kind of conveyance, everybody singing songs and enjoying themselves.

While on the subject of transport, and dances in particular, perhaps this is the right place to include another story. On occasion, the estate coffee store would be cleaned out, decorated and turned into a ballroom. However, if the planter's bungalow was palatial enough, it would be used as a ballroom and the coffee store would act as a dormitory to accommodate travelling planters, bachelors, grass widowers and the like.

Nobby and the Four-Poster Bed

This particular story, about 'Nobby', is told in my previous book and the only excuse I make for telling it again is because of popular request by a certain number of ex-Ceylon planters, and two from India that I recall. Certainly, it captures the life and times of those who lived on the coffee estates.

Although one might not think it, a coffee store was a very comfortable and dry place at which to stay, providing one had the foresight to come prepared. One planter, who, after long experience, knew the form at such meets, is said to have turned up at the designated estate complete with all that he deemed necessary for the questionable salubrity of a coffee store. He appeared upon the scene riding beside a bullock-cart on which he had loaded a four-poster bedstead, a mattress, a tin bath, a carpet and other essentials to a man's comfort, including a rifle. After the unloading of his cart, his creature comforts were carried by eager Tamils into the coffee store where he pegged out his claim on the ground nearest to the door, on account of the air being fresher there. Just before dusk, having settled in, quite a party developed among the inmates of the store who, having imbibed a little more than was good for them at such an early hour, then endeavoured to negotiate a change into evening dress. The proud owner of the bedstead, affectionately known as Nobby – on account of the brass knobs on the four corners of the said contraption – proceeded to tank up faster than most, until he became a nuisance. Luckily for everyone it was not long before he passed out, after which a certain calm prevailed while the others gathered themselves for the climb through the coffee to the big bungalow farther up the hillside.

As the ladies had been allotted different bedrooms in the married planter's bungalow, it was necessary that the party be brought to a close at a reasonable hour in the morning, so that they could retire to the comfort of their beds in peace. The rest of those present turned out and stumbled down the hillside in the bright moonlight to the coffee store which, being situated in a hollow, was enveloped in a white ground mist to about waist high.

Upon a sudden impulse, a small group formed around Nobby's bed and, with one heave, bed and inmate were lifted and carried outside and unceremoniously dumped in the middle of the flat coffee drying grounds with only a blanket as cover. Back at the store, candles were lit, singing commenced and the party went on until it was quite light. Meanwhile, with the first glimmerings of dawn the apparent corpse on the bed slowly regained consciousness. Finding himself in a cloud, with only the golden knobs of his four-poster bed visible above him, and the singing of many angels coming from close by, he thought he had passed on. It was only when the bungalow staff got on the move that one of the house boys, looking down, was attracted by the four golden orbs catching the rays of the rising sun. Recognising them for what they were – for Nobby had been this way before – the boy hurried down the hill, and walking through the still waist-high mist, presented on a silver salver a cup of hot tea. Nobby, seeing only the top half of the apparition standing before him, wondered a little; the suspicion grew upon him that he had not passed through the Pearly Gates after all and, upon being asked if he would care to partake of a cup of tea, knew that it was only a bad dream, turned over and went to sleep again.

A short digression into the complicated life of a certain young planter. (Totum = Estate)

The Tale of a Tea Planter

Christopher Rupert Aloysius Pilles

Managed a Totum all covered with hills
The worst of the matter to Christopher P.

Poonagalla bungalow and garden

With views away to the sea – a paradise for exotic birds

Poonagalla Tea Estate garden and bungalow. (*Photos 1969, courtesy Tony Gottelier.*)

Rothschild Tea Estate garden lake. (*Photo 1960, courtesy John and Joan Turnbull.*)

In 1988 I came upon a large flock while standing in tea adjacent to Glenkairn bungalow. After wheeling above for a not inconsiderable time, the whole flock shot off, as one, to settle in a large tree close by, putting up an incessant chattering before finally darting off.

The Ceylon Parakeet, or Hill Parrot, inhabits all of the mid and up-country tea districts up to and above Maturata. It associates in flocks of between 20 and 40, is a very noisy and restless bird uttering its harsh 'crake' on the wing while darting at arrow-like speed up and down the valleys.

(*Hand-coloured plate from Legge's Birds of Ceylon, 1881*)

▶ was the fact that the Hills were all planted with
    tea.
The above mentioned Mountains were so very
    steep
That they fairly made Christopher (R.A.P.) weep.
To his Agents one morning our Christopher
    wrote
'These cliffs are unclimbable, please send one
    goat'.
The Agents who thought him a bit of a fool
Said:'No! What you want is a good-looking
    mule.'
So Christopher ordered a Mule V.P.P.
Which duly arrived to his infinite glee!
The Mule looked quite docile, and Christopher
    strode
To mount him – and found himself flat on the
    road!
Advancing more cautiously near the brute's
    head,
He got a good bite on his – well enough said!
With Protractor and Compass he next took a
    line
To the middlemost spot on that animal's spine.
He leapt like a grasshopper straight at the spot
But found that the distance he'd quite over-shot!
But C was a lad of undoubted resource,
He refused to be rugged by the Son-of-a-Horse!
Beneath a great shade tree he had the beast led,
And dropped from a branch on the back of its
    head.
The Mule was so dazed from the impact and
    shock
That Christopher mounted him – firm as a rock.
And now O'er the Mountains he daily can roam,
But the Mule always 'shows him the way to go
    Home!'

(From Times of Ceylon, 1937)

It is, perhaps, true to say that the happiest and most settled times for the British planter was from the 1920s
until about 1950, but by then a certain gloom had
descended upon the European planting community
with the ugly head of nationalization of the estates a
distinct possibility.

An increasing number of planters were married and
their children would return to Britain to be educated,
though the Hill School at Nuwara Eliya was an excellent preparatory school for boys and girls. After school-
ing, a good proportion of the sons returned to Ceylon
to take up a career in planting, often many generations
in a family carrying on what they knew best. After all,
a doctor's son will probably follow his father's profession, likewise the Tamils, the backbone of the tea industry, carried on from father to son, many being
employed on a particular estate for over a hundred
years. One wonders how the plantation industry could
have managed without them.

It is all in the day's work for a planter to receive
numerous calls at his office and more occasionally at
his bungalow: perhaps a contractor with his tender to
cut and remove timber, by elephant, from a 100-acre
block of estate jungle, earmarked for a new tea or rub-

'The Dimboola pack gets its revenge'

'E. Palliser had at one time the luck to have a fair turn up with a
leopard with the dogs and hunting-knife. At that time he kept a
pack at Dimboola, about nine miles from my house. Old
Bluebeard belonged to him, and he had a fine dog named
Pirate, who was the heaviest and best of his seizers.

He was out hunting with two or three friends, when suddenly
a leopard sprang from the jungle at one of the smaller hounds
as they were passing quietly along a forest path. Halloa-ing the
pack on upon the instant, every dog gave chase, and a short
run brought him to bay in the usual place of refuge, the boughs
of a tree.

However, it so happened that there was a good supply of
large sharp stones upon the soil, and with these the whole
party kept up a spirited bombardment, until at length one lucky
shot hit him on the head, and at the same moment he fell or
jumped into the middle of the pack. Here Pirate came to the
front in grand style and collared him, while the whole pack
backed him up without an exception.

There was a glorious struggle of course, which was
terminated by the long arm of our friend Palliser, who slipped
the hunting knife into him and became a winner. This is the only
instance that I know of a leopard being run into and killed with
hounds and a knife.'

That great sportsman, Sir Samuel W. Baker, describes this
hunting incident in the early 1870s, a few weeks after an old
faithful, Bluebeard, had been lost to a leopard.

ber clearing; or perhaps an applicant for the post of Cook, who would arrive at the bungalow with his *tundu* (chit or note) from a past employer saying how good he is. Those whose business was in the culinary department of the bungalow might, on occasion and in the absence of any decent credentials, resort to a professional 'letter writer' in the local bazaar, who could be guaranteed to write a suitable letter – at a price. The more literate the vendor of letters the higher the price to be paid.

Whether the following letter is the product of such a letter writer or the good man himself, a Tamil hailing from Ootacamund in South India, it is hard to say. It was received by an estate Superintendent and was passed on to the *Ceylon Planting Gazette* for publication in January 1914:

PETITION TO A P.D. (Peria Dore = Big Master)

Most Honoured Sir,
Understanding that there are several hands wanted in your Honour's Department, I beg to offer my hand as to adjustment. I appeared for the Metric Exam in Ooty, but failed, the reason for which I describe to being with my writing was illegible, this was due to climatic reasons for having come from a warm to a cold climate, found my fingers stiff and very disobedient to my wishes. Further I had received a great shock to my mental system in the shape of the death of my only fond brother Mr. C. Viraswami besides honoured Sir I beg to state that I am in very uncomfortable circumstances being the only means of support of my fond brother's seven issues consisting of three adults and four adulteresses, the latter being bains of my existence owing to my having to support my two wives as well as their issues, of which by God's misfortune the feminine gender predominates. If by wonderful good fortune these few humble lines meet with your highnesses kindness and favourable turn of mind, I the poor menial shall ever pray the long life and prosperity of yourself as well as your honour's posthumous olive branches.

Soon there would be those back in Britain who regarded the life of a planter as being one of pure indolence and luxury: a lovely climate, an attractive bungalow and garden, with two or three servants, and the Club, as a last resort – and so it was, but the running of the estates was efficiently carried out by men who now not only worked hard but played hard too. They and the country had inherited much from the pioneers.

It would be enough to say here that for the planters of the 1920s and 1930s there was a bewildering variety of pastimes to pursue at week-ends: to the traditional sports of hunting, shooting and fishing were added cricket, golf, squash and of course tennis and billiards at the Club – not forgetting dancing.

One can imagine the conversation at planters' Clubs at week-ends, both in old and modern times. Unlike the pub in southern Ireland, especially those that are situated in the general vicinity of the great pike fishing waters – where stories abound and have done so for many long years about the whoppers that got away – in the clubs throughout the planting districts very different stories are told. This one comes from the early years, when there were no cars, and concerns a well-known and famous planter (a Scotsman) who caught his Assistant sleeping under a tea bush. The Assistant, having had a blinder at the club the night before, arrived back on the estate just before morning muster, when the creatures of the night were still plainly audible and even the birds had not got out of bed. Electing not to go back to the bungalow and sleep it off and having attended muster, he trudged wearily around his Divisions. Later, as the sun got up high in the sky and the wild-life took refuge, he picked out a large tea bush and was soon asleep. His Manager had, by chance, happened to ride by and, to the Assistant's considerable embarrassment, he awoke to find 'Faither' surveying him with a frosty eye from the back of his trusty steed. Scrambling to his feet his Manager waved him back with the cutting remark, 'Lie down again, Laddie, ye're doing nay harm there.' Such were Managers in those days – not half bad characters! I have, on occasion, found myself in a similar position but sitting comfortably on a steep hillside of tea with legs in a silt-pit under a Dadap shade tree (*Erythrina lithosperma*), with its lovely brilliant red flowers against a deep blue sky. Yes, planting was a good profession!

Then there was the story of the gushing young lady, with auburn hair and green eyes, who was just out from England, and a well known so called sportsman, who, when out on a shoot was not only a hopeless shot but a danger to all those who were with him. It so chanced the two found themselves sitting next to each other at a dinner-dance. When in due course the snipe was served, knowing that he was a keen shot, she charmingly said, 'And did you, sir, shoot this?' – to which the great man replied, 'Yes, I did. What's the matter with it? Isn't it dead yet?'

Before World War II European planters numbered around 2000. Then came the 1939-45 war when most of the younger planters left for the Services, with older men shouldering the responsibility of looking after several estates. Those that returned in 1946 got down to the job once again and life went on much as before.

As well as those returning from the war to take up their old billets, others were coming out to start what they imagined would be a lifetime in planting. I myself was one of those who arrived in the island in 1950, at a period when the future was just beginning to become clouded for the European planter by the uncertainty that the industry might become nationalised.

On the assumption that the story may occasionally be interrupted by something other than tea, here is a true story – every word of it.

The Wild Boar

'Presently I heard the rush of the boar in the jungle, coming straight up the hill towards the spot where I was standing' …

(Sir Samuel W. Baker, 1872.)

Stalking (*Lithograph 1853.*)

Some varied wildlife

Boar hunting from F. Marryat's 'Ceylon'. (*Drawing c. 1835.*)

Ceylon Spur Fowl. (*Hand coloured plate 1881 from 'The Birds of Ceylon' by Legge.*)

A pioneer's hut.
(*Watercolour by S.R. Fever.*)

Noosing wild elephants

'In constructing the corral itself, care is taken to avoid disturbing the trees or the brushwood within the included space'

(*Sir J. Emerson Tennent, 1867.*)

Elephant corral. (*From I. K. Prince, drawing c.1840.*)

Typical tea country
Foreground. Mature tea bushes under Grevillea shade trees.
Below and right. Shaded nursery beds.
Left. New clearing work in progress. Silt pits in this replanting area
have already been cut, to hold up the valuable top soil during
monsoon rains in later years.

Right and beyond. Another more advanced new clearing in which
the newly planted clonal tea can be seen.
Left and beyond. The estate factory.
(Photo late 1960s, courtesy Tony Gottelier.)

► ## *The Ship's Doctor tries his hand at Dentistry*

Half way through the 20th century I took passage to Ceylon to start my career in planting. As this book is all about tea and planters, at the expense of a small digression, let me tell you about the time when I performed the duties, quite unofficially of course, of an acting, unpaid dental assistant.

I had boarded the British India cargo-passenger vessel *Chilka* at Tilbury Docks in 1950, bound for Colombo. It was *Chilka's* maiden voyage and she had accommodation for twelve passengers, her main priority being cargo. There were five of us planters, or planters to be, on board, some returning to Calcutta from leave.

I will not bore you with a long account of the many ports of call during our passage, except to say that it was while steaming up the Persian Gulf that I took on the duties of a dental assistant; in fact, to be frank, I was merely able to give the ship's doctor a helping hand when he most needed it.

One day after lunch the young doctor caught me and said that if I had nothing better to do, I might like to pop in to his surgery at 4pm, as he had to remove the tooth of one of the crewmen, a Lascar. I spent a pleasant hour looking forward with great anticipation to my trip to the surgery. The young doctor had just completed his medical training, and no doubt wanted some moral support, as he admitted that he had not pulled a tooth before.

I turned up a little early and found him thumbing his way through a massive medical book, trying to work out which of a battery of grim looking instruments in a glass case, he would select for the job. Purely as a partial bystander, and not a patient, I found it all extremely interesting.

From the look of the patient when he arrived it was obvious that the tooth was just about driving him mad, as he had probably been putting off the evil day for quite some time. The doctor had by now taken me into his confidence and we were together studying the medical book, whilst he again explained that having never taken a tooth out before, he wanted to get things right, which seemed most sensible.

There were some wicked looking hypodermic syringes and a batch of even more vicious looking forceps all lined up on the table by now, at which the more than frightened patient was rolling his eyes. The first injection didn't seem to go too well, as the needle squirted the serum - if that was what it was - all around the inside of the man's mouth, as well as over his face, and as I happened to be leaning forward, I caught some too. It was obvious to see that the first injection wasn't any good, so the Doc had a second go, squeezed, and as nothing came out this time, all well and good, or so it seemed. We then had to wait an agonizing ten minutes or so for the second injection to take effect.

The doctor picked up one of the wicked looking forceps from the table, told the patient to open his mouth wide and then, as far as I recall, spent the next few minutes trying to get a good hold of the correct tooth, which he had previously marked with a pencil. The moment he started some serious pulling the patient gave an awful cry, or gurgle, and seemed to shoot up out of the chair a foot or more. I was in an agony of indecision as to whether to help by holding the man down in his seat. I said, helpfully, should I get on his shoulders and press downwards which seemed a very logical thing to do, to which the doctor agreed. Enjoying the doctor's confidence I became very daring and took the liberty of placing a small table behind the patient on which I climbed and from there was able to hold and push downwards on his shoulders; one might say he was kept steady.

By this time the poor Lascar was shaking like a leaf and we were all sweating profusely. The doctor suddenly said 'Ready' and had another pull, and I was hard pressed to keep the man in the chair, but this time the triumphant doctor was proudly holding the tooth in his pliers. The second injection obviously hadn't worked either but he did pull the right tooth out, which was something. The patient was so relieved that he shot off without even a thank you.

It seems quite amazing to realize that both the doctor and I were acting in the patient's best interest, but even in this more modern day and age operations do go wrong, even in the best of hospitals.

By sheer coincidence, the very next day one of the crewmen was buried at sea. Being in general an early bird, and having washed and shaved, I chanced to be taking a walk on deck when I became aware the ship was reducing speed. I soon heard voices coming from the port side of the ship and making for the spot arrived just in time to witness a small service and the consignment of the body to the deep. I distinctly remember wondering if by some strange chance it could have been the body of the crewman who had had his tooth pulled, but later, asking the doctor, was relieved to find it was another man.

Little did I know that I would soon be in a similar position, when a Sinhalese dentist pulled out one of my own teeth and his injection did not work either!

Just Tea Estates

From the coffee days, when estates averaged 200 acres or so, and with the continuing opening out of yet more jungle first time to tea, many estates had become giants.

Nowadays a Group of say 1500 acres of tea consisting of three or four Divisions, might have a resident population of about 3750 souls, of which about half would provide the working labour force, the balance being made up by dependents. The Group is a compact tightly-knit community often with many generations of the same Tamil families, going back to the days when its Divisions were individual coffee estates. The difference in the elevation of tea fields within a Group, as on Spring Valley Estate, could be almost 4500 feet between its top and lower Divisions. This being often the case, it is a labour intensive industry in Sri Lanka, where hand-plucking is the only option on land that is generally on the steep side.

Collection of the green leaf by mechanical harvester, which is practised in the tea fields of Japan and some other countries, is not workable in Sri Lanka, though it has been estimated that up to 25% of the tea acreage is on a terrain that would allow knapsack harvesting in the latter country.

Various types of leaf harvesters are manufactured in Japan, from small hand-held ones to tractor-driven machines, smaller but similar to the combine-harvesters that we see in the wheat fields on our farms in Britain.

Mechanical harvesting of the green leaf was first carried on Dickwella Estate by Basil Fay and these trials lasted for some years, but were eventually stopped owing to labour trouble brought about by the fear of job losses.

The Tea Research Institute carried out trials during the 1960s on special plots on St. Joachim Estate and Hapugastenne State Plantation, but owing to the amount of coarse leaf and stalk harvested, which had later to be picked out, the operation was considered uneconomic. The amount of made tea was considerably less from machine-harvested plots than that from hand-plucked plots. So the attractive scenes shown on our packets of tea, with pluckers in colourful saris, will not disappear.

In April 1954 the Queen and Duke of Edinburgh made a most successful visit to Sri Lanka. She and the Duke had a full itinerary which involved a wreath laying ceremony at Colombo, with visits to Polonarua and a Garden Party at the King's Pavilion in Kandy, where it poured with rain. Then on to visit the up-country planting district and in particular the Radella Club where the royal couple met planters. The Duke visited Pedro Tea Estate in Nuwara Eliya, where he met the Superintendent Mr. N. M. Sanders and estate staff in the factory and at the labour lines.

After the War and continuing up until 1955 the number of European planters actually increased, and then, as the threat of nationalization became more evident, there was a steady decline in numbers – the ▶

Frotoft Group. Plucking does not stop for the rain and is a wet job when you realise the tea bushes are soaking too. The plucking Kangani (overseer) usually carries an umbrella – a symbol of his authority. After World War II Kanganies often sported, and cherished, the discarded jackets and army greatcoats of planters; this was a mark of high esteem, recognised by all.
(*Photo mid 1960s, courtesy Alan and Elizabeth Sharp-Paul.*)

Completed in 1832, the Satinwood bridge was constructed entirely of satinwood, without the use of a single nail or bolt in it, the whole of the massive woodwork being merely dovetailed together. (*Drawing by permission of the British Library.*)

Bridge building on Spring Valley Group. (*Sketch by and courtesy of Charles Brooke-Smith.*)
Inset: An elephant working on a road on Balangoda Group. (*c.1920, Photo, courtesy Joan Turnbull.*)

A factory boiler on its way to an up-country tea estate after a long sea passage. (*Photo 1890s.*)

You can't get far without an elephant

'Porky' Balfour's Bridge, Spring Valley Group. (*Photo 1935, courtesy Charles Brooke-Smith.*)

Manufacture of instant tea - Ceytea factory

Originally owned by a German tea importing firm, Haelssen and Lyon, Hamburg. By 1970 ownership had passed to the Unilever Group, Lipton Ltd.

Ceytea Factory. L to R Herbert Braune, Engineering Officer, Ceytea Ltd.; Romesh Llangakoon, Ceytea; M. D. Banda; Gordon Gunesekara, Ceytea Ltd.; Alan Sharp-Paul, Whittall Bousted, Agents and Secretaries.
(Herbert Braune served in the German army through the Stalingrad cauldron during World War II.)

Pluckers from surrounding fields.

Inside the factory. Herbert Braune; M.D. Banda; Baku Mahadeva; Dr. G. Iriyagolle, Ministry of Agriculture.

The Ceytea factory.

Machinery inside the factory. Gordon Gunasekara; M. D. Banda; Romesh Llangakoon.
(*Photos 1967–70, courtesy Alan and Elizabeth Sharp-Paul.*)

The elephant receives a present. During the construction of Hapugastenne Tea Factory, in 1928, an elephant was employed to assist in lifting the heavy Ruston Hornby engine onto to its bed of concrete inside the factory. After its exertions it was suitably rewarded with a 'santosum' (present) of sugar cane. It was on this estate that the first trials using mechanical harvesters were tried during the l960s. *(Photo 1998, courtesy Frances Salvesen.)*

▶ white planter was, finally, on his way out.

Numbers of European and Ceylonese Planters

	European	Ceylonese
1950	797	940
1955	859	–
1959	419	1408
1963	276	–
1965	175	–
1972	106	–

Journeying into the 1950s there was the 1958 Emergency, with many shortages and what was generally called rationing. The Army became very officious, poking guns at everyone, including of course some of the planters and their wives, and the curfew caused problems on the estates. Transport including estate Land Rover was requisitioned, with not a few planters having their private transport taken too. All this was very unpleasant while it lasted.

During the late 1940s and early 50s there was a period when planters were ambushed and shot at when returning to their estates with coolie pay. We would drive into town in a convoy of three or four cars, collect the cash and then drive back to the estates with some of us riding 'shot gun'. This worked well and the pay was dropped off at the offices of two or three different estates. Of course everyone in the district knew we carried rifles with us and this was enough to stop any thoughts of an ambush. Sense prevailed.

I have been reminded by Tony and Joan Gottelier, late of Poonagalla Estate, of some of the murderous attacks that were made on planters during their many years in the planting districts. There has always been trouble on estates with the labour force and every planter would tell you that in most cases it could be overcome with reasonableness and tact. Murder in the heat of the moment is one thing, but murder for gain is different.

Before World War II the Manager of Stellenberg Estate, Mr. Pope, was waylaid on the estate cart road when taking the monthly pay-roll back. He was stopped and beaten to death with iron pipes and the money stolen. The Manager of Talgaswella Estate, Mr. Blumer, was returning to the estate with cash for the labour force when he too was waylaid and killed on the spot.

Then there was the case of the rogue office Clerk. 'Chatty' Godfrey was on an estate in the Kotmale area and was going through the estate accounts when he came across a discrepancy. He called the Clerk into his office and showed it to him. The Clerk, having no explanation, excused himself on the pretext of going to the lavatory, returned with a shot gun and shot 'Chatty' in the back.

Yet another murder occurred in 1948 when the Manager of Madampe Estate, Rakwana, was returning to the estate with the pay-roll, which had been collected from a bank in Colombo. While returning along the Ratnapura road, just by a sharp bend, a group of men jumped out as the car approached and shot Mr. Whitehouse, who was sitting in the front passenger seat. Mrs. Whitehouse, who was driving, courageously swerved through the ambushers and drove on to Palmgarden Estate bungalow, where Mr. Cole-Bowen was Superintendent. The pay-roll was intact but Mr. Whitehouse was dead on arrival.

In the mid 1950s a good friend of mine was attacked when he went to pin up a Notice to Quit on the line door of one of the labour force. This man, with his family, had caused much trouble on the Division and in this particular case had been stealing his line neighbour's chickens. My friend suddenly felt the weight of a man on his back who promptly bit him on the shoulder, quite severely. It surprised my friend as he was over six feet tall.

Like Ceylon, planters in India had similar problems with their labour force. When there are a couple of thousand or more workers on an estate there is bound to be trouble, on occasion.

Going into the late 1960s, Joan Turnbull, whose husband John was Superintendent of Rothschild Estate, has some interesting recollections:

> Rothschild was a very 'good' labour force, however in the late 60s, for some reason I cannot remember, the factory labour force went on strike suddenly, leaving all the previous day's leaf on the tats. John decided that the leaf would be manufactured come what may. He got hold of the two S.D.s, Teamakers and office staff plus the odd lorry driver, K.P., etc., and they started. The senior S. D.'s wife and I decided to help, we were followed by several wives from the rest of the staff and we got the tea manufactured. It was pretty awful but we did it. By late afternoon all the factory labour were back, looking sheepish, and not another word was said about the striking.

As mentioned previously the estate is a tightly knit group of people who would muck in when the necessity arose; this time Joan Turnbull and her helpers save the day but take a rocket from the Superintendent, her husband, in doing so:

> On one occasion I had an S.O.S. from the office, 'where was "Sir"' one of the lines was on fire. 'Sir' was away on top of the top Division. So I piled into the Land Rover, taking a couple of clerks with me, stopped at the factory and demanded some extinguishers, piled in some labourers and we tore off to the lines. Chaos! It was only firewood in the attals on fire, but was spreading right along the line. Everyone had a wonderful time extinguishing it and themselves. We were soaked. John had seen the smoke and appeared as we got the fire out. I got a sound telling off for removing the extinguishers from the factory.

Mention has been made of Edwin Arnold's account of the truly grim conditions that prevailed on estates during the 1870s, and in Ceylon the planter's wife was an asset to the labour force, in days gone by. Joan Turnbull:

> I think most of us born in Ceylon had learned to cope with what came. In earlier days there wasn't even a Dispensary on the estate, as was the case with many of the smaller estates. Doraisany (lady) was expected to see to all the wounds and small ills of the labour force. (Until Unions got big, then we had to refuse to treat anyone and send them off to the nearest hospital.) I remember the fuss that sometimes went on, why didn't we treat them, if they went to hospital they would die. How life changed!

Here is a story that ex-planter Bill Atkinson told me. I should first explain that the planter was, in most cases, his own man, a thoroughly independent fellow generally not influenced by his fellow man, as those who live in the big cities often are. Most often he is a character ▶

Putting the hounds into covert

THE daylight is breaking,
The dew-drops are shaking
On each blade of the grass, as they wave in its ray.
In the gorge far below
The jungle cocks crow
And the myna's shrill piping announces the day.

" No fear of a bungle
To-day in the jungle!"
Is each sportsman's thought, as he views the fair scene;
And striding on quickly,
Thro' scrub thick and prickly,
They soon reach the edge of a gloomy ravine.

And now with wild bounds,
Nine couple of hounds,
The jungle's thick fringe dash merrily round;
There's " Sanguine" and " Spangle,"
" Fly," " Frantic," and " Bangle "—
Just see how they feather and cover the ground.

" Loo into it, Pilot!
Yooi in boy ! loo, loo !"
And the eager hounds fly thro' the jungle away ;—

" By Jove, we're in luck,
Here's the slot of a buck,
Still muddy and soft struck deep in the clay !"

And now nought is heard,
Save the cry of some bird,
That startled, flies screaming away far below ;
Or Teddy's " Hi--loo !"
As he draws the bamboo—
" Yooi in ! little Ringwood ! Yo, Melody, yo !"

Hark ! was that a find
Borne down by the wind ?
Each heart stops its beating in tumult divine.
But anon they beat fast,
For a loud ringing blast
Proclaims that old Ranger has hit on a line !

What joy each one felt
As he tightened his belt,
Is far beyond my humble pen to expound.
No music, I ween,
To the forester keen,
Can rival the silvery voice of a hound !

Drawing 1881 from 'Scenes in Ceylon' by Hamilton and Fasson.

▶ loved by all, except, on occasions by his labour force. Admittedly bachelors were sometimes lonely, made pets such as monkeys and praying mantis and did strange things. This story is about a planter who made his Appu (Cook) place a .22 pistol beside his solitary dining chair every night. This, he explained, he needed to shoot 'gekkos' which kept up an incessant and constantly irritating chatter, upside down on the ceiling. I can, myself remember spending hours sitting looking up at these quaint little fellows, who came out as regular as clockwork each evening. They would congregate around the electric lights, if you had any, greedily snapping up moths. Occasionally they would fall, landing on the polished cement floor with a loud 'plop', when quite often their tails dropped off; these continued to wriggle for some time afterwards. They played exactly the same trick in Malaya, where they are called 'Chi chars'. I have a couple of ornamental silver ones in my home to this day.

The Tea Research Institute

Those of us lucky enough to be drinking – on average – our 3$\frac{1}{2}$ cups of tea a day owe it in no small way to institutions like the Tea Research Institute of Sri Lanka. They and their like in different countries around the world are experts in the business of growing tea effectively while keeping at bay pests and diseases that could, if unchecked, wipe out the tea industries in producing countries.

Those in the tea industry will know, only too well, the history of the fatal leaf disease (*Hemileia vastatrix*) that killed the once great coffee industry in Ceylon over a hundred years ago, and there will be many who remember today, that second equally virulent leaf disease, Blister Blight (*Exobasidium vexans*) which first descended upon the tea fields in 1946. Had it not been for the T.R.I., who can say what dire consequences there might have been for the country and its great tea industry? The dedicated scientists at the T.R.I. had a battle royal on their hands but this time the battle was won. This all goes to show that growing tea is not just a matter of sending out pluckers – those one sees on television and on packets of tea in the supermarket – there is an awful lot more to it than that.

During the years since its establishment in 1925, the T.R.I. has contributed in many ways to the industry in combating pests and diseases. Taking a light-hearted view of all the insects that fly and crawl around in the tea fields, perhaps you have heard the story about the Cockchafer grub, the Shot-hole borer and the Tortrix caterpillar? Now, the Tortrix caterpillar, which emerges from the eggs of the moth, is a leaf-eating pest which, like the Indian Looper caterpillar, does the same job on a field of tea, if unchecked. The Tea Research Institute combated this little monster by the introduction of a predator (*Macrocentcentrus homonae*) which was imported in large quantities from Java and when released effectively controlled the Tortrix. In the western world we have the minute mealy bug which, if it gets a hold in a conservatory, is very hard to eradicate, except with a predator. In this case the Australian Ladybird (*Cryptolaemus*) does the trick and is just one of the many predators that we use today. This little charmer, the Ladybird, has done some sterling work in my own conservatory wiping out an infestation of mealy-bugs.

By way of introduction to the Shot-hole borer, there is the story of one Basil Fay, a Visiting Agent, who was considered an expert on this nasty pest. B.F. was one who never took prisoners and while doing his rounds on Wevekelle Estate, Namunukula, this portly gentleman, feeling the need of a rest, sat down on a large tea bush which promptly collapsed around him. He explained in a loud voice to the Superintendent, John Turnbull, who knew that Wevekelle was pretty free of the pest, 'There, I told you so, Shot-hole borer,' and was promptly told, 'Nonsense, it is 16 stone of Basil Fay – you have ruined my tea bush!' Of course the story went the rounds of the Clubs!

Some of the pests mentioned are today less active than they used to be in the tea fields of Sri Lanka. The three 'bug poems' are a light-hearted approach, and I have to admit they are my very own copyright – with apologies to the scientists at the T.R.I., Talawakelle. Having had no success with the publication of any of my previous poems, it is hoped the reader will forgive my slipping these in here, for if it ever gets out that I have been writing poems, it will cause me no little embarrassment and no decent person will talk to me.

The Shot-hole Borer

The Shot-hole borer is by name
yet another dreaded pest,
When busily engaged, his works proclaim,
that he is one of the best,
With tight circles around solid stems, he
    perforates,
the branches half shot through,
The planter comes around to estimate
what work he has to do.
Nothing much that can be done
has not been done before,
Chances are, that you've half won
by pruning evermore.

The Cockchafer Grub

Oh Planter, watch out for the Cockchafer grub
As far as pests go he's the number one thug
For, just when you think you are doing alright,
Comes the Cockchafer grub plus his
    huge appetite
And, with never a 'May I?' or much less a 'Please'
he and his family will ringbark your trees
Then, as a result of their persistent chewing
The damage they do may well be your undoing.
So the minute you see them apply lethal spray
and, if that does not work, you will just have
    to pray

▶

The Tea Research Institute of Sri Lanka

St Coombs Estate, Talawakelle

Director Dr. M. T. Ziyad Mohamed (2004)

The TRI opened on St Coombs Estate in 1928

Total tea acreage	410 acres
Present factory built	1928
Type of manufacture	Orthodox–Rotorvane
Total scientific staff	114
Total estate labour force	784

Main laboratory complex of the TRI.

Looking ahead with the TRI

Aerial view of the main laboratory complex of the TRI in 1985. *(All photos courtesy TRI.)*

Experimenting in the field, laboratory and factory

The analytical laboratory of the Soils and Plant Nutrition Division.

Interior laboratory of Technology Division.

Tea Research Institute

The factory of St. Coombs Estate and TRI
Laboratory buildings in 1931.
(Photo courtesy the TRI.)

Almost the same angle of view but taken
from a higher elevation in 1961.
(Photo courtesy the TRI.)

Landscape view of the imposing laboratory
complex of the TRI in 2004, showing part
of the area allotted to trial plots. The total
area under tea in Sri Lanka today is
189,000 hectares on 495 estates. Of this
amount 58% is old seedling tea and 42%
clonal vegetative propagated tea.
(Photo courtesy the TRI.)

A splash of colour in tea country at around 4000 ft above sea level. A typical scene showing pluckers after leaf weighing in the field, which will be followed by a final one at the factory at the end of the day.
(*Photo 1982, CAW.*)

Experimental plots on St. Coombs in 2004. The bushes that separate the trial plots are Assam cultivar TRI 2043; the shade trees are *Grevillea robusta.* (*Photo courtesy TRI.*)

Manual uprooting of 80–85 year-old tea for replanting on Brownlow Estate.
(*Photo 1982, CAW.*)

▶ that Divine inspiration will think up a plan
For a way to put paid to the Cockchafer clan.

The Tortrix Caterpillar

By night the Tortrix eats the flush
which on all good estates is ever so lush.
Our planter loses so much leaf
he declares the Tortrix is a thief!
The life of the caterpillar is just five weeks
and during this time it eats and eats.
600 lbs of leaf an acre, is a lot
but what do you do if you haven't got
a predator who will eat eggs and pests
and lay the little beast to rest.

Talking of caterpillars and things reminds me, not of a monoculture like tea, but of the more varied life on a farm in the British Isles and of my boyhood days when the aforesaid, together with moths, butterflies and birds used to claim my undivided attention, not to mention any stretch of water whether flowing or still, with its dragonflies, great-crested newts, moorhens and fish; all have given me the right background upon which to base my knowledge of caterpillars! As to fish, I recall that, when quite young, I was taught by an old farm-hand to tickle trout, a most rewarding activity up fast flowing, boulder-strewn streams; one simply works upstream against the current feeling carefully under boulders until one's hand comes in contact with the trout which is then cradled, lovingly, in the upraised palm of the hand(s) and then brought infinitely slowly away and up to the surface, or almost, whereupon the grip tightens around the body and it is flung out, a flash of wriggling silver onto the grass bank. As they say north of the border: 'Hav ye nae gay goodled trout under the steines?' (Have you not gone guddling trout under the stones?') Ah well, happy days – Gumping and Guddling.

Tusker in the Tea

I must include one more story; I think you will agree it is worth telling. Here is an interesting story for Sri Lankan planters, especially the younger ones, who would probably tell you that an elephant in a tea field is highly unlikely, today; well so it is, but this happening occurred hardly 30 years ago. During the pioneering years when there was patana and jungle land everywhere, our good friend the elephant was used extensively on the coffee and later, tea estates; in fact right up until recent times, but a wild untrained one, in your tea field, is another matter.

One of the lower Divisions on Poonagalla Group had its boundaries adjoining jungle to the south and east, towards Wellawaya. While resident on Poonagalla Joan Gottelier, writing in 1971 for the Loris *Wildlife Magazine*, gave this entertaining account. It is nice to be able to include it here:

What would be your reaction if you were doing a watcher's round of a tea estate at 6.30 am and came face to face with a wild elephant in the tea? That is what happened to a Poonagalla watcher on the 10th January, but history does not relate which of them got the bigger fright. Word was sent to my husband at the office, who was told that, on seeing the watcher, the elephant had turned and run back the way it had come along the field road and into the patnas and gums ¼ mile back. This is at the saddle at the base of Trig Hill on the estate side, which overlooks Broughton factory, main road and hairpin bend on one hand, and down on Ballagalla Ella and Leangawella on the other, and can be clearly seen from that part of the Bandarawella-Poonagalla road. On the other side, it looks across the Moneragala range of hills, and is at an elevation of 5000 feet. Trig Hill and its base hill rise up almost sheer from the new Ella-Wellawaya road.

My husband rushed back to the bungalow, grabbed his camera, binoculars and me in that order, and off we shot in the Scout to this point, about 1½ miles up from our bungalow, parking the Scout on the estate road and walking on the track that leads round the base of Trig Hill where it meets the tea. I must admit that we thought it may have been a hoax, but sure enough, there the elephant was – and a Tusker at that! A stocky 7-foot male elephant, thought to be the Swamp Elephant, with a pair of fine tusks, very white, thick and symmetrical, and about 2½ feet in length. It was a cold morning with mist swirling around. A crowd was watching the elephant from the patna and a dog, who was fearless enough to warrant his name of 'Tiger', was barking furiously at it. When we appeared, it turned and lumbered down into the gums on the top of a lower and adjacent hill, 'Tiger' following close on its heels and being threatened every now and again. We were concerned that it might have gone down this gum hill and landed up on Broughton estate road and so on to the main road at the hairpin bend. It was in such a belligerent mood, obviously very frightened, that it would have killed anyone it came upon, and there were already cries from the crowd that it would have to be shot. They would not listen to my husband's pleas to keep quiet and give the elephant a chance to get away quietly. After a while it came out of the gums and rushed up at us, falling forward on to its knees once in the effort, and we had to make a quick get-away. Later on, it made another charge at us, getting on to the track level with us, whereupon it came straight towards us. My husband tried to run uphill, lost his wind and could not move, and I am sure all the events of his past life must have floated through his mind while the elephant pounded on to about 15 yards. The crowd shouted at it harshly and loud, and 'Tiger' rushed out at it, and this stopped it in its tracks whereupon it turned and went back to the gums. It really was too close for comfort, and gave us all quite a fright, whereafter we retreated to a safer distance. It trumpeted as it went back again to the top of the gum hill, pushing down sizeable trees in its rage as if they were matchsticks. One 'clever Dick' started to walk up towards it as it stood in the gums, and when he was fairly close it charged him down the hill. It was a very close thing, and I am sure he thought his number was up, he then decided that discretion was the better part of valour and returned to the crowd. My husband sent for a tom-tom beater to try and 'beat' the elephant back on to the track and around the hill, where it would have been able to return to the Ella jungles, but that did not have the desired effect, and the elephant remained in the gums at the top of the hill. A crowd of about 20 with the tom-tom beater volunteered to 'beat' up the hill en masse and attempt to drive it on to the track. We saw the elephant hiding in the gums at the top and shouted to them to be careful, but the tom-tom and their hoos and haas drowned our warning, and they were near the top of the hill and almost on top of the elephant before they saw it, a split second after it had seen them and started to charge. I was always under the impression that an elephant could not charge downhill as it would then be top-heavy, but what came next dispelled that impression. It charged the men downhill for about 150 to 200 yards, a gradient of about 1 in 6, through gums, grass, hidden rocks, uneven ground, as surefooted as anyone. It almost caught up with one man and could not have been more than 10 feet from him when he came to a deep wide drain, and this undoubtedly was his salvation, as he cleared it and the elephant stopped at it. It had gained on the men steadily and I was so certain it would notch up one dead body that I had my hands ready to clap over my eyes, quite forgetting I had a camera in my hands and could have got a remarkable photograph. I did get three or four shots earlier, one as he rushed up at us, and hope results will be good, although there will probably be quite a bit of 'camera shake'! By then my husband had made the crowd realise that taunting the elephant would not help, and the poor animal had to be helped, and prevailed upon to keep quiet. 'Tiger' was tied up, and eventually the elephant walked slowly back up the gum hill, over the small ridge and onto the track where we were. It had one or two half-hearted looks our way, and it seemed very tired by then, with reason, then it turned away and walked along the track around the hill, when it would have gone on down the patna land into the jungle. This track is often used by buffalo and wild pig.

This operation took close on two hours, and having seen the elephant safely round the hill where it would have turned its back on civilisation, we felt we had done our job. We did not allow the crowd to follow it up, as there were no escape routes that way, and we did not want it further harassed, and probably undo all the good we had done. My husband informed the Wild Life Department in Colombo who immediately arranged for the Ranger stationed at Hakgala to come over if it was seen again, but after it had been seen again that evening just out of the jungle at the bottom of the estate whereupon it turned back again, that need never arose. I understand that it was one of a small herd trapped between Buttala and Passara, and two days later it was seen with 3 other elephants on the 10th mile of the new Ella-Wellawaya road, so we assume it has now returned to the comparative safety of the jungle and will have decided that civilisation and two-footed animals are not its way of life.

A few days later my husband and I walked to the top of Trig Hill, which is approximately 5500 feet elevation, and two-thirds of the way up, on the steepest ridge of the hill, we found elephant droppings, so the elephant must have come over the summit and down the ridge, and would have been silhouetted against the treeless skyline at some time of the early morning. What would be your reaction if you were returning from the Club in the early hours of the morning, and found a wild elephant silhouetted against the skyline above you?

How can one follow a story like that? – well, with another!

30 Years Later

Jumbos Back at Poonagalla Estate

In February 1997, elephants, once again, put in an appearance on Poonagalla Estate, and a wild-life team enlisted the help of some 200 estate workers in driving some of the elephants down towards the Wellawaya road. With opposition coming from villagers in the Wellawaya region, Dr. Nandana Atapattu, the Deputy Director of the Wildlife Department, had planned to tranquillise the elephants and air lift them, by helicopter, down to a wild life sanctuary in the lowlands. Owing to the difficulties involved in tranquillising elephants on the steep terrain around Poonagalla, the 1997 airlift never got off the ground.

In 1998 a herd of a dozen elephants were back on the Poonagalla and Macaldeniya estates, where eight people were killed, tea trampled, coconut, plantains, Jak and del trees destroyed. Among this herd were five bull elephants. The estate labour force, their lives at risk, hid in their line rooms at night fearful of the marauding elephants.

Any present day planter returning from the Club in the early hours, nicely lubricated, had better beware, for if he imagines he has seen a pink elephant it could just possibly turn out to be the real thing. A census conducted by the Wild Life Department in 1998 shows the elephant population of Sri Lanka at between 4000 and 4500.

Before leaving Poonagalla Estate it may be interesting to know that two leopards were caught in the trap (illustrated in the next chapter) in which a live goat was used as bait; first the mother, then her cub, when fully grown. When still in the trap, each leopard was shot behind the ear by the Superintendent, Tony Gottelier.

Besides having their cattle killed, the labour force in the lower Division that bordered the jungle at Wellawaya, were naturally fearful for their small children. Dogs are certainly a favourite prey for leopards. One of the estate workers spat on the dead leopard, as it had killed four of his cattle.

Nationalization

By the time nationalization of the estates had been completed in 1975, the tea industry had suffered many years of cut-backs by British companies in expenditure on costly replanting programmes. This lack of investment by foreign owned companies went back almost 25 years to the early 1950s, when nationalization was far from being the declared aim of any government. This, however, did not stop ministers talking about it in public, which naturally scared the tea companies.

With approximately 590,000 acres of tea in 1970, of which over 500,000 were foreign owned (British), about a quarter was old seedling tea that had been planted before, or just after the turn of the century. Only a comparatively small acreage had been planted up with high yielding vegetative propagated tea. Crop dropped drastically and this state of affairs reduced the country's world market in made tea from 30% in 1970, to 23% by 1980.

After nationalization replanting fell even further behind but started to pick up during the 1980s, when the industry received help from the outside world in the form of loans from the World Bank and Asian Development Bank. This is all dreadfully dull for the general reader who is probably, anyway, familiar with the misfortunes that occur when an old established industry is taken over, be it the British Teak industry in Burma, or the Tea industry in Sri Lanka.

The assistance provided by the Asian Development Bank, alone, amounted to a $12.8 million concessional loan for the Third Tea Development Project. This Bank Loan was for a period of 40 years, including 10 years grace, having a service charge of 1 per cent per annum.

On the political side, but affecting the plantation industry, there has been considerable unrest amongst the Tamil people who work on the estates. The Tamil Liberation Front was formed in 1972, to look after Tamil interest on the Island. Terrorist violence persisted throughout the 1970s and 1980s, and sadly still does. During the late 1980s conditions on the tea and rubber estates deteriorated to an extent when 1500 troops were sent to protect estate factories. The leftist Peoples Liberation Front burnt down 23 tea and rubber factories, killing 25 estate workers and burning thousands of kilograms of made tea. Shortly after, another five factories were burnt down by subversives and completely destroyed in the Uva District, which was managed by the Janatha Development Board. Such tactics are well within the capabilities of saboteurs to not only derail trains - as outside Hatton in 1939 - but to cause great damage and havoc to both the tea and rubber industries, which are the main economy of the country - though the tourist and clothing industries have been increasing year by year.

Sri Lanka's tea acreage is decreasing and stood at 543,000 acres in 1992, of which 151,000 acres, or 28%, were small holdings of less than 50 acres.

Many an old planter might wonder, like we all do at times, what the modern generation get up to, such as converting tea factories into hotels! Yet there is one of these oddities, and in case you would like to get some first-hand experience of living in a tea factory, the Heathersett Tea Factory is the name, and it is situated in the Nuwara Eliya district. A friend of mine has stayed there and the 'staff' welcome tourists with open arms. Not half bad is the verdict.

The commercially important tea camellia, both the China and Assam varieties of the plant, have been spread far and wide throughout the world (the first tea seed to Ceylon in 1839) and to-day this great industry gives employment to millions in the tea growing countries.

With Australia going into the 21st century growing and producing its own tea, it is time for our good friends to say, 'No worries, it's not just the Poms that drink the stuff - <u>we</u> even grow it!'

CHAPTER VII

AN ILLUSTRATIVE RECORD OF TEA PLANTATIONS OF THE WORLD

India
Sri Lanka
Kenya
Bangladesh
Malawi

China
Taiwan
Japan
Indonesia
Australia

Like a combine harvester in the wheat fields of England or North America, a Valiant Tea Harvester (MC-10) crops green leaf from orderly, well manicured tea fields. The view shows Mt. Kaimon in the Kagoshima Prefecture on southernmost Kyushu Island, Japan. (*Photo 1997, courtesy Matsumoto Kiko Co. Ltd., Japan.*)

BANGLADESH. Tea pluckers going out to work on Lungla Estate. (*Photo 1998, courtesy Duncan Brothers [Bangladesh] Ltd.*)

Into the 21st century

Life and conditions on the plantations today

Compared to living conditions on the tea estates in the past, the welfare of the resident labour force is very much improved today, as one would expect.

In the early days of the tea industry, started by the British and Dutch in India, Java and Sumatra, and Ceylon during the early 19th century, the labour force on estates lived in crude bashas made of split bamboo and sometimes plastered with mud and ekra, with a thatched roof to top it off. These low hovels nestled closely together – one might almost think for safety in numbers – in small clearings hemmed in by jungle, a good example being the photograph on p. 40 *A Living Community in the Jungle*.

Wild animals abounded and the bites of snakes posed a very real threat to those engaged in opening out jungle with the axe, yet it was far more likely that, of all the hazards, the minute malaria-carrying anopheles mosquito would give them a good dose of fever. Then there was always black-water fever, dysentery, cholera and smallpox to contend with – all this with no hospitals or medical attention of any kind – and less serious ailments such as hook-worm caused by soil pollution in and around the labour lines.

The highly researched watercolour drawings showing *The Early Stages of the Assam Company's Headquarters at Nazira* and the map *Pioneer Country North of Nazira* in Chapter II, so admirably depicted by the artist Sidney Fever, give us an excellent indication of how countless small tea estates were opened. One might express astonishment at the meagre dwellings in which the labour force lived, not least the European planter in his 'bungalow' who generally resided, through necessity, cheek-by-jowl with a labour force which, finding life intolerable, would sometimes sneak off to some other godforsaken spot when the opportunity arose.

The single- and double-'line' dwelling then evolved, with rough stone walls and mortar under a corrugated iron roof, which accommodated six to twelve families on each side in 12 x 10 ft rooms. This type of dwelling was the norm until the 1970s, and later on some estates.

To remind us of the truly awful conditions on the tea, coffee, sugar and cinchona plantations in India, Ceylon, Mauritius, Java and Sumatra during the 19th century, planter Edwin Arnold, writing in the late 1860s, has this to say of the mortality rate of the labour force on his estate in South India:

> Many cases were past the mending of any earthly doctor, and in one week fourteen coolies died in the 'lines' within a stone's throw of my bungalow. They dropped out of the ranks to be buried in the nearest strip of jungle, and nobody knew when they came, or where they were.
>
> The Coolie graves in the jungle nearby were at this time growing terribly numerous, and the jungle was becoming thickly marked with the little hillocks which denoted the last resting place of the poor wretches; there were more already there than we had opened acres, and the numbers increased daily.
>
> Many of the graves were made shockingly shallow, and the wild dogs and wolves tore open and partly dismembered the inmates.

By then the rapid expansion of the planting industry had far-reaching effects upon a wide range of people, giving employment to millions. It continues to do so today and the estates' resident labour force are housed in small individual dwellings, most of which have piped water on hand. Each family – as indeed often in previous years – has a small plot of estate land on which to cultivate vegetables, plantains, manioc and the like. Now, when the plucker and her husband go out to work in the fields or in the factory each day, their young children are either looked after by their grandparents or go to the estate crèche or school.

The estate hospital, its doctors and nurses provide all the health care that is required: the new Camellia Duncan Foundation Hospital on Shumshernugger Tea Garden, Bangladesh, being as up-to-date as any in that country. Westerners need not now commiserate with the conditions of those who work on the estates.

Indeed few realise the enormous benefits that have been derived, over the years and to this day in some tea growing countries, through the involvement of large plantation-owning companies such as the Camellia Group P.L.C.; Williamson Magor & Co. Ltd.; George Williamson & Co. Ltd. and James Finlay P.L.C. – some of whose tea plantations are illustrated in this chapter. These tea companies bring employment to millions.

The Camellia Group's interests are principally in tea, with a total cultivated area of 78,000 acres (32,000 hectares), making it one of the largest producers in the world. Many companies within the Group are well over 100 years old and on the Indian sub-continent the Group's history goes back to 1868, when Alexander Lawrie set up Balmer Lawrie & Co. in Calcutta – while its tea holdings in Africa – in Kenya and Malawi – are of more recent times.

The great Agency House of Williamson Magor was formed in 1869 as a partnership between James Hay Williamson and Richard Magor, who were working in Calcutta and Assam – the former having been a paddle-steamer Captain and Superintendent of Cinnamara Tea Estate, which was opened in Assam in 1854. Williamson Magor, with its headquarters in Calcutta (now named Kolkata) is run by the Khaitan family. Mr. B. M. Khaitan became managing-director in 1964 and from 1965 has been chairman. The tea section of the group is made up of 51 estates covering Assam and the Dooars belonging to McLeod Russell India Limited, the Bishnauth Tea Co. Ltd.; Williamson Tea Assam and the Doom Dooma Tea Co. These Companies comprise the largest single tea group in India, producing some 70 million kilos each year.

The large tea companies, in some cases based in the U.K., play their part in the tea growing countries by ensuring a proper health regime and welfare services, often well beyond minimum government requirements, for all who work on their estates, both on the Indian sub-continent and in Africa.

In fact, their labour forces are fortunate to work and live their entire lives in the 'Company Family', well looked after and cared for.

The five estates making up PT. Indorub Sumber Wadung's Group, some of which are shown in the Indonesian section, do not have their own hospitals but have a staffed polyclinic to which a visiting doctor comes two or three times a week and then, if necessary, sends patients on to hospital, the estate bearing the costs.

There are also good schools on PT. Indorub SW's estates. Each estate has a kindergarten and primary and often even up to secondary schools, supplementing and surpassing Government standards. All in all once again their labour forces are well looked after in the plantation family community.

This last illustrative chapter on tea plantations is perhaps the first attempt to show just what is happening today in the different tea producing countries around the world as we enter the 21st century – including, for instance, tea that is grown and manufactured in Australia and the United States, albeit in small quantities. Having looked back in time at how the pioneers

lived, worked and played – through the many early photographs and Indian scene paintings, some with a nostalgic appeal – it is hoped this final chapter will provide an insight into the modern working lives of those on the tea plantations. In future you will appreciate how tea got into a chest and then into the packet that you have just bought from the supermarket. So enjoy the photographs which appear on each country section and which will give you a visual and I hope comprehensive insight.

The Tea Camellia under Commercial Cultivation

A picture is worth 1000 words

The tea plant belongs to the genus *Camellia* which includes some 80 species, all of which are indigenous to south-east Asia, but it is the commercially important tea camellia – the two varieties of which are *C. sinensis* and *C. assamica* – that concern us here. The bushes, whether grown on plantations in India, China, Africa, Sri Lanka or South America, are kept to a uniform height of about 3 ft in the fields for easy hand-plucking, or to accommodate the riding-type tea harvesting machine. However, left to its own devices, the tea plant will grow into a tree 60 ft in height, with a 40 inch circumference at ground level. See next page 166 which shows one such ancient tea tree in Vietnam that must be a few hundred years old.

Monsoon period – tea growth

The only large tea growing region not affected by the monsoon is that in Indonesia (Java and Sumatra).

The tea growing regions in Bangladesh, India, China and those in Sri Lanka and Japan are all affected by the south-west monsoon which breaks at the beginning of April with the Small Rains, and this is followed by the full monsoon about a month later. The busiest time on estates is during the monsoon proper, from the middle of June until the end of October. During these months plucking rounds are stepped up so that the green leaf is taken from the bushes more frequently and plucking goes on every day of the week.

During these hectic months manufacturing conditions are at their most difficult with the heavy crop coming in overloading factory capacity, and with all machinery working every day for 16 hours or more at a stretch.

Productive life of the tea bush

The commercial life of the tea plant is between 50 and 70 years during which time it is pruned every 3 to 5 years, depending upon its 'jat', or type and the conditions under which it is grown: climatic conditions and elevation – from 500 feet up to 6500 feet – play a big part in yields, as does the 'clone' of the plant, also whether it is the China or Assam type.

The China tea plant (C. sinensis)

The erect, small-leafed China tea plant, which grows best when planted at higher elevations, has a slower rate of growth and because of this produces a better quality of made tea. China bushes are pruned every 5 to 6 years and sometimes the pruning cycle is even

Big tea plant in Northern Vietnam (about 8 m in height). (*Courtesy the World Green Tea Association*).

longer. The commercial life of the China variety is longer than that of the broad-leafed varieties, *C. assamica* and *C. manipur*, often being as much as 80 years before yields drop sufficiently to make uprooting and replanting necessary. The China tea plant and hybrids are grown on plantations throughout China, Japan and Taiwan, also in some up-country districts in Darjeeling and the Nilgiri Hills of South India.

The Assam tea plant (C. assamica)

The horizontal broad-leafed Assam variety is planted throughout much of the tea producing countries of the world – China and Japan excepted, the latter having a very small acreage. Its useful commercial life, again depending upon conditions, is, on average, 60 years. Black Tea is manufactured from the Assam variety

while Green Tea is produced from the China variety.

After a life of yielding their green leaf, 'flush', the bushes end up as firewood for the estate labour force when a field of old, poor yielding tea is uprooted for replanting. Each estate maintains a strict rota for both pruning and uprooting old uneconomical tea in its many fields of different ages.

The future

In this final chapter the reader will see the shape of things to come with respect to the changing methods of harvesting the green leaf and manufacturing. The traditional hand-plucking is still carried out in China, India, Indonesia, Sri Lanka and Africa, but other countries use modern machinery such as the riding-type tea harvester, portable machines for two persons and hand-shears. This green leaf harvesting machinery has been designed for both flat and hilly terrain and can be seen to great advantage in the Japanese Tea Culture section, p. 267.

There are probably upwards of 600,000 acres of flat-grown tea in Assam and the Dooars which is admirably suited to the riding-type harvester instead of the present hand-plucking. If it was ever decided to 'go mechanical', such a change could only be brought about slowly over a period of many years, when old poor yielding tea is uprooted and all new plantings can be put out in straight rows and at the right distance apart for the machines.

Such a saving in labour costs would put hundreds of thousands of estate workers out of work – and not only pluckers as the application of fertiliser to the tea fields and the pruning of bushes can also be done efficiently by machinery. The Governments of some tea producing countries are opposed to mechanical harvesting for this reason but riding-type machines will doubtless eventually be used in North-East India. Nor will the estate workers always wish to spend hours in the field in the hot sun or shivering in the rain.

Though tea harvesting machinery cuts leaf, shoots *and* stalk, it cannot possibly beat a good pair of hands when it comes to selective plucking of 'two leaves and a bud', as required for the manufacture of optimum quality tea.

Comparatively speaking a very small amount of 'new land' is being opened to tea, except in Africa. In Java and Sumatra the position is somewhat different in that 'old tea land' – previously abandoned and having thereafter reverted to scrub during and after World War II – is being brought back into production with high yielding clonal plantings, and a great increase in acreage.

However, the tea industry is passing through a phase where many estates – particularly in Darjeeling as well as in Indonesia – are having to close down. Management and labour costs on estates are rising continuously while tea prices are not – in fact they are often depressed as they are at present.

These rising costs just cannot be contained and there seems to be no prospect of change in the tea market as Kenya, in particular, continues to produce ever more tea each year. World-wide there is far too much tea on the market and buyers take full advantage of this, avoiding sharing the responsibility by paying more for their teas. Indeed, some buyers have the cheek to check and see if estates are looking after their workers properly and not taking advantage of them.

Meanwhile the tea companies and their estates remain responsible for the livelihood and welfare of hundreds of thousands of people; many estate workers know no other way of life, a good proportion having forbears who worked on the estate(s) for the past hundred years.

Production and area of tea in the world (FAO, 1999-2000)

(Sources: Shizuoka Statistics & Information Centre (*SSIC*), Kanto, MAFF).

Bearing in mind the vast difference in the cost of living in the Western world and that of the people in tea producing countries, the social welfare enjoyed by estate communities is today a top consideration for tea companies – as shown in this last chapter.

Finally not many people realise the important role the tea plant plays, not only in giving us our daily cup of tea, but in combating the 'greenhouse effect', leading to global warming. In simple terms tea, with its lush green canopy, is most effective when it comes to photosynthesis, the process by which plants use sunlight to convert carbon dioxide into new cells. Tea plants and their shade trees absorb the harmful carbon dioxide and give off oxygen in its place.

As will be seen from the chart, at the turn of the century there were approximately 2,400,000 hectares or nearly 6 million acres of tea grown worldwide. This colossal acreage of tea is, as far as one can predict, assured for the future as no rain forest can ever be.

'Opening out'

Before proceeding to the illustrations showing life and work on present day tea estates – which in the case of those in India and Java have been established for over 170 years – it may be interesting to understand just how all these estates were formed, in nearly all cases from virgin jungle (in the case of British and Dutch development of tea in Asia) while China and Japan have been cultivating the tea camellia for approximately 5000 and 800 years respectively, but not on the same plantation scale.

Perhaps if I share and re-live my own happy experience of opening out 105 acres of estate-owned land in Ceylon, in this case for rubber, just 50 years ago in 1955, it will provide a small link with what our forbears were doing under far worse conditions when introducing a variety of plantation crops to the East such as tea, coffee, rubber, cinchona and cocoa.

During the 1950s – unlike the great pioneering

years – there was little new clearing work in Ceylon. Mid- and up-country tea estates had been fully developed to their maximum acreages. In the Southern Province, however, the position was slightly different in that there were still new clearings being opened up from estate-owned jungle, mainly for rubber. One was indeed fortunate to have the chance of doing this particular work.

The new clearing – hard at work

It had been arranged with a native contractor to fell and clear away all the trees on a 50 acre block of jungle, leaving the balance of 20 acres of jungle and 35 acres of scrubland to be cleared by the estate labour force. The expense of such an operation is great for, whereas it is three years before the tea bush is brought into plucking, it takes seven years before the rubber tree reaches a girth of 21 inches at three feet from the ground and is ready to be tapped.

The contractor and his men had come from a village about 18 miles away, and arrived one morning complete with a ramshackle old lorry and, only a little later, with two elephants which had been ridden all the way. In his 50 acre contract block were many good timber trees which were suitable for furniture making. A large sawing hut was soon erected by his men, to which most of the timber was brought. Once they had started, the men worked seven days a week, except on full moon, or 'poya day', the Sinhalese monthly holiday. It was necessary for two estate watchers, who each carried a gun, to keep an eye on the felling, otherwise some good timber trees would also have disappeared from the adjacent estate-owned jungle; I would also visit the estate jungle which lay close to the contractor's felling area on Sundays and at odd times of the day to see that all was as it should be.

Many of the jungle trees must have been over 150 feet in height, and at ground level their great roots spread in all directions to anchor the lofty giants. Massive trunks rose perfectly straight, without branch or limb, for a full 100 feet to the canopy above, seeking the light in competition with the rest of the forest. The steady click of axes falling upon hard timber and the occasional mutterings and shouts of the men when a tree was about to fall went on all day. On some of the forest giants the axes, sharp as they were, bounced back as if they had struck on iron. When felled, the long straight trunks of the very tall trees were cut into more manageable lengths of 20 feet or so, depending upon their girth and weight, and a man would cut a hole in the end of each of these shortened lengths through which a strong chain could be passed to enable the elephants to drag the timber.

There were numerous small villages close to the boundaries of the estate, and from these a good number of Sinhalese would come daily to work on the new clearing; many of their wives and daughters were already employed by the estate, either as ancillary workers or as tappers.

A few weeks after the arrival of the contractor's men, work was started by the estate labour force on the remaining acreage. The estate had just received three Australian 'monkey grubbers', which were going to be used to open out the 20 acres of heavy jungle. Before the monkey grubbers could be used to good effect, the forest floor had to be roughly cleared. A gang of men – all Tamils – worked their way through the jungle, cutting down all the undergrowth and small trees up to a girth of 18 inches; this left the floor of the jungle comparatively clear and open, ready for the monkey grubber men to start their work on the remaining larger trees.

A group of three Tamils worked each machine, which was a simple portable contrivance made of steel with a highly-geared winch, carrying on its drum about 200 feet of steel hawser. Prior to winching, the tree's wide lateral roots were exposed and then cut through with an axe; this helped the work, for the tree was then not only more easy to pull over but, when it finally crashed to the ground, the remainder of its root system could be levered and ripped out of the ground. An extra large tree would be selected to which the monkey grubber was anchored at its base, the steel hawser was then run out to the tree that was to be pulled down – the hawser being placed around the tree at about 10 feet from the ground – then the winching would begin with two of the coolies pushing and pulling a lever backwards. The steady click-click as the winching men vigorously moved the lever would only be interrupted by the noise high above of the tree canopy shifting slowly and then smashing its way through the branches of adjacent trees, until it would gradually heel over and fall with a reverberating crash amidst a shower of leaves and broken branches.

Each day I would visit this part of the new clearing and listen to the sound of axes shattering the solitude of the surrounding jungle, occasionally driving out an owl or a group of flying foxes from their slumbers. The smell of resin was pleasant and, as the sun rose higher in the sky and beat down upon the fallen forest, my thoughts would turn to the day when the trees would be dry enough to 'fire'.

Over in the contractor's block of jungle, the distant sound of axes, followed every now and then by the crash of trees, went on all day.

It was while clearing the 35 acres of scrubland that we came upon a small area that had previously been planted with tea. After the land had been cleared of its tallish undergrowth and scattered trees, one could plainly see old supervision paths that had once been traced on the land. The paths were in pretty good condition, and only required cutting out a little. This portion of land had probably been opened out from virgin jungle some 50 or 60 years before, and for one reason or another had been abandoned. It was strange to walk along these forgotten paths in the footsteps of the men who, long ago, had cleared the original jungle, planted tea and tended it. The conductor told me that, according to some of the very old coolies, there had once been a tea estate in that part, as well as a small factory. This news so whetted my appetite that we proceeded to the place the very next day, and found amongst the undergrowth and trees the clearly discernible ruins of the factory.

A big fire - a call at midnight

A few months later I had my first experience of a big fire. We had already successfully set fire to the by then dry 20 acres of felled jungle, with no damage to the adjoining jungle on one side or the estate rubber across a cart road on the other. Now the separate block of 35 acres of scrubland and semi-woodland was to be fired. By dusk the fire had run its course over a good two-thirds of the area, leaving behind smouldering tree trunks and hundreds of small patches of flickering flames which made a pretty sight in the gathering gloom. A pall of smoke rose above the clearing into the evening sky, and the smell of burnt wood was everywhere.

One small area was still burning furiously as night fell, and before returning to my bungalow, I saw to it that two good Tamils were left to act as night watchmen. They had instructions to keep an eye on the spread of flames, especially along one particular part of the estate which had a common boundary with a small, native owned, rubber holding, and to let both me and the conductor know if anything untoward should happen.

It was close on midnight when my boy woke me. One of the Tamils had just arrived to say that the flames had jumped across our boundary and were spreading into the next rubber property. As I ran across the drive to the garage, I quickly became aware of an ominous red glow in the sky coming from beyond a

Opening out – extending the estate.

large block of jungle that rose high against the skyline. Taking my motorbike, I was soon speeding along under the rubber at breakneck speed, feeling for the very first time in my life that all the cares of the world were upon me. As I drew nearer, my heart grew heavy; I had never seen a sky quite like this before. A deep glow not only filled the sky, but also spread over the whole land-scape. When I finally reached the fatal spot, I saw with some relief that the conflagration was mostly on the estate side of the boundary, just within the new clear-ing itself; nonetheless at half a dozen points the flames had crossed and were spreading through the rubber trees on the other side. Even though these seedling rubber trees – growing amongst thick weeds and bush-es – were about 40 years old and on their last legs, the fire had to be stopped, and quickly.

The conductor and a small group of men came towards me as I pulled up, and we immediately set off down the slope below the cart road which led to a small stream. Water was just what was needed, and a fire-break. Being a rubber estate, there was no difficul-ty in obtaining buckets since every tapper had one to carry the latex. Returning to the road, I told the con-ductor to jump on the pillion seat and we shot off to the nearest lines to wake the inmates. About 40 men were quickly pressed into service and set off towards the fire, carrying between them about three dozen buckets and axes.

Back at the new clearing, I once again made my way down to the stream and stood looking up the opposite hillside to where the boundary ran. I knew that the

men would not arrive for at least another ten minutes, and, as I could do nothing without them, I tried to decide where it was best to cut the fire-break in the adjacent property leading up the hill. By now the flames had crossed a good length of the boundary and were running through the undergrowth beneath the old rubber trees, setting the trunks of some alight. By the time the men arrived, I had formed a plan. All avail-able hands were put to clearing a seven foot wide fire-break all the way up the steepish hillside, about 20 yards inside the adjoining property and some 15 yards ahead of the advancing flames. Amidst a lot of shouting and hullabaloo, they set to furiously slashing the under-growth and pulling it back. With 30 or more able men thus employed, the fire-break soon extended to the limit of the immediate danger zone, which covered in all about 100 yards along the boundary.

Meanwhile, the remaining men had been carrying their buckets of water up the hill, and were doing the best they could against the advancing flames. As the fire-break was now complete, it was further widened along its entire length. Time passed without our know-ing it; the men worked with a strength and fury although they were all very hot, both those carrying water, and those slashing at the undergrowth. I spent my time stumbling up and down the slope, keeping an eye out for any danger points that might break out and generally speeding up the difficult job of the water car-riers. During the cutting and slashing of the fire-break, hundreds of small sharp pointed branches were left sticking up from the ground, and these caused many cuts to the ankles and bare feet of the men, lit only in their work by the flames.

Sometime later, the conductor arrived with more men and buckets and thereafter there must have been upwards of 60 buckets of water being thrown down in front of, and along, the entire length of the fire-break every four or five minutes. By dawn the boundary area was safe. Notwithstanding the five hour fight, about 80 rubber trees from the adjoining property had been badly scorched.

As daylight came I mustered the men on the cart road. Tired, scratched and bleeding from cuts, they had done a good job. All were to be given a full day's pay. They were a good bunch of men. I, like the workers, was covered in scratches, cuts and charcoal marks as I made my way back to the bungalow to shave, wash and breakfast. For me the day's work was just beginning.

When I returned to the scene of the night's activities about two hours later, smoke was rising peacefully upwards over the whole of the now blackened land. The first two rows of seedling rubber trees belonging to the smallholding looked a sorry sight. On our side, scores of small subdued pockets of flame smouldered, and a pall of light blue smoke hung over the clearing, drifting slowly into the nearby jungle to disappear amongst the tall lush green leaves. I walked a few paces onto the blackened landscape, and the heat of the ground was such that I quickly beat a hasty retreat back to the road. Everywhere white ash lay thick on the ground, while the blackened stumps of trees still smouldered on. In a couple of days, when the land had cooled, a small gang of axemen would go over the whole area cutting and piling up the partly burnt wood which would be rekindled again. The clearing was then ready for the cutting of cart roads, paths, drains and silt pits, and then for the lining of the ground, pegging and holing.

The first task was that of tracing and cutting cart roads for supervision purposes and, where possible, to connect with an already existing road. It was after the line of the road had been traced, more often than not on a steep slope of land, that, during the subsequent cutting of the road, one would sometimes come upon a massive granite boulder in the very path of the road, unearthed by the road cutting men. As with the cutting of latrine pits, a special Tamil would be brought in to bore an 18" or 24" hole in the rock, and I would then place my sticks of dynamite and blow the rock apart. If necessary, the 'borer-man', as he was called, would bore further holes and this method would be continued until enough of the rock had been removed to take the road through.

In a new clearing at this stage there is always the need for many small gangs of men, whose job is to cut up and roll aside any unburnt tree trunks or root systems that may straddle and hold up the road, path, drain, and silt pit cutting works. As these different works progress, the burnt surface of the forest floor changes; red soil is thrown up everywhere, and the whole clearing takes on a more orderly appearance.

Ravines, down which the water of a thousand monsoons have tumbled, would now be blocked by huge rocks, or choked with half-burnt tree trunks and root systems of fallen trees. These, too, had to be cleared out to afford a free unobstructed passage for the rains. These natural jungle ravines are turned into what are called 'leading drains', and it is into these that all the silt pits and side drains lead. Then, when heavy rain falls as it can only do in the tropics, it does not simply rush down the steep slopes over the cultivation area, but is channelled off, first into silt pits, then into side drains, and finally into the main leading drains. There is no shortage of stone for the building of terraces and the construction of leading drains, for it is found everywhere in the clearing. The Sinhalese stone mason excels at this particular job, and it is always a pleasure to stand and watch the work.

Silt pits, which are used to hold up the valuable topsoil, were unknown in the days of the early pioneers, who knew little about soil conservation; theirs was a big enough fight to merely exist while opening out hundreds of thousands of acres of dense virgin jungle. In later years, when it was seen just how much rich top-soil was washed off the steep slopes down to the rivers below, the cutting of silt pits became standard procedure.

The whole clearing is a scene of wonderful activity when works are in progress: dark glistening bodies cutting silt pits and drains, mumaties poised above heads for a moment before coming down with a crump into the earth, scores of small fires burning all over the clearing, and the constant chink of the stone mason as he hammers, chips and shapes his large stones, while his two helpers wage war with their heavy sledge-hammers upon nearby granite boulders. In such surroundings, with smoke climbing slowly upwards into a clear blue sky, it was indeed hard to drag oneself away.

As the different works progressed, the tidying up of the land continued until, at last, cart roads, paths, silt pits, drains, terracing, and planting holes had been cut and, with the filling of the holes, the new clearing was ready for planting when the monsoon came.

Note: A new clearing for seedling rubber in Ceylon can be seen on p 124; a new clearing for clonal tea on Huberta Estate in West Sumatra on p 274 and on Havukal Estate in South India on p 209.

Tea plantations shown

INDIA

ASSAM: PAST TENSE   The Assam Company
Margherita Tea Estate (W)
Bukhial Tea Estate (W)
Bhooteachang Tea Estate (W)
Pertabghur Tea Estate (W)

WITH EVOLUTION OF TEA MACHINERY
Hunwal Tea Estate (W)

DOOARS: Leesh River Tea Garden (G)
DARJEELING: Lingia Tea Estate
NILGIRI HILLS: Havukal Tea Estate

BANGLADESH: Shumshernugger Tea Garden (D)

AFRICA

KENYA: Nandi Hills District (O)
MALAWI: Lauderdale Tea Estate (O)
Limbuli Tea Estate (O)
Likanga Tea Estate (O)
SOUTH AFRICA: Middelkop Tea Estate (O)

SRI LANKA: Great Western Tea Estate
Rothschild Tea Estate
Spring Valley Tea Estate
Poonagalla Tea Estate
Frotoft Tea Estate

CHINA and TAIWAN: Chinese Tea Culture
JAPAN: PAST TENSE   Japanese Tea Culture
21st century Tea Culture

JAVA & SUMATRA   Huberta Tea Estate (P)
INDONESIA   Patuahwattee Tea Estate (P)
Alkaterie & other properties (P)

MALAYSIA   BOH Tea Estate (X)
Bukit Cheeding Tea Estate (X)

AUSTRALIA   The Pioneering Cutten Brothers
Glen Allyn Tea Estate (X)
Madura Tea Estate

SOUTH AMERICA   Estableciento Las Marias, Corrientes
Argentina

Special layouts for the Tea Research Association, Tocklai, Assam and the Tea Research Institute of Sri Lanka are shown in chapters IV and VI respectively on pages 88 and 156.

KEY TO MAIN PLANTATION OWNERS

W   Williamson Magor & Co. Ltd.
D   Duncan Brothers (Bangladesh) Ltd.
X   J. A. Russell & Co. Sdn. Bhd.
O   Eastern Produce Malawi Ltd.

G   Goodricke Group Ltd.
P   PT. Indorub Sumber Wadung Tea Plantations
O   Eastern Produce Kenya Ltd.
O   Sapekoe Estates (Pty) Ltd.

NILGIRI HILLS, *SOUTH INDIA*

LOADING TEA, COCHIN HARBOUR,
*SOUTH INDIA. A Tantea photo courtesy
Tamil Nadu Tea Plantation Corporation Ltd.
Coonoor, India*

*TEA GROWING COUNTRIES OF
THE WORLD*

MALAWI (*NYASALAND*)

SOUTH AFRICA

South
America

SOUTH AMERICA – ARGENTINA

SRI LANKA

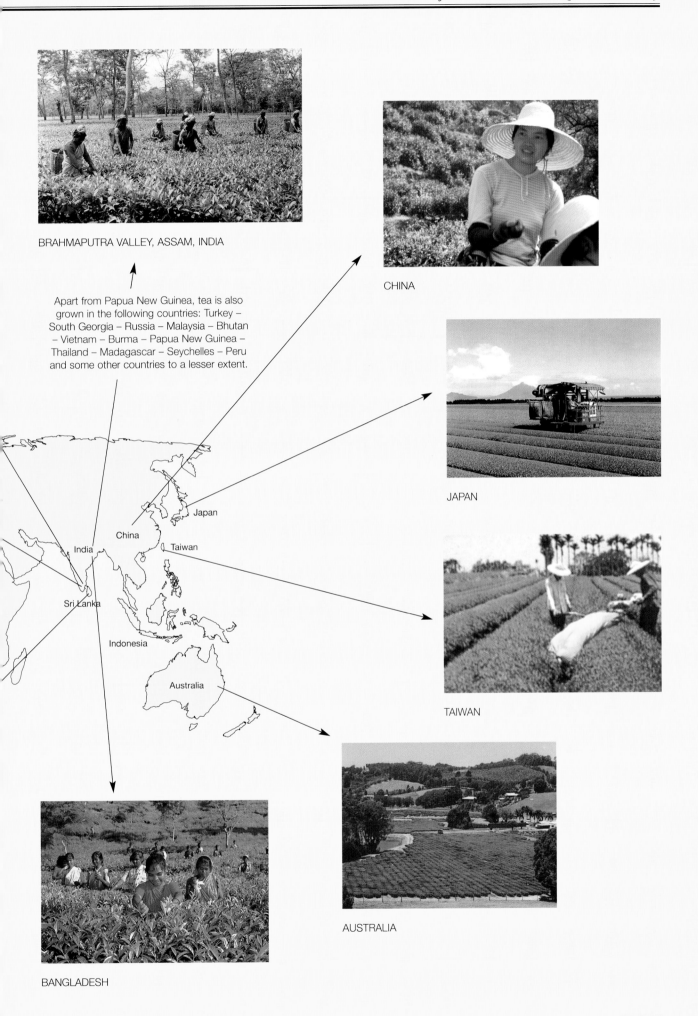

BRAHMAPUTRA VALLEY, ASSAM, INDIA

CHINA

JAPAN

TAIWAN

AUSTRALIA

BANGLADESH

Apart from Papua New Guinea, tea is also grown in the following countries: Turkey – South Georgia – Russia – Malaysia – Bhutan – Vietnam – Burma – Papua New Guinea – Thailand – Madagascar – Seychelles – Peru and some other countries to a lesser extent.

Japan

China

Taiwan

India

Sri Lanka

Indonesia

Australia

This stunning photograph showing a moonlit Mount Kanchenjunga, 28,146 feet, has been taken from Darjeeling Hill which is above the town. (*Photo c. 1912*)

Pluckers on Chubwa Tea Estate. This famous old estate was developed from one of the original tracts of indigenous tea that C.A. Bruce found growing in their wild state and which he 'worked up' during the late 1830s. See maps inside back cover and on pages 34/35. (*Courtesy Tetley GB, Tata Tea Group, 2007*).

VIEWS IN AND AROUND PLANTATIONS IN PRODUCING COUNTRIES

India

Assam	*Past tense -*	*The Assam Company*
		Margherita Tea Estate
		Bukhial Tea Estate
		Bhooteachang Tea Estate
		Pertabghur Tea Estate
		Evolution of tea machinery
		Hunwal Tea Estate
Dooars		*Leesh River Tea Garden*
Darjeeling		*Lingia Tea Estate*
Nilgiri Hills		*Havukal Tea Estate*

Bangladesh

Shumshernugger Tea Garden

1839
The Premier British Tea Company

The Assam Company

Illustrations published by *The Graphic* in 1875 from sketches made on the Company's gardens.

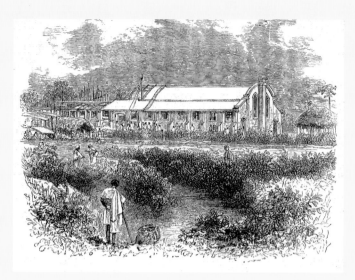

Construction of a new Tea House. Mazingah.

Cherideo Tea Garden.

Darjeeling planter (*Photo 1868, courtesy Royal Geographical Society.*)

These three gardens, and Galakee, were originally formed in 1840 from rich tracts of indigenous tea found growing under heavy jungle.

Plucking on Makeepore

Galakee Tea Garden. Weighing at factory
(*Photo c1950 courtesy Inchcape plc.*)

Tea plucker, Assam
(*Photo by permission
of the British Library.*)

Galakee Tea Garden.

Plucking on Makeepore Tea Garden
(*Photo c1950 courtesy Inchcape plc.*)

Williamson Magor Plantations

Assam

---

*Routine daily works in the field
– in the factory – in the air*

*In the field on Margherita,
Bukhial, Bhooteachang and
Pertabghur Estates*

The Manager of Margherita Tea Estate, Upper Assam.

At the end of the day.

An ideal setting; pluckers' saris make a splash of colour against a sea of green. (All photos for *In The Field* c 2001, *courtesy Williamson Magor & Co. Ltd.*)

During the monsoon period leaf growth is rapid and every effort is made to pluck the bushes every 7 days. During the main monsoon months of July to October near 60% of the crop is produced, i.e. up to 15% in each month. The July production in the factory is made from a high percentage of Third Flush leaf and is superior in quality to the Rains Teas of August, September and October. The highest quality tea is manufactured during the Second Flush which appears during May and June.

A medium prune.

Bhooteachang Tea Estate. Skiffing – a level off skiff (LOS) is done to level the plucking
surfaces of the bushes after a season's growth and some 35 plucking rounds.

In the field

The application of fertilizer.

Pertabghur Tea Estate. Some very expert eyes among the tea.

Bukhial Tea Estate. Shade trees. A moderate canopy is beneficial in certain tea growing districts in that it reduces light intensity and leaf temperature as well as conserving soil moisture. Importantly, most shade trees are leguminous and provide, through nodules on their root systems, valuable nitrogen to the soil. Leaf-fall and prunings also provide green manure which benefits the soil. Thinning, replacement and removal of old shade trees damages the tea bushes but also provides fuel for the estate labour force to use in their homes. The planting of shade trees was first started in Assam during the 1880s.

Evolution of tea machinery

In the factory, manufacture: withering – rolling (withered leaf processing) – fermenting – firing

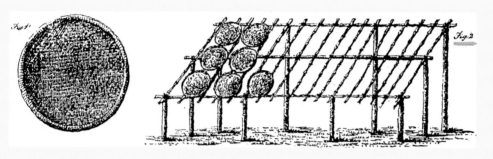

The method employed by C. A. Bruce during the late 1830s in Assam, of withering the plucked (indigenous) leaf in the sun.
(Drawings by C. A. B. 1839. *By permission of the British Library*.)

Withering the leaf in the sun, Ging Tea Garden, Darjeeling.
(*Drawing 1876.*)

Withering

Withering on 'tats'. Darjeeling factory.
(*Photo c1895.*)

Enclosed trough withering allows the fans to blow a current of air through the bed of leaf from below and above. The picture shows a trough being loaded when leaf is thrown in the air to separate handfuls of shoots brought in by the pluckers. Physical and chemical changes occur during the withering process; the former brings about a loss of moisture and the latter alters the taste of the tea. The leaf is allowed to remain in the troughs for some 12 to 18 hours. Loss of moisture makes the shoots flaccid and the cells are then more easily ruptured during 'processing' to bring about fermentation. The fully withered leaf is then ready for the next stage of manufacture.

Rolling

Early method of hand, foot and wrist rolling the withered leaf.

Hand rolling on an estate in the North-West Province. Rolling by hand in India was on the way out by the late 1870s, except on small outlying estates in the northern hill districts. (*Drawing 1883, The Graphic.*)

Table rolling was followed by the more hygienic machine rolling. An early model of Jackson's cross-action roller, introduced during the 1870s. (*Photo courtesy Inchcape plc.*)

A Marshall's Roller; this type remaining in use throughout the 20th century. (*Photo courtesy Ralph Callander.*)

Today, because not only rollers but rotorvanes and CTC machines are involved in processing the leaf, this stage of manufacture is known as withered leaf processing.

SPREADING LEAF FOR FERMENTATION   For Nectar Tea Co

The date of this drawing, tinted in watercolour, is about 1900 and shows the method of fermentation when, in those days, the rolled leaf was spread out under damp cloths until fully fermented. Until the end of the 20th century leaf has been fermented on a variety of surfaces such as cement floors, ceramic tiles and aluminium.

CTC processing and fermentation

At the end of the century continuous fermenting machines were developed to bring about a continuous system of manufacture as opposed to batch processing

Continuous fermenting machines are the latest development. This picture shows a Rotorvane, at right, feeding a triplex CTC formation (Crush, Tear and Curl) where three cuts are given and the leaf is conveyed to a flat bed-like continuous fermenting machine shown in the top left hand corner of the picture.

A drawing by C. A. Bruce *c*1838, showing his adaption of the complicated Chinese method of manufacture, firing; the tea leaves (about two pounds) being put into a cast iron pan and placed over a stove.
(The Method of Making Tea, by C. A. Bruce, 1839, *by permission of the British Library*.)

A line of brick/stone built charcoal burning 'chulas' (ovens), Assam c1860s. (*Courtesy Inchcape plc*.)

Charcoal burning ovens in a Darjeeling factory. (*Photo 1880, The Graphic*.)

Firing

'Sirocco' Endless Chain Pressure Tea Driers installed in an Assam factory in the 1950s.

The impressive Kilburn Vibro Fluid Bed Driers (VFBD) produce some 300 kg and 450 kg of CTC tea per hour depending on the model. These machines operate for some 12 to 16 hours a day during the monsoon months in Assam. The picture shows a VFBD discharging fully dried tea onto a conveyor belt for continuous sorting. (*Photo 2002*.)

Selim Tea Garden, Terai. The background shows cleared forest land on which huts have been erected for housing the labour force. A small group of women are seen demonstrating hand-sorting with Chinese bamboo sieves. (*Photo 1865 courtesy Royal Geographical Society*).

Sorting

The British followed in detail the method of tea making in China when starting their own tea industry in India – as did the Dutch in Java.

Hand-sorting in a Darjeeling factory.

Early sorting machinery, showing an early model of a Jackson's Cross-action roller in background, at right.
(*Drawings, The Graphic 1876 by permission of the British Library*.)

The single tray Trinick Sorter is fitted with 5 segments of various mesh sizes and was developed for the continuous sorting of CTC tea direct from the dryers. The first prototype machine was made by Steelworth, Tinsukia, Assam in the late 1960s and developed under the guidance of Mr. J. M. Trinick, Tea Taster and Manufacturing Adviser to Williamson Magor Group. The Trinick Sorter is now used widely in tea factories throughout the world.

John M. Trinick, nearly 60 years in tea.

Packing

Once tea has been dried and graded it is stored in dehumidified bins to prevent uptake of moisture. Tea is a hygroscopic material which will deteriorate rapidly if allowed to pick up moisture from the atmosphere. After drying, the moisture content is 3 to 4% and around 5 to 6 % when sold to buyers for retail purposes. The picture shows tea being packed in multi walled paper sacks.

In the air

Pertabghur Tea Estate – an aerial view of the complex with tea factory, offices, hospital, school staff and labour houses.

WM Chairman, B. M. Khaitan.

A Cessna aircraft owned by George Williamson (Assam) Limited. (*All colour photos, including WM machinery c2001, courtesy Williamson Magor & Co. Ltd.*)

Tea tasters at work in Williamson Magor's offices at Four Mangoe Lane, Kolkata.

Assam - Railway Boom - and elephants during the 1880s

Depiction, railway elephants

When people call this beast to mind
They marvel more and more
At such a little tail behind
So large a trunk before.

(Hilaire Belloc)

During the pioneering years elephants were a capital asset. Among everyone there was a buzz of excitement during the 1880s – the coming of the railways in India.

Assam, like other districts being opened to tea, had its problems of transport and communications and it also had its share of planters who, in some instances, became Railway men; Oscar Lindgren was one such man (1857-1945).

With the approaching railway 'boom' and with it requirements for timber for cutting into sleepers for the new railroads, some planters – their contracts being completed with their tea companies – sought pastures green, grazing under the Railway authorities as sleeper-contractors and sleeper-cutters. The first railroads in India were pushed through some very inhospitable places where wild animals and disease went hand in hand.

'On the March' with tents and stores. (*Photo courtesy Guy Arnold.*)

The Railway authorities employed their own elephants and their Mahouts and the trace of the actual line over suitable terrain through jungle was the job of the Railway District Chief Engineer; for all other work the planter, turned Railman or sleeper-contractor, together with *his* men and the railway company's elephants, were more than capable.

Before the elephant can do its work the heavy undergrowth together with all the tree saplings up to about 10 feet are cut down, thus opening out the ground floor of the forest; next the Nepalese axemen can

The extraction of timber. Elephant 'straightening out'. Floating heavy trunks down river to a sawyers camp. (*Photo courtesy Guy Arnold.*)

get to work on the forest giants which, when felled and the upper canopy branches cut, are dragged by elephants to a nearby river for floating out or to a sawyers pit within the actual clearing.

Those of you who know Makum in upper Assam might like to know the founder's name, Oscar Lindgren, who else; he tells us in his own words:

So I selected a place called Makum some three miles from Tinsukia, and moved my Nepalese and Assamese sawyers there. But first I said goodbye to my good Miri friends, without whose help I could not have worked the earlier contract. The place was chosen because of its sleeper possibilities, and for no other reason. At this time I had charge of eighteen elephants which belonged to the Railway. These were used for hauling logs to the saw pits, work which nothing but elephants could perform.

It is no boastful spirit that I lay claim to be the founder of Makum, which has been noted for ill-health for a long time. I merely wish to undercut criticism. Do you know Lindgren? Yes. Mad as a hatter. He was the fellow who founded Makum.

Yes, 'Mad as a hatter' and off his trolley, but a planter through and through, and a good man to have with you in such places:

In due course the trace of the line from Makum to Margherita was commenced. To carry out this work some hundreds of very wild looking Nagas came down from the hills, each armed with a murderous weapon for slashing jungle undergrowth.

In time the railroad was pushed through dense jungle to Margherita (Tea Estate), which 120 years later is the subject of our photograph showing the tribal 'Jhomur' dance on this Williamson Magor estate, in the year 2004.

Dooars

The stretch of land that runs south of the foothills and mountains of Bhutan is known as the Dooars: the western Dooars, bordering what was Selim Tea Garden, near Jalpaiguri, and the Eastern Dooars which runs east into Assam. It is a flat strip of fertile country averaging some twenty miles wide into which numerous fast-flowing rivers flow down from Bhutan.

When this district was first opened to tea, being similar to that of the hot steamy Terai, it had heavy tree jungle which fostered malaria and black water fever. The first tea garden was opened in 1874 at Gazaldubi by one Dr. Brougham who had also purchased land and opened one of the first tea gardens in Darjeeling some fifteen years earlier. The Gazaldubi tea was worked and managed by Richard Houghton who is credited with being the pioneer of tea in the Jalpaiguri District.

Though felling and clearing tall jungle by axe was a considerable undertaking there were great benefits to the owners of the land in the amount of good timber that could be extricated. Jalpaiguri was a bustling town and the centre of all manner of enterprises in those early days of the tea industry, including many large sawing mills.

The expansion of tea in Darjeeling, followed by that in the Terai to the south, was then carried eastward through the Dooars eventually to join up with the tea gardens that were being opened on the North Bank of the Brahmaputra, in Assam. By the late 1870s a dozen or more tea gardens had been established in this forest wilderness that ran along the plains below Bhutan, among them Leesh River Garden, in 1876, the subject of our illustrations. As tea was extended further eastward the need for transport and communications grew, not only in the Dooars and Assam but throughout the whole of the vast sub-continent of India.

Great numbers of garden workers were required to work the ever-increasing tea acreage in the Dooars. At first Nepalese (who already worked on the gardens in Darjeeling and the Terai) were employed but it was soon found that even greater numbers were needed and this labour was drawn from some distance away, in Bihar. The recruitment of labour for tea gardens in India and Ceylon (Sri Lanka) has been and still is conducted by a sort of Recruiting Sergeant, a Sirdar in the former country and a Head Kangany in the latter. However, the enticement of workers from one garden to another has always been a problem for Managers.

Like the tea gardens in Darjeeling and Terai districts, those in the Dooars were at first planted up with the China variety of tea. Today, hybrids of the Assam and China plant are put out but do not produce the same quality of made tea as those in Darjeeling.

The modern tea garden, as on Leesh River, has excellent facilities for the treatment of its workforce, with qualified doctors, dispensaries and schools where tuition is provided free, and all the workers' houses have piped drinking water.

The Dooars Tea Industry, started 130 years ago, has now grown to a little over 155,000 acres on 150 gardens which provide nearly 20 per cent of India's total tea production. This contributes greatly to the Dooars economy, employing 233,000 workers on the gardens with a further 40% finding derivative employment in subsidiary jobs throughout the country.

Darjeeling

The district of Darjeeling was formerly part of the Kingdom of the Rajah of Sikkim. The Directors of the Honourable East India Company wishing to obtain the site of Darjeeling as a sanatorium, authorised General Lloyd to open negotiations with the Rajah of Sikkim, and on 1st January 1835 the following transfer Deed was completed:

The Governor General, having expressed his desire for the possession of the Hill of Darjeeling on account of its cool climate for the purpose of enabling the servants of his Government, suffering from sickness, to avail themselves of its advantages, I the Sikkimputtee Rajah out of friendship for the said Governor-General, hereby present Darjeeling to the East India Company, that is all the lands south of the Great Rangeet

▶

Hunwal Tea Estate

Brahmaputra Valley, Assam

Manager Sanjay Batra (2004)

Estate first opened	1861
Total tea acreage	2107 (853 ha)
Present factory built	1952-1956
Type of manufacture	CTC/orthodox
Total estate labour force	2010
Resident estate population	6715

Estate school and hospital medical staff 7, one doctor.

Ransomes Single Tine Sub-soiler, with seed drill attachment. See below on plinth.

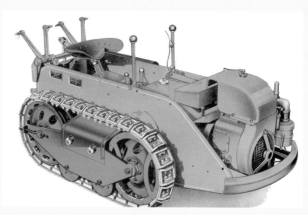

Ransomes 'Crawler Tractor'. This model built from 1952 onwards. Both this and the Sub-soiler were in use on Hunwal until 1959. (*Photo courtesy Ransomes Jacobsen Ltd.*)

Inside these five bays are the withering troughs; the factory is just out of the picture at left.

A 75-year-old Rain Tree, *Pithecolobium saman*, stands at the entrance to the Manager's bungalow (built in 1928), and with the vivid red-flowering *Ixora singaporensis*, right, provides a most attractive setting.

Managerial staff L to R. Field Operations: Vivek Seth (Deputy Manager), Amal C. Bora (Senior Assistant), Sanjay Batra (Manager), Hitesh Maadan (Welfare Officer and in the factory). The tea is 36 years old and the shade trees are *Acacia lenticularis* of the same age.

Entrance.

The hospital complex with bungalows for medical staff.

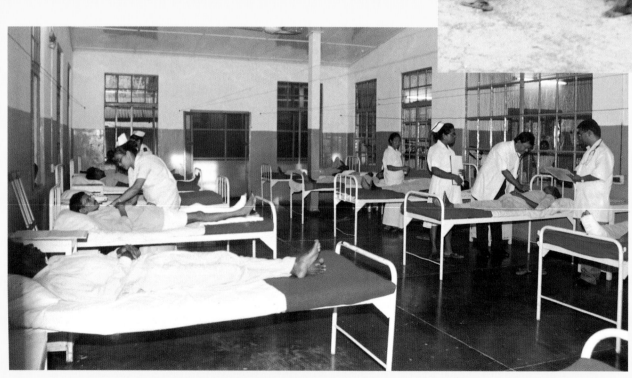

Male Ward. Patients are cared for by qualified doctors and nurses. Many will be surprised to see the level of care that is taken for all who work on the estate. Everything is very smart, clean and tidy.

An attractive scene on Hunwal. Individual dwellings of the workforce have pretty gardens with flowers, palms, plantains and fruit trees.

Welfare of estate workers

The tea estate is a close-knit community and some families have been employed on Hunwal for over one hundred years.

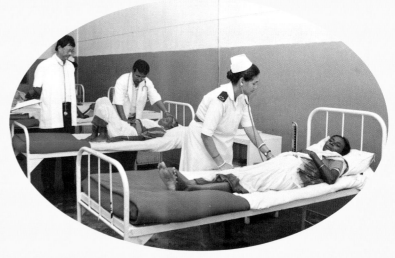

Part of the female ward.

Vegetative propagation. Clonal single-leaf cuttings in polysleeves are kept under high Agro Mesh netting which allows 60-70% sunlight to filter through.

Cuttings once they grow up to 5-6 leaves are removed from the Agro Mesh area and kept outside for sun-hardening to establish into ready plants. Once the plants are 30-40 cms. tall, they are taken into the field for extension planting, replanting or infilling of vacancies in the mature tea.

Mature tea fields generally contain between 12,000 and 13,000 bushes per hectare

60 years is the economic life of a tea bush

Once tea areas cross 60 years in age and gradually begin to lose commercial viability, the bushes are uprooted by a tractor-mounted winch. In the past elephants were used to uproot old tea bushes, which are distributed to workers' families free of cost as statutory issue firewood.

Some of Williamson Magor's other estates

Line chowkidars (watchmen) who are given the following day's 'kamjari' (work allocation) the previous evening, visit the workers' lines/dwelling area at dawn the next day and announce loudly where the labour is to be deployed.

Estate school and hospital: medical staff 8, 2 doctors.

BOGAPANI ESTATE. The labour force rise well before dawn to take their 'Chota Hazri' early morning tea and biscuits.

Giri Sodhi, Visiting Agent for WM estates.

Celebrating the Tribal 'Jhomur' dance on Margherita Estate in upper Assam. Estate school and hospital; medical staff 4, 3 doctors.

MIJICAJAN ESTATE. Pluckers with their leaf at the Divisional weighment shed.

A young English Assistant in Assam during the early 1900s said this about his overbearing Manager and leaf weighing: He drives out in his tum-tum round the work and at each section grumbles and nags. Then the leaf weighing, which he regularly attends, becomes the nastiest bit of the day's work when it should be the most pleasantest, for is it not the end of the 'bela'? Not a woman brings in leaf fit to be seen; poor devils, it is not for want of 'hazri' cutting and 'gallikaroing'. Then a round of the teahouse and the man there – God help him!

Estate school and hospital; medical staff 6, one doctor.

(*All photos of Hunwal and this page 2003/4, courtesy Williamson Magor & Co. Ltd.*)

Life in the 21st century in tea, school & hospital with Williamson Magor

A line dwelling provided for the labour force.

Weighing the green leaf in the field.

Phulbari Estate Central Hospital.

A class at the Assam Valley School (AVS) established by the Williamson Magor Group in 1990s.

The art class at the AVS.

Rushing from one class to another at the AVS.

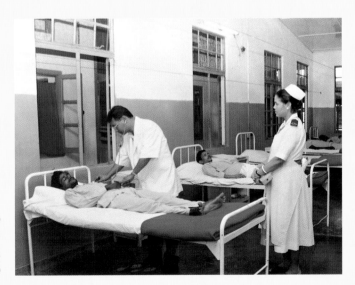

Men's ward at the Hunwall Estate Hospital. (*All photos 2000, courtesy Williamson Magor.*)

An Assistant's bungalow in Assam, with quite probably an interior earth floor, photographed in 1858. Almost 150 years separate the photos above and below. (*Courtesy Inchcape plc.*)

Goodricke Group Ltd.

Leesh River Garden, Dooars

Garden opened	1875
Total tea acreage	1566
Present factory built	1876
Type of manufacture	CTC
Total estate labour force	1693
Resident estate population	5810

The present Manager's bungalow and Manager Mr. Kalyanbrata Palchoudhuri on Leesh River Garden in the Dooars.

Shade trees, especially when in flower, add a luxuriant appeal to the gardens.

Plucking on Makeepore Tea Garden
(*Photo c1950 courtesy Inchcape plc.*)

Young shade trees (that have been interplanted between rows of young tea bushes) will shortly be uprooted for planting out in newly replanted fields of tea.
(*All colour photos by A. S. Hobbs, courtesy Goodricke Group.*)

► River, east of Balsun, Kahail and Little Rangeet Rivers and west of the Rungpee and Mahanuddy Rivers.

In the Darjeeling district tea cultivation was first started in a small but compact area around and below the town itself. By 1857 several thousand acres of forest had been felled and cleared, of which sixty to seventy had been planted out with tea. Some of the first tea gardens to be opened were those of the Darjeeling Company, the Tukvar Tea Company Ltd and the Soom Tea Company, during the early 1860s.

When the tea industry was started in this region there was a great demand for tea seed. By then the Assam Company had more than sufficient seed, both Assam and the China variety, for its own needs in Assam; it was therefore able to supply large quantities of China seed to the newly developing tea gardens in the Darjeeling District, which it had obtained from original importations of China stock. Nurseries were established in various parts of Darjeeling in which many tons of seed were sown, either the resultant seedlings being planted out in the new clearings, or the seed itself put out directly in the field as seed-at-stake.

In these northern latitudes plucking takes place for about seven or eight months of the year. The valuable first plucking of the new season (First Flush) is made in early March followed by the Second Flush – also good quality tea. The production during the monsoon is much inferior but is followed in October by the choice Autumnal teas. During the 1960s and 1970s Russia took nearly 52% of all Darjeeling teas, which was then mixed with the country's own tea, grown in Georgia. Germany and Japan have continued to pay high prices for the teas made in the quality periods.

Darjeeling has a distinct disadvantage in lying 27° north of the equator. From the day tea is planted it takes seven to eight years to bring it into economical bearing, compared to about five years in the Nilgiri Hills of southern India, where sunshine hours are longer and plucking goes on throughout the year. Because of these factors, together with steep slopes, small leaf and many vacancies in old tea fields, the average yield per acre of Darjeeling tea is about half that of the rest of India.

It is a fact of life that in the Tea Trade a great deal more of the much sought after 'Darjeeling tea' is bought on the open market than is actually manufactured!

Tea planter, Darjeeling, 1860s. (*Courtesy Royal Geographical Society*).

Replanting on steep slopes in this region is extremely costly and often results in the loss of much valuable soil. When uprooting between 2500 and 3000 old, poor yielding China tea bushes to every acre, the valuable top soil – that has been held up for over a hundred years by the extensive root systems of the bushes – is loosened and is at risk from heavy rainfall, for with no cover, the exposed soil is subject to erosion and is washed down steep mountainsides to the rivers below, before the root systems of the newly replanted tea can spread and anchor the soil. Nowadays, and for many years past, soil rehabilitation is carried out with legume cover crops and weeping grass is planted, after uprooting old tea, to prepare the soil for the young tea plants.

Landslides are common in the district. In the great flood of 1968, nearly 2500 acres of tea was lost or buried during massive landslides, when continuous rain fell for just three days; another 2000 acres of land suitable for tea was either totally or partially destroyed. This was a terrible setback for the industry. Quite apart from the loss of this acreage of tea and land, the damage caused on gardens to factories, roads, bridges, culverts and dwellings of the labour force, as well as staff bungalows, amounted to Rupees 98 Lakhs – equivalent to £600,000 Sterling.

There are now approximately 44,000 acres (18,000 hectares) of tea on Darjeeling's 96 estates, which range in elevation from 1500 ft, in the deep valleys, to 6500 ft.

South India

Like Darjeeling, during the early years of the 19th century, the Nilgiri Hills and Ootacamund in southern India were a temporary haven for the fever-stricken British, jaded by the heat of the plains. This lovely hill region was not, however, just a sanatorium, it was also eminently suitable for growing tea, with just the right climate, elevation and rainfall.

It is known that some of the best coffee is grown in the Blue Mountains of Jamaica, so too the hills of southern India produce fine teas, where, under certain conditions on a hot day, the hills turn a misty cobalt blue – Blue Mountain Tea!

The history of tea in South India goes back to the year 1836, when a consignment of 2000 young China tea seedlings reached the Nilgiri Hills in the Madras Presidency. These plants had been germinated at the

Botanical Gardens in Calcutta – under the direction of the Superintendent, Dr. N. Wallich – from seed that came from the original shipment of 80,000 tea seeds brought from China by G. J. Gordon the previous year.

During the early years little success attended those first trials with the China plant, which was put out at

A moonlight ford on the way to the hills.

the Government's experimental farm at Kaity, and on other small plots of land thought suitable by officials.

It was some seventeen years later, during the early 1850s, that some of the first adventurers arrived out from Great Britain to make their fortunes in tea and coffee.

The journey, from the small then uncharted ports along the southern part of the Malabar coast, such as Calicut and Cochin, up to the central hill district during the 1850s was, for the pioneers of the tea and coffee industries, a wild and beautiful one.

From the coastal region the journey inland was made by the slow bullock cart until the foothills were reached, when some serious climbing became the order of the day. Paths and tracks strewn with rocks and lianas, amidst massive out-crops of granite boulders, threaded their way through dank virgin jungle in which tiger, elephant, panther and everything else you could imagine, watched, unseen, the slow progress of the small band of men as they toiled upwards, soaked in sweat.

This was how it all started; the beginning of the tea and coffee industries in South India – at first a small trickle of men, then over the years an ever increasing number would follow in the footsteps of the first pioneers.

With the arrival of the first tea pioneers the industry expanded slowly, alongside that of coffee, until the 1890s, when a mere 11,000 acres of forest had been felled, burnt, cleared and planted with tea. However, from that date on the tea industry increased rapidly to the extent where, by 1930, 130,000 acres of land was under tea.

The cultivation of tea in South India resembles that on the estates in Sri Lanka, as do the methods in field and factory which have been introduced, to some extent, by Ceylon planters, including that country's early tea and coffee men, who crossed the Palk Strait to carry on their chosen work in the hills of southern India.

The tea districts in South India include the Eastern and Western Ghats which come to an end at the Nilgiris with abrupt, almost vertical precipices. The tea estates in the Nilgiri district range from 4000 to 6000 feet, while those in the Wynaad are situated lower down. South of the Nilgiris and the Palghat gap, at an elevation of about 1000 feet, the land rises again steeply to the Annamalai and Cardamon Hills, which rise up to the Kanan Devans, another important High Range tea region.

Today, there are 207,000 acres (84,000 hectares) of tea in South India. The estates are composed, equally, of the Assam broad-leafed and old China hybrid.

The Toy Train

Engine No. 782, Darjeeling Himalayan Railway. The 2ft gauge railroad runs from New Jalpaiguri, at an elevation of 500 ft, up to Ghoom Station at 7500ft, before descending to the town of Darjeeling. The 52 mile journey takes just over 7 hours. For the man who rides in front of the engine – whose job is to sprinkle sand on the lines to gain traction for the wheels on the steeper inclines – it is often a cold job.

Lingia Estate

Darjeeling

Nepalese pluckers make a pretty sight under the 'weighing up shed'. The plucked leaf has to be picked over to remove coarse leaf and excessive stalk before weighing.

Estate workers' 'lines' are, these days, neat little dwellings for individual families.

A Sirdar (foreman) in charge of tea pluckers.

The pluckers he supervises. (*Photos 1996, courtesy Reichmuth von Reding, Hanspeter Reichmuth, Switzerland.*)

Lingia Tea Factory, Inset: T. M. Raj, 3rd generation teamaker on Lingia.

90-year-old China bushes cling to steep slopes.

Darjeeling teas command high prices and have that elusive muscatel flavour. The cost of production is very high due to low productivity and very low yields, owing to a large proportion of the bushes being over ninety years old. Another factor is that the small leafed China bushes (*Camellia sinensis*) are difficult to pluck. Some 6000 shoots, each with two leaves and a bud, go to make one pound of manufactured tea, whereas the larger broad-leafed Assam and Manipuri varieties produce the same amount of tea from only 3000 shoots.

Marigolds and cannas bring a touch of colour to the estate workers' dwellings.

Firewood for the factory.

'The goods' ready for dispatch from the factory. Tea chest markings, T.G.F.O.P., denotes the grade of tea packed: Tippy Golden Flowery Orange Pekoe.

Map showing the extent of the estate's tea fields and their acreages.

Inquisitive Nepalese children prepare for lessons in the estate school house.
(*Photos 1996, courtesy Reichmuth von Reding, Hanspeter Reichmuth, Switzerland.*)

A carpet of tea under pollarded Grevillea shade trees.

Views on Havukal

Pluckers, waist high, make a pretty sight.

A new clearing of young tea plants. Steep slopes require the cutting of silt-pits between stone terracing to stop the valuable top soil being washed down the mountainside. The Stone Mason excels in the art of building terraces and leading drains.

Foreground: mature tea and shade tree, while beyond the young plants get some H_2O.

Havukal Tea Estate

Kotagiri, Nilgiris, South India

In the field

The first China Jat tea plants were put out in the Nilgiri hills in 1835 at the experimental farm at Kaity.

A close-up of a new clearing: young tea plants (put out at 5000 to the acre) with a cover crop of strawberry plants in between under polythene sheets. Polythene strips are used so that the strawberries do not touch the earth.

Vegetative propagated clonal cuttings under high intensity shade nursery.

Clone Craigmore 60i7.

Pluckers carry their green leaf to the upper floors for weighing and trough withering.

The old-type tea chest, made of plywood lined with aluminium foil usually measures 19 x 19 inches and holds 90 to 110 pounds of leaf grades to 130 of broken grades.

Multi-walled paper sacks are in common use on tea estates in all tea producing countries

Havukal Tea Estate

First opened in 1918
In the factory

Total tea acreage	400
Present factory built	1920
Type of manufacture	Orthodox/CTC
Total estate labour force	400
Resident estate population	1000

Trough withering.

The flaccid leaf is sent down chutes to the rolling room and rolled in an old Britannia roller.

The factory tea tasting room. Manager Deram Jayaram. Frequent tasting of teas provides a check on manufacture. The 'roll' is then put through a roll-breaker (not shown) before it is ready for the next process of manufacture, fermenting.

The 'dhool', lying on smooth polished concrete or ceramic tiles, is lifted when fully fermented and carried to the driers and placed on an endless revolving chain of wire trays for 'firing'. The last process is sorting, grading and packing.

Havukal estate school – children are tidy and happy.

Mature tea shaded by pollarded Grevilleas, with Havukal factory against a back-drop of the Blue Mountains of the Nilgiris. The elevation of this estate is between 5000 and 6000 ft.
(*All previous photos of Havukal and this page, 1995, courtesy Reichmuth von Reding, Hanspeter Reichmuth.*)

The estate field officer, pruning Kangany (supervisor) and pruners at work in a field of Assam jat (variety) tea. The task for each pruner is 250 bushes a day. (*Photos this page 2000, courtesy Deram Jayaram Thangavelu.*)

Doctor and midwife at the estate hospital.

Estate labour force lines – each houses five families.

Bangladesh

Shumshernugger Tea Garden, Bangladesh

Including Lungla and Karimpore

The beginning of tea cultivation in Bangladesh dates back to 1840 when experimental planting was started in Chittagong. However, the commercial production of tea only commenced in 1857 with the setting up of a tea garden in Malnicherra in Sylhet district. As with the other tea regions, it was British planters who opened the gardens there.

Two famous men came to this region: one an Irishman, Samuel Davidson, planter and inventor of tea machinery, the other a Scotsman, Walter Duncan; both made their names in tea. Samuel Davidson left Belfast in 1864 to become a planter in Cachar where, just four years later, he took out a patent for his newly invented tea-drying machine, the NO. 1 SIROCCO DRIER. By the following year he had designed a new tea roller. In 1881 he gave up planting and returned to his native Belfast, where he set up the engineering firm Davidson & Company Ltd., makers of tea machinery for nearly a hundred years.

Walter Duncan was the founder of a famous tea company which still bears his name today, Duncan Brothers (Bangladesh) Ltd. This company has developed from early beginnings when in 1858 Walter Duncan sailed from Southampton to India, where, the following year, he started a business in cotton under the name Playfair, Duncan and Company. Later, upon the arrival of his brother William, they formed Duncan Brothers and Company, in 1875.

For those who like statistics, here are some! The phenomenal development with regard to Bangladesh tea is the emergence of a strong internal market of 140 million people, which consumes 65% to 70% of the total tea production. In order to deal with the increasing domestic consumption, small holding tea cultivation in the northern region and eastern hill districts has recently been commenced. Under the plan approximately 1600 acres is expected to be planted by 2007.

The major export destinations for Bangladesh tea are Pakistan and Afghanistan, where more than 60% of the country's exports are shipped. Apart from direct export, tea is sold through weekly auctions at the port city of Chittagong, which caters for both internal and external markets.

The labour-intensive tea industry employs more than 100,000 people. Unlike other sectors of the economy, tea-based workers comprise 80% ethnic minorities, mostly Hindus, who migrated from other parts of the Indian sub-continent in the early days of tea cultivation. Half of the workforce is female, which gives the industry unique characteristics and plays a pivotal role in making the industry a disciplined one.

The industry's contribution to the national economy is also demonstrated through the generation of additional employment, as different post-plucking processes employ about 600,000 people. Besides which, the industry makes seasonal employment for about 35,000 workers in plucking, the most important field activity of tea manufacture.

For the past fifty years the export of tea from Bangladesh, Sylhet, Cachar and surrounding regions – that used to go out by way of the Meghna River to Calcutta – has been dispatched down to the Port of Chittagong. Chittagong Warehouses Ltd. was formed in 1948 by Balmer Lawrie & Company Ltd., which built the new warehousing facilities that exist today. Duncan Brothers, who had always been actively connected with this warehousing company now own the controlling interest.

Bangladesh tea has not only weathered unfavourable situations at different times but has also flourished with sustainable development, particularly higher yields, and is well poised to cope with the challenges of increasing globalisation.

Living conditions for labour and planters alike. (*Depiction 1840 period, watercolour by S. R. Fever.*)

Past tense

Where the labour force lived

'It was no uncommon thing to have 50 per cent of one's labour force down with malaria, without counting stomach complaints, which are always large items among coolies in jungle areas.'
Assam planter Oscar Lindgren, 1870s.

The two smaller sheds house the labour force and are constructed of split bamboo uprights under a thatched roof. The larger 'Tea Making House' has mud and ekra walls. (*Depiction 1840 period, watercolour by S. R. Fever.*)

Today, dwellings of the labour force nestle along tea fields on Lungla Estate.

Present tense

In and around some of Duncan Brothers' gardens in Bangladesh.

The communal lines of the pioneering years have been replaced with neat hygienic houses for the estate workers.

A typical labour house on Lungla Estate. (*Photo 1995.*)

Fuel efficient smokeless stove introduced in all dwellings. (*Photo 1995.*)

Camellia Duncan Foundation Hospital, Shumshernugger Tea Garden, Sylhet.

Welfare of the garden work force Bangladesh 1990s

Built in 1994 this attractively designed hospital has a pathological laboratory, x-ray department and theatre. It has 5 doctors and 10 nurses.

Children at the crèche at Karimpore Tea Garden.

Line Health Workers (LHWs) provide promotive and preventive health care at the household level.

LHWs collecting data on primary health at Shumshernugger.

The 50 bed hospital provides for a healthy workforce, and is the centre of the Lawrie Group's medical services in the region.

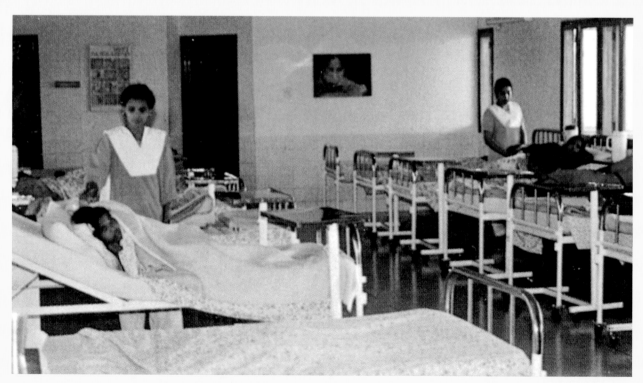

Female Ward at the CDFH.
(All colour photographs, courtesy Duncan Brothers (Bangladesh) Ltd.)

VIEWS IN AND AROUND PLANTATIONS IN PRODUCING COUNTRIES

Africa

Kenya   *Estates, Nandi Hills District*

Malawi   *Lauderdale Tea Estate, Mulanje District*
                   Limbuli Tea Estate, Mulanje District
                   Likanga Tea Estate, Mulanje District

South Africa   *Middelkop Tea Estate, Limpopo Province*

Africa

An ever increasing acreage

On can be forgiven for thinking the tea we buy in the supermarket comes from the traditional producing countries like India, Ceylon, China and Indonesia. During World Wars I and II, the British were drinking thousands of gallons of it – in fact we still are. It is interesting to know that, in 1940, India and Ceylon produced over 80% of the world's tea and that this share of the market has now declined to less than 40%, owing to large increases in the tea acreage of other producing countries.

Africa is now a big player in the tea business with approximately 175,000 hectares under tea, and now produces at least 50% of all the tea we drink in the United Kingdom. Kenya, Malawi, Zimbabwe, Tanzania, Gambia, Mozambique and South Africa are all tea producing countries on this vast continent. African tea is blended with teas from other producing countries, repacked by small and medium size companies with household names such as Twinings, Lipton, Brooke Bond and Tetley, some of whom have since been acquired by large multinationals such as Associated British Foods, the Unilever Group and the Tata Group.

For the future, full mechanization will be an important consideration with ever-increasing labour costs. New highly efficient machinery is always being developed for work *in the factory*, but there are still many methods of applying machinery *in the field* which need developing: by various riding-type machines that can be used for cropping the green leaf, for pruning the bushes and for the application of fertiliser – not to mention individual hand-held shears for taking the green leaf. These will surely be introduced in the near future as hand-held shears are already in use in the country.

Spot the baby. A little head is just visible at his mother's back. This estate worker also carries a bundle of old tea that has been uprooted from nearby fields; root stocks and branches make good firewood. (*Photo 2002, courtesy Eastern Produce, Malawi.*)

Elephant on the Shire River fired at from Livingstone's launch the Ma Robert. Oil painting by Thomas Baines 1859. (*Courtesy Royal Geographical Society*).

Kenya

In Kenya, seeds of the tea camellia were first introduced from India in 1903, and during succeeding years further importations of Assam and Manipuri seed were extensively used during the 1920s and 1930s. By 1954 4450 hectares of land had been planted up by the white settlers on estates around Limuru and Kericho. The latest figures show that there were 120,429 hectares of land planted with tea in Kenya in 1999, most of which (about 71%) is in the smallholder sector, managed by the Kenya Tea Development Authority. Large western companies such as Camellia Group, George Williamson & Co., James Finlay and Unilever, hold a significant acreage (29%) on up-country estates in the Kericho and Nandi areas.

The right climate for all year round plucking, good

A steam launch typical of the type used on the Shire and Zambezi rivers for the transport of tea, coffee and cotton off the estates. (*Photo courtesy Central Africana Lt., Balantyre.*)

soil and altitude give Kenya a distinct advantage over many other tea growing countries. Tea production on the large company-owned estates is considerably greater than that on the smallholdings. A tremendous increase in yields over the past thirty years has come with the introduction of Vegetative Propagation.

Long before vegetative propagation (V.P.), planters have known that certain bushes in a field of tea were more productive of leaf (Flush). Many years later, when vegetative propagation was first commenced, tea leaf cuttings (clonal cuttings) would be taken from such high yielding mother bushes and then grown on in polythene sleeves in high intensity shade nurseries; the resultant plants being identical to the parent. For the past 35 years this has been normal practice.

With many trials and rejections during the nursery stage it is a lengthy business and takes in the region of fifteen years to fully evaluate a particular clone's potential with regard to its vigour, high yield and quality, and its resistance to disease – among other important characteristics – before the young clonal plants can ever be released for planting out in the field. It is enough to say here that it is a long and complicated process to produce a good clone. The yield per acre on Kenya's large company owned estates is among the highest in the world.

Future prospects for the expansion of tea in Kenya alone are enormous, with upwards of half a million acres of suitable land for tea still available. An indication of Kenya's growing importance is that she now produces around 300 million kg or 300,000 metric tonnes of made tea per annum.

Eastern produce plantations

Kenya

Nandi Hills district

Altitude 1750 to 2000 meters
7 estates comprising 5500 hectares of tea
Fuelwood plantations 2500 hectares
Average number of employees 10,000
Average yield – 3000 kgs of made tea per hectare per year

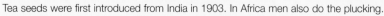
Tea seeds were first introduced from India in 1903. In Africa men also do the plucking.

A typical up-country tea-scape with neat hygienic houses makes for a healthy, happy work force. Approximately 4^1/$_4$ kgs of green leaf –
when manufactured (made tea) – produces 1 kg of black tea, the sort those in the western world drink.
(*All photos courtesy Eastern Produce Kenya Ltd.*)

An idealistic form of suburbia in the hills!

Malawi (Nyasaland)

Today, Malawi has some 40,000 hectares of tea which is situated in the two main growing areas in the Thylo and Mulanje Districts, and this gives employment to over 42,000, the industry being the largest employer of labour in the private sector. Small-holdings also play an important part in the industry.

The first white settlers – one of whom was ex-Ceylon coffee planter Harry Brown – arrived in the early 1890s and planted coffee in Mulanje. As in Ceylon, the early planters experimented with tea and various other plantation crops including tobacco and cotton. Some of the original tea bushes, now over a hundred years old, can still be seen on Lauderdale Estate.

The tea industry in Malawi plays a significant part in Africa's total tea production, being second to the largest tea growing country, Kenya. Tea seeds were first planted on a commercial basis in the Mulanje District in 1893 along a stretch of land below and around Mount Mulanje on Thornwood and Lauderdale estates.

Being a land-locked country, Malawi's early settlers had great difficulty in getting their tea or coffee out before the coming of the railway. At first ox-carts and rivers played their part. In the early 1900s chests of tea were carried off the estates by ox-carts along miles of rough tracks down to the lower reaches of the Shire River, where it was loaded onto native craft to continue by way of the mighty Zambezi through Mozambique and eventually out through the port of Beira on the Indian Ocean.

Today the industry is centred in the south of the country in Mulanje and Thyolo districts, with just one large estate, Kawalazi, situated in the north. Here too, as in Kenya over the past thirty years or so, all replantings have been made with high yielding vegetatively propagated clones. Nevertheless only about 19% of Malawi's tea is clonal, the balance being old seedling tea. Only about 1% of its old poor yielding seedling tea acreage is replanted each year.

Eastern Produce Malawi Estates

Lauderdale Tea Estate

Total tea acreage	1059
Manufacture	LTP (Lawrie Tea Processor)
Total estate labour force	1400 peak season
Resident estate labour force	750

Ex-Ceylon coffee planter Harry Brown plants the first tea in Malawi in 1893

The Mount Mulanje massif dominates the tea estates in the Mulanje district which are themselves at an average elevation of 660 meters. 100 years separates the main picture and the small sepia one and here we see a country that has just celebrated its 100th anniversary in tea and where, on fertile land below and around Mount Mulanje, the first tea camellias were planted on Lauderdale and Thornwood estates during the early 1890s.

Flamboyant. Flame Tree *Poinciana regia*, with seed pods 18" in length, is spectacular when in flower.

Lauderdale estate in 1893.
(*Photo, courtesy Central Africana Ltd., Blantyre, Malawi.*)

Lauderdale

This good stand of healthy china type bushes is now over 90 years old.

Hand-held shears, with plastic containers, are used on the small leafed China hybrids from the 2nd year after pruning because of the greater number of shoots (compared to clonal and the larger, broad leafed Assam varieties), which makes them more difficult to pluck by hand.

Villagers in the Mulanje District supplement the estate's labour force.

Standing close to the site of the pioneer's old Lauderdale bungalow (previous page) are members of the Mulanje Mountain Trust.

Eastern Produce Malawi Ltd Estates

Mulanje District

A flame tree frames Likanga Tea Factory which is no longer used to produce tea, having been converted to a Coffee Hulling Plant during the mid 1980s. However, tea is still grown on Likanga Estate and is processed at Lauderdale Factory.

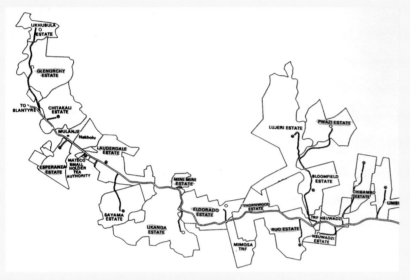

Map showing positions of some of the estates that are included here.

Limbuli. Future young workers' sports day.

Wood fuel stack. Limbuli.
(*All photos 2002, courtesy Eastern Produce Malawi Ltd.*)

Limbuli. The man with a cap, at left in pit, lifts, the other sawer pushes down.

South Africa

Apart from early trials when a small number of tea plants imported from Kew Gardens were put out at various sites, the South African tea industry was launched on a commercial scale in 1877 by Sir Liege Hulett on his Kearsney Estate near Stanger, where he planted out Assam-type seed. Following his example, others took the field and the first tea was manufactured in 1881 and by 1886 80,000 pounds of black tea was produced in Natal.

During the early years of the industry indented labour from South India was employed on the tea estates in Natal, and by 1907 there were over 5000 acres planted up with the tea camellia. During the late 19th and early 20th centuries hundreds of thousands of Tamil and Telegu workers from the east coast of Southern India left their impoverished land to live and work on the plantations that were being developed – from Malaya, across to the shores of Ceylon and beyond to Mauritius and South Africa. This vast area was an agricultural hot-house most suitable for growing a variety of plantation crops such as tea, coffee, rubber and cocoa. The rapid expansion of the planting industry had far-reaching effects upon a wide variety of people.

The Southern African tea industry grew slowly but political and social influences put an end to the influx of indented labour from India when the price of tea dropped on world markets. These two factors combined to make the tea planters turn to a less labour-intensive crop – sugar, and the tea industry was abandoned in 1949.

Its rebirth came during the early 1960s and coincided with rising tea prices world-wide and, importantly, the arrival of Kenyan immigrants who brought with them the latest knowledge and methods in the cultivation and manufacture. With the establishment of a large tea plant nursery in the Eastern Transvaal, the industry was set to take off again.

At its peak in 2002, there were approximately 6200 hectares of tea in Southern Africa which, during the growing season, provided employment for 22,000 people. Wages, hospital care, dwellings and benefits for the workers were up with the best in the tea growing countries of the world. The South African estates produced 50,000 tons of green leaf which, after manufacture, resulted in approximately 10,000 tons of made tea; this met about half the local demand.

The South African tea industry suffered an irreversible setback in 2003 when not only were import restrictions imposed but minimum wage levels were introduced and the currency strengthened. The combination of these factors resulted in major losses and the closing of estates in early 2004. At the present time no plans are in place to operate these estates, and it is considered unlikely they will ever be reopened as tea estates.

Other African countries

In Africa there are a further 6800 hectares of tea in Zimbabwe (Rhodesia) with lesser acreages in Tanzania, Zambia and Mozambique, the last of which has seen its progressive tea industry shattered by the War of Independence and Civil War, its tea fields – strewn with mines – reverting to scrub jungle, with estates abandoned and factories destroyed.

But today, if the total production of all African countries is taken together, Africa has become the third largest tea producer in the world – after India and China – and is now ahead of Sri Lanka.

Sapekoe Estates

Tzaneen, Limpopo Province, South Africa

Middelkop Estate

Estate first opened	1963
Total tea acreage	1238
Present factory built	1968
Type of manufacture	CTC
Total estate labour force	430–1000
Resident estate population	1000

Two leaves and a bud are taken by the pluckers who carry bamboo canes, which they place across the bushes to 'pluck to a level'. Each plucker gathers about 150 pounds of green leaf a day which, after passing through the various stages of manufacture, produces approximately 29 pounds of made tea. (*Photo 2003, courtesy Sapekoe Estates (Pty) Ltd.*)

Pluckers bring their leaf to one of the weighing stations in the fields where it is weighed and an account taken by the worker dressed in blue (*Photo 2003 courtesy Jane Moncreiff.*)

Tea bushes clothe a part of Middelkop like a fitted carpet. (*Photo 2003, courtesy Sapekoe Estates (Pty) Ltd.*)

Seed was used for the first plantings in 1963, which was supplied by George Williamson Estates Kenya and Tanganyika. To date there are 481 hectares of seedling tea and 20 hectares of clonal tea. The bushes are pruned every three years.
Note: In December 2004 Sapekoe announced it would close all its tea operations as they were no longer financially viable. This decision was the result of the impact of the strength of the Rand and removal of import protection. Opportunities are being investigated to identify alternative uses for the land.

The plucked leaf is put into lug boxes and loaded onto the estate trailer for transport to the factory. (*Photos 2003 courtesy Jane Moncreiff.*)

VIEWS IN AND AROUND PLANTATIONS IN PRODUCING COUNTRIES

Sri Lanka

Great Western Tea Estate

Rothschild Tea Estate

Spring Valley Tea Estate

Poonagalla Tea Estate

Frotoft Tea Estate

Into the 21st century with Great Western Tea Estate

Total tea acreage	1012
Present factory built	1928
Type of manufacture	Rotorvane/CTC
Total estate labour force	1064
Resident estate population	3500

Nursery. Young tea plants nearing readiness for planting out. Crèche in background.

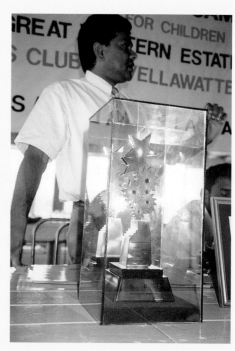

The National Development Bank Productivity Awards, March 1998. As winner in the large category division, Great Western Superintendent, Maithri Liyanage, receives the Award Trophy for improvements to G. W. Factory, one of Talawakelle Plantation's 19 tea estates (managed by the Hayleys Group.) (*All photos 1997/98, courtesy Maithri Liyanage.*)

Fields of clonal tea, with the Superintendent's bungalow right, and estate offices below left.

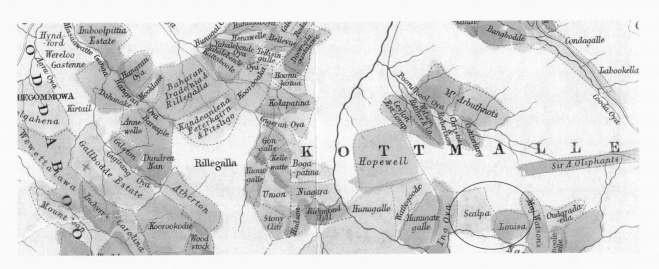

Map showing the positions of Louisa and Scalpa coffee estates which became part of 'Great Western' Estate, so named by J. A. Rossiter in 1866.
(Map *'Showing the Positions of Coffee Estates in the Central Province of Ceylon' by J. A. Arrowsmith, 1859.*)

Grevillea robusta, or Silver Oak, is native to Australia and was introduced into Ceylon in 1856; it provides shade for the tea, and is also planted as a wind-break.

The 'old' factory. Tea carts wait for chests of tea for transport. (*Photo c1894.*)

Tea chest markings B.O.P.F. denote the grade of tea packed: Broken Orange Pekoe Fannings.

The cup that cheers.

Great Western 'new' factory seen from almost the same position as top of page.

The Notice Board says: A Combination of Worker Co-operation & Management Dedication.

Great Western Tea Estate

Tea tasting room.

Factory officer T. Nadarajah.

Cleanliness in the drying room.

Rolling Room, with 'dhool' lying on fermenting beds. (*Colour Photos 1997, courtesy Maithri Liyanage, Manager, Great Western.*)

A part of Colombo harbour. A sketch depicting the old landing jetty pre 1950s, with booking office above; beyond that, across the road, is the Grand Oriental Hotel (G.O.H.); to the right of the jetty are the tea customs sheds; the vessel at anchor is the M.V. *Chilka*. (British India Steam Navigation Company) (*Pencil sketch by S.R.Fever 1985.*)

Rothschild Tea Estate

In the field

Early experiments were conducted with the tea plant on Rothschild 160 years ago when it was a coffee estate. Today, Tamil pluckers stand in the footsteps of the coffee pickers of long ago.

One of the spraying gang.

Pluckers bring in their leaf for weighing up in the field.
(*All photos, except map, courtesy John and Joan Turnbull.*)

240

Spraying two-year-old tea plants with copper fungicide against Blister Blight in a newly replanted field.

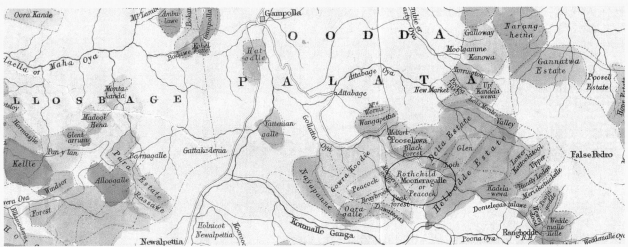

PIONEERING COUNTRY. Map showing Rothschild & other coffee estates. (*Detail from map drawn by J. Arrowsmith, 1859.*)

Pruning tea bushes takes place at periods varying from three to four years, depending upon elevation.

Rothschild factory.

Foundation stone, laid in original coffee store or factory in 1839.

In the factory

Total tea acreage	673
Present factory built	1939
Type of manufacture	C.T.C. w.e.f. 1993
Total estate labour force	725
Resident estate population	2371

Modern 'C.T.C.' machines that crush, tear and curl the green leaf, replace the old orthodox tea rollers.

Roll of Honour.

The estate lorry, c1965.

(All photos 1998, courtesy Joan Turnbull.)

'C.T.C.' machinery operating.

The latest method of weighing the green leaf as it arrives in coir sacks from the fields for manufacture.

Ready for dispatch, the made tea that we drink.

Poonagalla Tea Estate

It is not known when Poonagalla was first opened (to coffee) as it is not mentioned in A. M. Fergusson's Directory *Statistics of Ceylon Coffee Plantations in 1857.*

In 1895 Poonagalla appears as a Group, including within it the original coffee estates of Lunagalla, Udahena and Cabragalla. By 1898 the records show that W. S. Coombe had become Manager of the property, having taken over from C. Bisset, and by the year 1900 the total acreage of land on Poonagalla Group was 2755 acres, of which almost half, 1237 acres, were planted in tea.

The coffee leaf disease had appeared in 1869, by which time there were 276,000 acres of land under coffee in the island; this colossal acreage of dead and dying coffee bushes had all but been uprooted and replanted with tea by the year 1900. By this time there were 380,000 acres of tea – some turnaround!

Interestingly, Rettie's Report shows that a small acreage of coffee was still being put out in 1894 and 1895 on Poonagalla; it also shows the extent of old abandoned coffee land which, to some extent, would have been the case on many of the estates in the country at the turn of the century. This old coffee land and Patna would very quickly have been cleared and planted up with tea – an easier proposition by far than the coffee planters faced when felling heavy tree virgin jungle back in the 1830s.

The name Coombe has been associated with Poonagalla from the late 1890s (W.S.C.) and later, when R. G. 'Thamby' Coombe retired, his son Gorton took over the management until he retired in 1960, followed by Tony Gottelier until his retirement in 1971. The Coombe family held sway on Poonagalla for 72 years, while the Rettie family were on Spring Valley Estate for a mere 66 years.

In the belief that Ghost stories are sometimes more interesting than facts about tea, here is an unusual account given to me by Joan Gottelier, who lived on Poonagalla for eleven years. The story is in her own words.

Poonagalla sitting room (*Photo 1998, courtesy N. Johnpillai, Superintendent Poonagalla Group.*)

The ghost of Poonagalla

Poonagalla Bungalow had its ghosts, and for those who are sceptical as to their existence, I give some incidents that happened. People asked me if this did not frighten me – to me, the Coombes were so happy on that estate and their lives so enmeshed on Poonagalla, I considered their ghosts as happy ghosts.

When Tony went up to the estate to take over from Gorton Coombe, he had the large Guestroom at the Eastern side of the bungalow. One night, and knowing nothing of the Resident Ghost, he heard books being thrown about in the lounge next door, and in the nursery-room next to his room he heard the clanging of wires (this room was used to dry off the ironing so had wires across the room) and when he went into the room to see what the noise was, the Coombe's Siamese cat had jumped onto the top of the wardrobe, 8 feet high, with no aid in getting up except straight off the floor. A later incident was when Tony's cousin's son was out from England for a holiday with us, and had that Guestroom. He knew nothing about the Ghost. At 2 am there was a knock on our bedroom door, which as at the other end of the bungalow, and Chris was there saying 'R.G. is here. Can I sleep in your room?' He was clutching a blanket, was as white as a sheet, so I made up a bed for him in another bedroom of ours. But it was the same pattern as David's experience. Some of Carson's Agency Staff refused to sleep in that bungalow, as they all knew of 'R. G. Coombe's Ghost'.

Two more incidents were even more realistic. Michael was only six when we first went to Poonagalla. One day when Tony and I were out, in the evening Rita the Nanny told Michael to run down the passage to the Drying Room to get his pyjamas before he had his bath and got ready for bed. He did this, but ran back very disturbed, hiding behind Rita, which was so unusual, as he was never frightened of 'things'. He told her, and I quote his words, 'A man was walking up the passage. He was tall, like Dad, he had white hair and he stooped like that.' (A demonstration here! And all the Coombes stood over 6 ft 4 in) 'He had a striped shirt with long sleeves and grey trousers. He had a walking stick and behind him was a little dog.' We had only been there a few months and had never mentioned the ghost to the Nanny or any of the servants, all of whom were new to the place, as we were. We told our friends, the Walls, who rented the other bungalow on the estate that had been built for R. G. when he retired, and they told us that after R. G.'s wife died in that bungalow, every evening he went for a walk with her little dog, and always entered the bungalow through the old billiard room and up the passage, with the little dog walking behind him. None of us had known R. G. but the Walls described him as being very tall, white haired and bent, always wore his shirt sleeves down, and walked with a stick. He took the dog out for a walk every evening, and would always have re-entered the bungalow through that back entrance.

Another really authentic sighting of the ghost was by our Tamil cook. He came to me one morning and I quote what he said. 'Lady, a funny thing happened last night. I locked up the kitchen and was walking down the road to my house' (which was in my big vegetable garden) 'and I saw somebody walking in front of me. I thought it was my wife come up to meet me and I called "Mary, Mary" but it wasn't her. It was a bright moonlight night and when I walked down, she walked in front of me. She was tall, like our Missie (meaning our daughter Jean) and had long hair like Missie. When I stopped at the gate of my house, she walked on and walked through the closed gate at the end of the road.' We again asked the Walls, who told us that a Coombe daughter had died in the bungalow of Typhoid aged 17. She was blonde and had long hair and was tall and slender. As none of us, let alone the servants, had ever heard of this girl or her death, it confirms the authentic sighting of an authentic ghost. No way could our Tamil cook have dreamt up such a real and vivid picture, as he had not been long on the estate.

Pluckers made a pretty sight in the tea fields.
(*Photo 1970, courtesy Tony Gottelier.*)

Each plucker takes 'two leaves and a bud'.

Poonagalla Tea Estate

3000 such shoots (Assam variety) of 'two leaves and a bud' go to make approximately one pound of made tea.

Picking over Black tea for stalk removal. (*Photo 1970 Brooke Bond, courtesy Tony Gottelier.*)

Poonagalla Tea Factory. (*Photo 1997, courtesy N. V. B. Johnpillai, Manager, Poonagalla Group.*)

Leopard trap and dead leopard. (*Photo 1971, courtesy Tony Gottelier.*)

The Poonagalla leopard is brought to book after killing 12 head of cattle belonging to the estate labour force.

Poonagalla nursery, holding 250,000 VP clonal tea cuttings. (*Photo 1971, courtesy the then Manager, Tony Gottelier.*)

Spring Valley Tea Estate, old factory. There were two tea factories on the estate. This, the larger one, was burnt down in 1943. This factory was on the site of the old coffee store, and was powered by electricity generated by water power (pelton turbine). The property was run by a resident Manager who communicated directly with the Company's Board in London. The Colombo Commercial Company acted as shipping agents. This arrangement continued up to December 1970.

Spring Valley Tea Estate

Two and a half million pounds of made tea from this estate in one year!

Spring Valley 'new' factory. Built 1944 to 1948. (Delayed by difficulty in securing materials at the end of World War II.) *Photo taken by C. F. Brooke-Smith about 1970.*
Elevation, 4800 ft. District, Badulla; Acreage in 1970, 2590; Tea, 2000; Estate elevation, 2200 to 6690 ft. Total Labour force 2750; Resident estate population about 5000; Opened c1845 as a coffee estate. Crop (made tea), manufactured per annum during the late 1960s averaged 2,650,000 pounds, mainly in Spring Valley ' New factory', but some in the small Kottagodde factory.

MANAGERS.

SPRING VALLEY COFFEE CO.

SIR WILLIAM REID	-1847
THOMAS WOOD ESQ.	1847-1865
A. T. RETTIE ESQ.	1865-1907

SPRING VALLEY CEYLON ESTATES LTD.

A. T. RETTIE ESQ.	1907-1914
W. T. RETTIE ESQ., M.C.	1914-1931
COL. F. I. S. SUTHERLAND O.B.E., M.C., E.D.	1931-1949
J. CRANFIELD ESQ.	1949-1955
C. F. BROOKE-SMITH ESQ., F.C.I.P.	1955-1970

The stone plaque erected in Spring Valley New Factory in 1970 by the last independent manager of Spring Valley Ceylon Estates Ltd., before he retired and the property came under the Ouvah Highfields Company. (*Photos 1970, courtesy Charles Brooke-Smith.*)
We wonder if only 8 managers in 125 years constitutes a record.

Frotoft Group

Ramboda

Frotoft tea factory.

Standing in the group are (L to R) Brian Ratwatte, the then Superintendent; Vernon Ratwatte in the foreground, the visiting agent.

Inside Frotoft shade nursery is Micky Abeyesekera, facing in white shirt, of Whittalls Estates & Agencies Ltd. In the late 1960s Frotoft was propagating half a million V.P. plants annually to supply its own needs and those of other estates. Experimentation of vegetative propagation of tea started on Spring Valley Estate, Badulla, in 1939, during the time of Charles Brooke-Smith. Experiments were resumed after the War in the selection of high yielding, disease resistant bushes during the 1950s.
(*All photos 1970, courtesy Alan and Elizabeth Sharp-Paul.*)

The interior of a high-shade nursery showing vegetative propagated clonal cuttings.

China and Taiwan

Chinese tea culture

Japan

Japanese tea culture
National Institute of Vegetable and Tea Science
past and present

Indonesia
Java, Sumatra

Huberta	Tea Estate, Padang, Sumatra
Patuahwattee	Tea Estate, Bandung, Java
Alkaterie	Tea Estate, Bandung, Java

China and Taiwan

The tea plant (*Camellia sinensis*) is indigenous throughout China and has been cultivated by the Chinese probably for about five thousand years on small plots of land around their dwellings (tea gardens) where the bushes were numbered in their hundreds, if not their dozens, each peasant farmer collecting his own leaf and producing his own palatable 'medicinal drink' – Cha. China is the classic tea country.

In spite of the fact that the tea camellia has been cultivated and its leaf prepared in China for so many years, accurate information about the methods employed did not reach the outside world It was not until the early 1600s that the Dutch and English East India Companies brought tea to Europe, Great Britain and north America, and it was only then that 'foreigners' started to learn something of the riches locked up in the mystical Celestial Empire – including Tea.

A little over two hundred years later, during the late 1820s and early 1830s, the Dutch and British commenced their own great tea industries in Java and in India and these – after a slow start pioneering a completely new tea industry (outside China) in the jungles of East Asia – came to dominate the world's supply of tea, chiefly owing to the tea that was being shipped out of British India from the Port of Calcutta, from the Kidderpore Docks – then known as the world's tea caddy. A direct result of the entry of Indian, Javanese and slightly later Ceylon-grown teas to the market in Mincing Lane, London was the decline and fall of China's once great export trade in tea.

Today, China, the sleeping giant of tea, has re-emerged and in all probability will soon become the world's largest producer of tea. Much of the tea produced, green tea, goes to a huge internal market with a comparatively small amount of black tea going for export. China's colossal acreage of land under tea – double that of India but by no means so productive or efficient – is undergoing a huge and progressive change. This will prove to be a considerable threat to the other tea producing countries in the near future such as India, Sri Lanka, Bangladesh, Indonesia and Africa. Even without China's progress, the global tea market is at present almost stagnant, with tea prices low and over production world-wide.

Tea cultivation throughout China today is proceeding at pace at all levels, with Government support and tea expertise coming from the country's Tea Research Academy, and with this the rapid growth of the industry by the opening of larger plantations with much greater efficiency, also because of the re-emergence of large cooperative farms. Soon, there will surely be a revolution in mechanisation in the tea fields of China on large plantations – as practised in Taiwan and Japan – and this in turn will lead to the manufacture of new tea machinery for greater efficiency in gathering the extra crop coming in from the ever increasing new plantings. The country's manufacturing industry is well equipped to do this.

Countless generations of small family farms throughout the country on which animal husbandry is often combined with a small tea area of tea bushes are bound to be swallowed up, amalgamated with others and consequently made more productive by output conscious entrepreneurs. The plucked leaf from such millions of small holdings is often carried great distances to processing factories where green tea (unfermented tea) is produced.

The uprooting of sparsely populated areas of tea bushes and replanting the land with high yielding hedge-planted tea will also increase yields everywhere as the young bushes come into plucking. Complete new areas of forest are also being felled and opened out to tea which, if on steep mountainsides, usually creates problems with soil erosion. Importantly Government subsidies are being offered with as much as half the cost being given for opening new tea farms, as well as the building of new tea processing factories.

Today, China is once again on the threshold of becoming the world's largest producer of tea.

Taiwan

Whereas the tea plant was introduced from China into Japan almost 900 years ago, it has only recently been brought over from the Chinese mainland to the island of Formosa, Taiwan R.O.C. – its introduction being some 200 years ago.

However, great strides have been made and the total tea acreage in Taiwan today is a little over 50,000 acres, equivalent to that in Japan, and similarly the industry has hedge-planted tea with mechanisation in the fields for harvesting the green leaf, for the application of fertilizers etc. The industry produces some 21,000 tons of black and green tea annually.

China

Homeland of tea Past tense

Chinese tea pluckers.
(*Drawing by Elizabeth Twining 1866.*)

Tea growing in China spans a period of 5000 years. China's tea area is the largest in the world and much of the tea is grown at high elevations in remote mountain regions on millions of small family farms where the tea bushes are often numbered in their hundreds. Today, tea is also grown on larger plantations and on workers' co-operatives.

A Chinese tea plucker.
(*From a drawing published in The Illustrated London News 1857.*)

Lithograph c1900, Cassell & Company, London.

The English mercantile agent's mission was tasting, pricing and buying the teas suitable for the British market.

The chests are supposed to contain a certain weight of tea and, when sold, are brought to be weighed in the presence of the buyer for shipment.
(*Sketches 1888 from The Illustrated London News.*)

Chinese tea culture
21st century

As in some other major tea growing countries where hand plucking has not given way to harvesting the leaf by machinery, pluckers are paid on the weight of leaf they take each day. Here we see an age-old custom of a plucker having her leaf weighed. See a similar scene in Assam on page 198. (*Photo courtesy Edward Eisler.*)

Chinese tea pluckers. (*Photo courtesy Edward Eisler.*)

Plucking the new season's spring flush in Fujian Province. From this first plucking with its tender leaves, the very best grades of tea are made.
(*Photo 2007 courtesy R. Twining & Co, Ltd.*)

China

Sleeping tea giant

With more land under tea than any other country, China will, once again, lead the world in tea production.

A pedlar carrying green leaf to a tea factory for processing. Such factories manufacture pan-fired steamed teas, also a certain amount of black tea and scented tea, the former for export to the Western World. (*Photo 2007 courtesy R. Twining & Co. Ltd.*)

White tea leaf being naturally sun-withered.
(*Photo 2007 courtesy R. Twining & Co. Ltd.*)

'Bai Mundan' white tea being hand sorted.
(*Photo 2007 courtesy R. Twining & Co. Ltd.*)

In this part of the world the food of the Giant Panda is the succulent shoots of the bamboo tree. Bamboo has many other uses including, here, racks for withering the green leaf. (*Photo courtesy Edward Eisler.*)

A typical tea scape.
(*Photo 2007 courtesy R. Twining & Co. Ltd.*)

China

In Yunnan province a small number of very old trees – over 100ft tall and some eight or nine feet in circumference, estimated to be over 2000 years old – have recently been discovered growing in jungle at over 8000 ft above sea level.

Rolling hills and hedge grown tea planted on the contours with vacancies in parts of the tea on hillside beyond. (*Photo 2007 courtesy R. Twining & Co. Ltd.*)

One of many tea pluckers.
(*Photo 2007 courtesy R. Twining & Co. Ltd.*)

Plucking on Dong Ding Mountain, Central Taiwan.

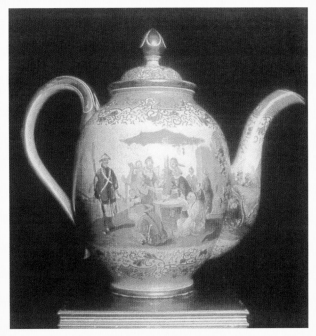

Twinings, founded in 1706, had this truly lovely porcelain teapot made for the Great Exhibition in 1851. It is probably the largest teapot in the world and holds thirteen gallons from which 1220 cups of tea may be poured.
(*Photo 2007 courtesy R. Twining & Co. Ltd.*)

Taiwan

The introduction of the tea camellia, from China, into the island of Taiwan occurred about 200 years ago.

Taiwan High Mountain Farm, 1800 metres. Taiwan Central Mountain Range. (*Photo 2007 courtesy Stephen Jack.*)

Views on Hangzhou Tea Plantation

with much forest for future extensions

Blocks of forest interspersed with fields of tea go well together in this exquisite landscape with stone terraces on many of the steep hillsides.

A peaceful scene where frequent mists envelop the hills wherein this attractive tea factory complex nestles – almost like a monastery.

Some reasonably flat tea fields with small dots in the upper field – 'coolie' hats are very noticeable in any tea landscape.

Tea ceremony and green tea at an office lunch in modern Japan. (*Photos courtesy The World Green Tea Association.*)

Japan

Full mechanization
in the tea fields

The history of the Japanese tea industry probably goes back to the 9th century when, it is said, the tea plant was brought from China to Japan by Buddhist monks and planted at Yeisan and Uji, near Kyoto. Certainly, it is known that a Buddhist priest named Eisai brought tea plants to Japan in the 12th century.

At first tea was taken as a medicinal drink but with the opening of the port of Yokohama in 1859, tea production increased rapidly up to the late 1890s. Previously all manufacture had been carried out by hand, as it had been in China, but with the introduction of new tea machinery production accelerated yet again.

The islands that make up Japan stretch for some 1600 miles from the top of Hokkaido in the north, to the southernmost part of Kyusho. Because of the high latitude of the northern part of Japan, tea is cultivated in the southern warmer districts where, nevertheless, there is still a long wintering period when the bushes lie dormant from the end of October until the middle of March.

The green leaf in the fields is usually harvested four times a year, with each cropping period lasting about two weeks: the first crop of green leaf is taken in late April to mid May; the 2nd crop in late June; the 3rd crop in late July to early August and the 4th crop in mid September. The first crop of the new season always gives the best quality and fetches the highest price.

In Japan, as in other tea growing countries, old 'seedling tea bushes' have been uprooted and replaced with high yielding vegetative propagated clonal tea. Up until 1960, 90% of Japan's tea fields were planted with old poor yielding 'seedling tea', whereas today, 90% of the country's tea acreage is clonal. The small leafed China variety, *C. sinensis*, is cultivated together with a limited acreage of the broad-leafed Assam variety, *C. assamica*.

The Japanese tea industry is small by comparison with other producing countries, but it is well organised and high yielding. Today, almost all the country's green tea production goes for domestic consumption, and from the early 1970s black tea production has practically ceased, owing to strong international price competition. The manufacture of green tea in Japan is made from the leaves of the China plant, with black tea – the type the Western world drinks – being manufactured from the Assam variety.

The Shizuoka Prefecture is Japan's greatest tea-growing region, within clear sight of Mount Fuji. Harvesting of the green leaf is carried out with hand-operated shears, portable machines, by machines that run on rails between rows of bushes, and by the use of riding-type harvesters on a flat terrain. Hand plucking is rare but this traditional method is always used for leaf that goes to make the finest grades of tea – Gyokura and Tencha green tea.

With the riding-type harvesting machines the shoots are cut and sucked into a separator, then into bags that are carried by the tractor, each bag holding 20-25 kilos.

The total area under tea in Japan today is approximately 50,000 hectares.

Acknowledgement to Dr. Hitoshi Yoshitomi of the National Research of Vegetables, Ornamental Plants and Tea, Shizuoka, Japan.

263

Japanese tea culture

Past tense

Statue of Buddhist priest Eisai, who is credited with having introduced tea from China to Japan in the 12th century. (*Courtesy NIVTS.*)

The first ever tea garden planted in 1194 at Kozanji Temple, north of Kyoto.

Plucking hedge-planted tea bushes with a field of young tea to the right. (*Photo, tinted, c1900.*)

Tea culture in Japan in 1874. When the young tea plants are three years old they yield their first crop of green leaf, the new flush being gathered at three or four pluckings between March and August, depending upon district and climate. A good plucker takes 40 lb of green leaf in a day and this yields 10 lb of made green tea. (*Drawings from the Illustrated London News, 1874.*)

Japanese tea culture

21st century

Young women plucking tea shoots in Kanaya-cho, Shizuoka. This traditional costume can only be seen in posters for advertising nowadays. (*Photo 1999, courtesy NIVTS.*)

Clonal propagation in the cutting bed.

Cutting bed after one year of planting.

Paper pot   Soil bed
Difference in roots

Paper pot cutting.

Mount Fuji Yama (12,391 feet) looks down on well manicured tea fields in the Shizuoka Prefecture, Japan's greatest tea growing district. (*Photo 1999, courtesy National Institute of Vegetable & Tea Science – NIVTS.*)

Zigzag planting of paper pot cuttings.

Young tea field (first year after planting).

Workers hand-plucking. (Kanaya-cho, Shizuoka.) In this highly mechanised industry hand plucking is a rare sight these days. In the past women pluckers wore traditional costumes in the tea fields which today can only be seen for purposes of advertising.

As Japan is a mountainous country, approximately 60% of the country's tea is grown on slopes. Small tea factories, like the one shown, can be seen in all the hill districts.

There are approximately 50,000 hectares of tea in Japan of which about 45,000 are planted up with high yielding propagated clonal plants of the China variety, of which one important cultivar, Yabukita, occupies some 86% of the total clonal area.

Countless small tea fields are scattered throughout the mountainous regions where high quality tea has been produced since long ago. (*Photos 1, 2 & 3 courtesy National Institute of Vegetable and Tea Science.*)

Rail-tracking plucking machine.

Riding-type harvester.
(*Photo 1997, courtesy Matsumoto Kiko Co. Ltd.*)

Methods	The amount of new shoots per day per person
Hand plucking	
Hand plucking	10 ～ 15kg
Hand-shear plucking	100 ～ 200
Mechanical plucking	
Portable machine for two persons	700 ～ 1,000
Riding machine	4,000 ～ 5,000
Self-rail-tracking machine	2,000 ～ 3,000

Green leaf harvesting efficiency.

Hand-shear plucking. (*Photos 5 & 6, 2001, courtesy World Green Tea Association.*)

Portable green leaf harvesting machines can be seen in most tea fields on steep slopes. (*Photo 1999, courtesy NIVTS.*)

The National Institute of Vegetable and Tea Science. The main building as seen from the entrance. This Research Station has many buildings, offices and trial plots of land for tea which cover an extensive acreage. The Institute started in 1896 as a laboratory for tea manufacturing process under the Ministry of Agriculture, and changed to a Tea Research Station in Kanaya, Shizuoka in 1919. (*Photo 1999, courtesy NIVTS.*)

Foreground, tea hedges that have been pruned by riding-type pruning machines.

The view also shows anti-frost fans mounted on tall poles. In the more northern parts of Japan in early spring, frost damages the young shoots of the first crop. In such regions there are three methods of frost protection: covering, freezing by sprinkler and air stirring by electrically powered fans. These fans prevent frosting by blowing/stirring warm air on to the tea fields.

Fuji and Numazu region.

A riding-type fertilizer-plower. (*Photos 2001, courtesy World Green Tea Association.*)

Pluckers pose for the cameraman. In mountainous areas the tea is planted along the contour and only portable plucking machines can be used. However, the portable plucking machine, dragging a leaf collecting bag, is too heavy for old farmers to operate and some steep tea fields will surely be abandoned when younger men cannot be found to use them. (*Photo 2001, courtesy World Green Tea Association.*)

The National Institute of Vegetable and Tea Science. (*Photo 1999, courtesy NIVTS.*)

Java & Sumatra
(Dutch East Indies)

During the early 18th century the Dutch East India Company had considered the possibility of starting its own tea industry in Java and Sumatra, as had the English East India Company during the latter part of the century in India. Nothing came of this for the Netherlands until J.I.L.L. Jacobson arrived on the scene.

J.I.L.L. Jacobson was the first European tea planter, pioneering the tea industry in the Dutch East Indies. By the time of his arrival in Java from Holland in 1827, where he had been a tea taster, Isadoris Jacobson had already a considerable knowledge of the finished product from China. While in the service of the Dutch Trading Company he was commissioned by the Dutch Government to collect all useful information on the cultivation of the tea plant.

Traders from the western world, the Dutch and English East India Companies, had for many years brought back to Europe and Great Britain tea, spice and porcelain from the Celestial Empire and this was taken a stage further in the early part of the 19th century when these two institutions decided, quite independently, not merely to import tea but to grow and produce tea on their own plantations in Java and in India. As it happened, these two great trading companies started their tea industries at almost the same time; the Dutch in 1827 and the English in 1834.

The Dutch Government imported the first 500 tea plants from Japan, which had by that time been cultivating the plant – originally brought from China – for about 600 years. These plants were put out at Buitenzor in west Java. Three years later, in 1830, Jacobson produced the first 'samples' of black and green tea from these 500 bushes. In that same year he brought tea plants from China which he would visit many times during the following six years, returning with seeds, plants and cultivators. China did not welcome the prying eyes of westerners and was extremely jealous of its tea trade; furthermore, it was often a dangerous commission for plant hunters to be sent to foreign countries – in this case to entice and recruit tea artisans while removing both seeds and the country's most famous tea camellia.

On a trip to China in 1832, Jacobson returned to Java with Chinese tea artisans and hundreds of thousands of tea plants, and the following year he succeeded in obtaining millions of seeds. While G. J. Gordon was in China in 1834 on *his* mission to secure tea seeds for the commencement of the British tea industry in India, he wrote to Dr. Wallich at the Calcutta Botanical Gardens saying that he had learnt from the Agent of the Dutch Company that they had three or four million tea plants with which they were establishing their plantations; botanical espionage between Holland and Great Britain!

In spite of this early start the Dutch tea industry did not progress at anything like the speed of that in Assam; in fact it virtually faded out; British India, having been endowed with the Assam indigenous tea plant, had the advantage. As far as the Dutch were concerned, it was not until the 1890s that – with the gradual elimination of their original plantings of the China variety – their tea industry got into full swing. The change took place with importations of seed from India and Ceylon. The first recorded planting of Assam seed was made at Gambung in western Java, in 1878.

Number of plantations, area under cultivation, and tea production in Indonesia in 1939

Island	Number of plantations	Area cultivated (ha)	Production (made tea, ton)
Java	299	105,162	51,113
Sumatra	38	33,226	18,753
Smallholder Plantations	–	75,000	12,548
Total Indonesia	–	215,388	82,414

Growth in the Dutch tea industry increased rapidly and by the year 1910 tea estates had also been opened on the island of Sumatra. By 1927 there were 116,000 hectares of tea in cultivation and just twelve years later this had risen to a colossal 215,000 hectares. At this time the Indonesian tea industry, with that of Ceylon, was the third largest tea producer in the world, after India and China.

After a dramatic setback during the Japanese occupation, when the country's tea crop could not be sold, bushes became overgrown, were uprooted to grow more important food crops and the tea plantations were abandoned. The industry has since made a steady if slow recovery and is now the fifth largest producer in the world. In 1958 the Dutch-owned tea plantations were nationalized by the Indonesian Government and by 1971 the area cultivated was as follows:

Island	Number of plantations	Area cultivated (ha)	Production (made tea, ton)
Java	112	48,500	33,898
Sumatra	8	10,800	10,812
Total Plantations	120	59,300	44,710
Java Small holdings	–	36,230	14,511
Total Indonesia	120	95,530	59,221

During the 1970s the Indonesian tea industry received loans from the World Bank as well as Dutch technical assistance for replanting old seedling tea. The 150th anniversary of the Indonesian tea industry was celebrated in 1976.

The types of tea produced are black, green and scented tea. To scent green tea the blossoms of two species of jasmine are used: *Jasminum officinale var. grandiflorum* and *J. Sambac*. The proportion of jasmine blossom and green tea, for scented tea production, is about one to ten and varies according to the quality of the flowers and the season. Most of the market for black tea, sold on sample at weekly auctions in Jakarta, is exported to the Middle East, the USA, Australia, Russia and Poland, the UK and the Netherlands, while green tea goes for domestic consumption. Indonesia is one of the oldest black tea producers and its tea is much used by British blenders.

Today, in spite of replantings with high yielding clonal tea, approximately 28% of the tea bushes are still seedling tea. New clones developed at the R. I. T.C. have a potential to produce 3500 kg of made tea per hectare in their third year. The potential for further expansion is good, with some 92,000 hectares of land suitable for tea, some of which had previously been under tea cultivation. Much of the tea in Java is grown on steep hills as in Ceylon (Sri Lanka) and is planted at elevations between 1000 and 7000 ft. As will be seen, the country's tea industry is still running below pre-war levels.

Area under cultivation and production of tea plantations in 1995 and 1996

	Area (ha)		Production (ton)	
	1995	1996	1995	1996
Government Plantations	51.993	53.558	86.415	93.061
Private Plantations	39.888	42.310	34.553	39.089
Small holdings	59.711	62.123	34.340	36.563
Total Indonesia	151.592	157.991	155.308	168.713

Source: Directorate General of Estates (1996)

However, the area under tea has greatly increased in recent years from 108,605 hectares in 1988 to 157,991 in 1996, with approximately 165,000 hectares under tea today.

Acknowledgement to the Director of the Research Institute for Tea and Cinchona, Bandung, Indonesia.

After the removal of all the good timber, the remaining top-most branches – that lie thickly everywhere – are burnt, supervision paths are traced and cut (top running L to R) and the whole clearing is tidied up for the next operation of lining, pegging and holing.

In this part of the world the habitat of the Orang-Utan is under threat from jungle clearance in Borneo and Sumatra. Vast areas of primeval forest are destroyed for logging, after which the land is planted with oil palms, tea and other crops. (*Photo Anup Shah/Nature PL.com.*)

'Opening out'

Land clearance for new tea extensions on Huberta Estate, Padang, West Sumatra

Estate first opened	1986
Total tea acreage	747
Present factory built	1997
Type of manufacture	Green Tea
Total estate labour force	400
Resident estate population	600

A hillside of newly planted tea. Infilling of vacancies in new clearings is carried out, while 'block infilling' in old tea areas is done after these patches have been rejuvenated with Guatemala as shown next page.

Lines of holes have been dug to receive the young plants from the nursery.

Above and below, young tea plants are carried from the nursery to mature areas in white coir sacks for infilling. Pests and diseases, drought and lightning strikes are the cause of small patches of mature tea dying.

Patuahwatte Estate

Maintenance of mature tea fields

Block infilling of old seedling tea with clonal tea.

Open patches of ground in mature tea ready for infilling.

When a complete field of 60-80-year-old tea bushes is uprooted, the land is planted with Guatemala grass and left for two years which rejuvenates the soil; after its removal the land is replanted with high yielding VP clonal tea.

Patuahwatte Estate Ciwidey, Bandung, West Java

The highest tea estate in Indonesia at 2400 M
Estate first opened   1911
Total tea acreage   1684

VP clonal cuttings – with Agro Mesh removed – for hardening off prior to putting out in the fields as 30-40 cm plants.

Young plants ready for transport to the fields.

Of the total tea acreage on Patuahwattee, 40% is old seedling tea comprising mostly Assam type and a little China which was planted pre 1940, the balance being high yielding clonal tea.
The percentage of old tea left on Indonesian estates overall is less than 30%.

A lovely setting amidst this high tea growing region in Java. This guest house and attractive garden is kept for staff from the company's Jakarta office for their routine visits and for other company guests.

Some of Indorub Sumber Wadung's other properties

Alkaterie Estate, Ciwidey, Bandung, West Java

Estate first opened	1911
Total tea acreage	1662
Present factory built	1997
Type of manufacture	CTC
Total estate labour force	805
Resident estate population	2500 +

and including HUBERTA and PATUAHWATTEE estates, below.

Huberta Estate, Padang. Towering over the surrounding tea fields is the volcanic mountain Mitra Kerinci.

Orthodox manufacture at Patuahwattee and CTC manufacture at Alkaterie

Patuahwattee Factory Orthodox.

Processing room Patuahwattee.

Alkaterie Estate, Bandung is just 7° south of the equator. Pluckers commence work at 6 a.m. when conditions, particularly in the high grown fields, can be misty and the bushes wet with overnight dew. Pluckers shed their protective clothing and other heavy sweaters etc. as the morning progresses and don their customary conical bamboo hats to shade them from the sun and also rain later on in the afternoons. The pluckers are paid based on a standard wage plus incentive so they work quickly in spite of the often very steep terrain and their average out-turn in the higher yielding blocks is around 40 kgs of green leaf per plucker.
(*All photos 2005. Courtesy Indorub Sumber Wadung Tea Plantations*.)

Alkaterie factory CTC.

Processing room Alkaterie.

VIEWS IN AND AROUND PLANTATIONS IN PRODUCING COUNTRIES

Malaysia

Boh Tea Estate
Bukit Cheeding Tea Estate

Australia

The pioneering Cutten brothers
Glen Allyn Tea Estate
Madura Tea Estate

South America

Argentina

Establecimento Las Marias

Malaysia

The first attempt to grow tea in Malaysia was a total failure. Dr. N. Wallich, Superintendent of the Botanical Gardens in Calcutta from 1817 until 1834, mentions a Mr. Brown trying to cultivate tea on Penang Island during the 1820s, using imported Chinese plants from Canton. Wallich, who had visited the Federated Malay States at that time, described the finished tea (manufactured) as very inferior. Brown was of the opinion the failure was due to the fact that Penang was a tropical country with its highest hills not exceeding 2500 feet, which leads one to think his plantings of the small-leafed China variety were possibly made at unsuitably low elevations in the oppressive heat.

Some 60 years later rubber (*Hevea brasiliensis*) made its appearance in Malaya when a consignment of young rubber plants was received in Malaya from the Royal Botanic Gardens at Kew. Kew played an important part in the starting of the cinchona and rubber industries in tropical Asia; (quinine is made from the bark of the cinchona tree).

In 1876 (Sir) Henry Wickham, a young botanist and explorer, collected a great quantity of rubber seeds from the Amazon and later that year the seeds – some 70,000 in number – were received at Kew, having been shipped out by the enterprising Wickham. On arrival disappointingly few plants had germinated but of these some 2400 were dispatched in Wardian cases to Ceylon. This was enough to start the great rubber industry in the East. A short while later plants and seed reached Malaya to be established at the Botanical Gardens in Singapore for distribution to some of the first men to take up grants for jungle clearance to establish rubber estates – my great uncle being one.

During the 1880s there were many new arrivals from Britain and Holland, responding to the urge to take up land as proprietary planters. As with all pioneers of a new industry they often came and went in quick succession, harsh living conditions and fever forcing many to return home with broken health. Others stayed on and some prospered with a wide variety of plantation crops – cocoa, tea, coffee, cinchona, rubber and latterly oil palms – and the tea estates in the older producing countries – India, Java and Ceylon – continue to this day. The huge numbers employed include many descendants of those who worked in the hard, tough pioneering years of long ago. The vast area from the Seychelles or Mauritius to the east coast of Malaysia became an agricultural hot-house of rapid expansion.

Tea in Malaysia is a comparatively young industry, coming almost a hundred years after the British and Dutch had opened the first tea estates in India and Java during the 1830s. Started in the Cameron Highlands by proprietary planter John Archibald Russell on BOH Plantation in 1929, several attempts were made by companies and individuals to plant tea in the lowlands, at around 500 ft during the 1920s, including the Bukit Cheeding Estate which survives to this day and is portrayed in the recently taken photographs.

Even during the 1920s and early thirties, when Russell started, it was a gigantic task to open out virgin tiger-infested jungle, clear and then plant the land up with tea, which in the case of BOH Plantation was put out as seed-at-stake. We learn from the BOH archives that nothing more than a single steam-roller, axe-men and mules were employed. Several other small tea plantations were opened in the Cameron Highlands during the early 1930s, including Sungei Palas Estate which today belongs to BOH Plantations and Fairlie and Bukit Cheeding Estates which also belong to J. A. Russell & Company.

Within ten short years all the tea that Russell (and others) had planted was abandoned when the Japanese invaded Malaya in 1941. Almost four years later, when the war ended, the tea fields were a sorry sight – the tea, having grown up to 20 ft, looked almost like scrub jungle. All the toil and sweat for nothing – but not quite. After 1945 the whole planted area on BOH was cut down and collar pruned and brought back into plucking. Today those same 75-year-old bushes are still yielding their flush, with no replantings of clonal tea so far.

At 5000 ft above sea level the Cameron Highlands is still a mainly jungle-clad region and has an ideal climate for high-grown tea, being similar to that in the hills of Darjeeling, Ootacamund and Simla in India, and Nuwara ▶

J.A. Russell & Co.

Mechanisation in Malaysia

High-grown tea in the Cameron Highlands

Boh tea plantation

Using a winch operated harvesting machine on steep slopes.

Tea was first planted in the Cameron Highlands in Malaya on BOH Estate in 1929 by John Archibald Russell.

Estate first opened	1929
Total tea acreage	1151
Present factory built	1933
Type of manufacture	Rotorvane
Total workforce	304

This Cresco aircraft is used for applying fertilizer on BOH. The airstrip at over 5000 ft above sea level is probably the highest in West Malaysia.

The Founder's son, Tristan Russell in this orderly panoramic view of tea fields bounded by virgin jungle. BOH is mainly pre-war seedling tea and most of the tea bushes seen here are 70 years old. From the early years the tea has been planted out on the straight 'up and over' system, not on the contour system.

A view of steep tea fields.

A similar view from the guest bungalow garden.

A 16 ft harvester cropping tea under palms.

A Universal machine equipped for inter-row weed control.

The Universal can also be adapted for fertilizer application, pruning and herbicide spraying.

Bukit Cheeding

Low grown tea – 50 ft A.S.L. tea & oil plantation

Estate first opened	1920s
(Purchased by Russell & Co. 1967)	
Tea acreage	511
Present tea factory built	1994
Total workforce	26 (Tea)

Rail mounted withering bins. These are mechanically tipped into the processing line.

Mechanically discharging green leaf from a field trailer with yellow cover (top) into a withering bin.

Oil palms provide shade for tea

First plantings on estate were made in 1967.

Fruit is sold to a nearby mill.

The shade provided by oil palms is very helpful in the establishment stage of the tea but some clonal tea grows well without it.

Loading oil palm fruit into a field trailer.

Mature oil palms on Bukit Cheeding under-planted with tea.

The method of harvesting the oil palm fruit with an aluminium harvesting pole with a very sharp sickle shaped knife.

Mechanically discharging oil palm fruit from a field trailer. Note the tractor-mounted grabber and scissor-mounted field trailer.

Palm oil is used for a huge number of purposes. Malaysia is the world's largest producer and exporter. Palm oil is the largest edible oil in world trade.
(All photos 2002, courtesy J. A. Russell & Co. Sdn. Berhad.)

▶ Eliya (New'ralia) in Sri Lanka. In the past these cool hill stations were a temporary haven for the fever-stricken British planters and Government officials as, though only 5° north of the equator, the mornings and nights are quite chilly with the sun pleasantly hot at midday.

Today, tourists who visit the Cameron Highlands can see in BOH Factory the various processes of 'tea manufacture' and at the estate's Visitor Centres they can buy packets of the company's named brand, BOH Tea. The workforce in Malaysia is a mixture of Tamils – descended from those who live on the Madras side of South India, Malays and Chinese, the latter being first employed on the rubber estates and tin mines established during the 1880s. The climate in the highlands is also excellent for growing fruit and vegetables, and the hundreds of small holdings run by Malaysians of Chinese descent have supplied their produce to markets in Kuala Lumpur and Singapore for nearly 200 years. At the famous Raffles Hotel and others from Singapore to Penang Island, you will be able to order strawberries and cream and have roses at your table, all fresh from the hills. The Eastern Hotel, Kuala Lumpur's oldest hotel, like its namesake in Calcutta, was for this reason a favourite haunt for planters when 'in town' in those far off days when there were no tourists – just working men.

In 1954 the founder's son, Tristan Russell, started work as a junior assistant to the then BOH Estate Manager, Bill Fairlie. In 1969 T.B.R. became Chairman of J. A. Russell & Co, which owns BOH Plantations as well as the three other estates previously mentioned.

Today, the company produces 70% of all the tea produced in Malaysia. The continuity that comes with a family concern is carried on by Tristan Russell's daughter, Caroline, as Chief Executive Officer, with her father Chairman.

Australia

Like the British, who have been drinking tea since the mid 1650s (albeit the rich ones), Australians have been drinking it since it was brought over by the First Fleet in 1788. Somewhat earlier, on the other side of the world in North America, British colonists had introduced the habit of tea drinking as they had in all their colonies. By the early 1770s a third of America's population drank tea regularly twice a day – until of course, the Boston Tea Party and that infamous night at Griffins Wharf in 1773, when the good citizens of Boston, Massachusetts, boarded the East India Company's tea ships and dumped their cargoes overboard.

Unlike the traditional tea-growing countries such as China, India, Sri Lanka and Indonesia, where the green leaf in the fields is hand-plucked and labour is cheap, giant harvesting machines are employed in the tea fields of Australia. As with the riding-type tea harvesting machines used in Japan, Malaya and some other countries, the green leaf is cut and drawn into bags or hoppers and then off-loaded into lorries for transport to the factory for manufacture.

The tea plant was introduced into Australia by one of the earliest English families to settle in Queensland, the four pioneering Cutten brothers. The total area planted in tea by the Cuttens extended to no more than about two acres and was put out as seed-at-stake at Bingil Bay, some 30 miles to the south of Innisfail, seed of the China variety being obtained from Ceylon.

Though the Cutten brothers abandoned their tea early on, they successfully grew a variety of other crops: coffee – erecting a Coffee Mill and Pulping House – oranges, chicory, tobacco, mangoes, bananas and of course, they established a large timber operation with Timber Mill for sawing planked wood, and not forgetting a coconut plantation. Much of this produce was shipped out by coastal steamers that plied up and down the coast. The stone breakwater-cum-jetty that the brothers constructed at Bingil Bay took only small sailing ships; heavy cargoes such as coffee, coconuts and bananas had to be rowed across a two-mile channel to Dunk Island to a receiving shed on the spit which had deep water anchorage, before loading onto

A traditional bush ballad

'The Billy of Tea'

You may talk of your whisky or talk of your beer,
I've something far better awaiting me here;
It stands on that fire beneath the gum-tree,
And you cannot much lick it – a billy of tea.
So fill up your tumbler as high as you can,
You'll never persuade me it's not the best plan,
To let all the beer and the spirits go free
And stick to my darling old Billy of Tea.

(Courtesy Australian Geographic.)
(The Sundowner, Bush Life c1910, courtesy Mitchell Library, State Library of New South Wales.)

coastal steamers.

The Cuttens had been at Bicton for almost 36 years, experiencing cyclones in 1890, 1911 and 1913; then came the great cyclone of 1918 and with it a massive wave that smashed into and across the entire Bicton property and its plantations from which the brothers would never recover. Scores of people along the coast were killed in this cyclone – designated hurricane force, but said by many to have reached 200 miles an hour – which left a trail of destruction everywhere.

In 1980, Rod Taylor, then a Director of Nerada, first visited the abandoned and forgotten tea that had been planted by the Cuttens almost a hundred years before, and says:

> Many people gave us clues and directions which led us on false trails. After an hour's fruitless search in this general area, we came upon our first clue when we found a white Camellia flower on the ground in deep shade under the forest canopy. Yes, it was *Camellia sinensis* unmistakably, a tea flower. Yet, nowhere nearby could we see a tea tree – no shiny dark green serrated leaves that we knew so well. We realised however, that the flower must have fallen from a great height, and that one at least of the nearby forest giants with straight trunks and no branches visible for fifteen metres, must be a tea tree, and its familiar dark green foliage was invisible to us, being lost in the jungle cover overhead.
>
> We were close then. We realised this at once, so continuing on we were soon rewarded when we saw one, then dozens, then thousands of tea trees – an absolute under growth of tea in which there almost seemed to be no other living plant than tea. Fallen tea seeds over the decades had sprouted into a wild nursery so virile, that it had become a thicket overpowering all the other young trees and plants of the forest.

Some months later, Rod Taylor brought Les Alexander (1893-1986), a nephew of the Cuttens, to see the old tea trees and he was of the opinion this was the original tea nursery planted in 1884.

Today, the original 120-year-old tea plants are plucked by the present owners of the property, Mr. and Mrs. Pontil, who make their own tea from the green leaf, having bought a book on tea manufacture.

Two present-day tea plantations are illustrated here; the first and largest is Nerada Glen Allyn Tea Estate with its four outgrowers situated in the Atherton Tableland in Queensland, the heartland of Australian tea growing. Figures from the Tea Council of Australia state that of the 1,600,000 kilograms of made tea produced per year from Australian grown tea, the Nerada group produce over 1,500,000 kilograms; this is about 10% of Australia's consumption.

It can be said that Australia's present-day tea industry was started towards the end of the 1950s, when a Dr. Maruff bought 320 acres of land at Nerada and started planting out self-sown tea seedlings that he had collected from the Cutten brothers' original planting at Bingil Bay. At about the same time a nursery was established at Nerada in which seed from the original China tea plants at Bingil Bay was used, as well as seed and seedlings from the Government-run Bureau of Tropical Agriculture at South Johnston.

By 1970 there were 80 acres of mature tea – in hedge form – growing on Dr. Maruff's plantation when – after interesting an Australian Trading firm, Burns Philip & Co. in the venture – the two came together to form Nerada Tea Estates Pty Ltd. In that same year a start was made on the construction of Nerada Tea Factory, but owing to insufficient green leaf being harvested from the comparatively small acreage of mature tea, it could by no means be fully operational. Importantly too, the 'mature' tea hedges had not grown sufficiently flat to accommodate the new harvesting machine which cut not only the green leaf, but much stalk too, leading to low prices for the made tea.

Seed that was collected from the Cutten brothers' original planting at Bingil Bay in 1884 has been used for all the plantings at Nerada as well as for those of the first four outgrowers. Today there are 1008 acres of mature tea belonging to the Nerada Group.

In 1985 J. A. Russell & Company, Malaysia, and James Finlay of Scotland entered the industry, buying land at Glenallyn and Taraquet respectively on the Atherton Tablelands. These two companies opened new plantations using high yielding clonal seed from their plantations in Malaysia, and Finlays tea plantations in the Kericho District of Kenya, Africa.

The other tea grower illustrated is Madura Tea, situated in Murwillumbah, New South Wales, who grow and manufacture tea which is then blended with tea that is imported from Assam and Ceylon (Sri Lanka). There is another small tea growing area in North Queensland in Daintree, up at Cape Tribulation.

The potential for greatly increasing the acreage under tea along the coastal region of New South Wales and Queensland is there. Whether further importation of Assam seed, taken from high yielding clonal mother bushes or seed-bearers, would benefit the industry remains to be seen. The large broad-leafed Assam variety *C. assamica* and its cultivars might prove infinitely more suitable for the conditions and elevations of the present tea growing areas.

So far as Vegetative Propagation with high yielding clonal single-leaf cuttings is concerned, it is interesting to see the illustrations taken on Williamson Magor's Hunwal Estate in Assam. The earliest experiments in Vegetative Propagation to be carried out in Ceylon were made on Spring Valley Estate in 1939 (see Frotoft Estate, Sri Lanka).

The history of tea cultivation and in particular tea drinking in Australia *must* include the 'Sundowner', who, like his fellow traveller the 'swagman', or swagaroo, was rarely to be seen without his billy as he traipsed the outback. Each day he walked 15 miles or so humping his billy, bags of tea, sugar and his meagre provisions – often hanging from his waist. The Sundowner, unlike the swagman, who would work for his keep, would arrive at a cattle station or homestead as dusk was falling, in the hope that the late hour would relieve him of the obligation to work, but grant a free meal.

Perhaps all Aussies, and many of their Pommie friends too, will agree – if we think about it – that this grand old character of the outback, the Sundowner, grabs our hearts like nothing else; who of us could resist a request for a full plate of tucker, work or no work! The writer has to admit that when leaving a planting career in Ceylon in the late 1950s, he and two brother planters thought seriously about becoming Jackaroos on a cattle station near Goondawindi, Durambandi; thereafter, and with some experience, pooling our capital and buying a 'small' cattle station. If we had done, I guess we'd still be Pommie b's. That said, all knowledgeable Poms realise this is a form of great endearment – most of the time!

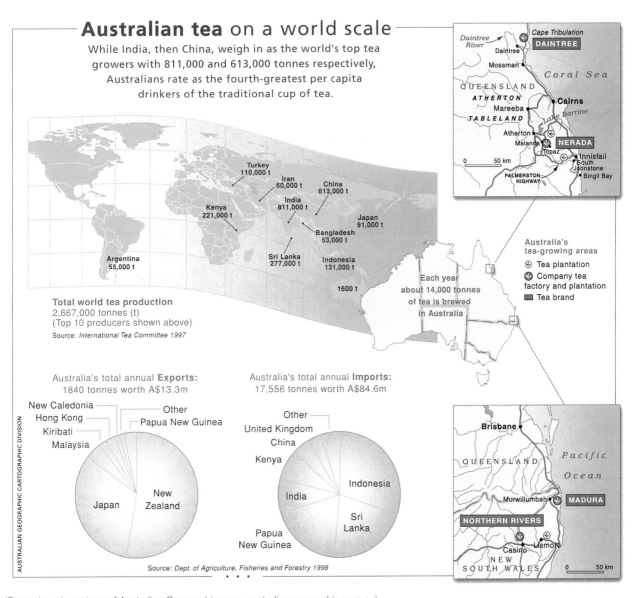

Australian tea on a world scale

While India, then China, weigh in as the world's top tea growers with 811,000 and 613,000 tonnes respectively, Australians rate as the fourth-greatest per capita drinkers of the traditional cup of tea.

Turkey 110,000 t
Iran 60,000 t
China 613,000 t
India 811,000 t
Japan 91,000 t
Kenya 221,000 t
Bangladesh 53,000 t
Argentina 55,000 t
Sri Lanka 277,000 t
Indonesia 131,000 t
1600 t

Total world tea production
2,667,000 tonnes (t)
(Top 10 producers shown above)
Source: *International Tea Committee 1997*

Each year about 14,000 tonnes of tea is brewed in Australia

Australia's tea-growing areas
- Tea plantation
- Company tea factory and plantation
- Tea brand

Australia's total annual **Exports:**
1840 tonnes worth A$13.3m

New Caledonia
Hong Kong
Kiribati
Malaysia
Other
Papua New Guinea
Japan
New Zealand

Australia's total annual **Imports:**
17,556 tonnes worth A$84.6m

Other
United Kingdom
China
Kenya
India
Papua New Guinea
Indonesia
Sri Lanka

Source: *Dept. of Agriculture, Fisheries and Forestry 1998*

AUSTRALIAN GEOGRAPHIC CARTOGRAPHIC DIVISION

Daintree River
Cape Tribulation
DAINTREE
Daintree
Mossman
Coral Sea
QUEENSLAND
ATHERTON
Mareeba
Cairns
TABLELAND
Lake Barrine
Atherton
Malanda
NERADA
Topaz
Innisfail
South Johnstone
Bingil Bay
PALMERSTON HIGHWAY
0   50 km

Brisbane
QUEENSLAND
Pacific Ocean
Murwillumbah
MADURA
NORTHERN RIVERS
Casino
Lismore
NEW SOUTH WALES
0   50 km

(Reproduced courtesy of Australian Geographic www.australiangeographic.com.au).

Herbert Frederick Cutten (1855-1930) was the father of the Australian Tea Industry. (*Photo c1880.*)

Australia's tea history and the pioneering Cutten brothers

Herbert Frederick Cutten planted the first tea at Bingil Bay, North Queensland in 1884/85

Bingil Bay, 2004. The low point of the hills is the site of the Cuttens' tea plantation.

Grave of Frederick Cutten and his wife Margaret.

The Cutten Empire and Bicton Homestead, Bingil Bay, c1900 painted by Mrs. Reuter from a photo by Mrs. Anthony Hordern of Sydney. (*Courtesy Rod Taylor.*)

Bicton 1895. Perched 80 feet above the beach at Bingil Bay, this was the Cuttens' 13 room homestead built from material on the selection.

Photo 1902. Part of a huge tree trunk, with young Cuttens atop, is transported from the Rain Forest by a team of 18 buffalo to the Cutten sawmill which they erected in 1890. Note the wooden wheels.

Jack Unsworth, the Cuttens' foreman working outside his hut at Bingil Bay *c*1890.

1912, before the terrible cyclone in 1918, showing at bottom – to right edge of the receiving shed – a small part of the flat stone breakwater-cum-jetty the Cuttens constructed at which small vessels could take on produce; from 100 acres of coffee came 250,000 pounds of clean coffee in one year, also 140 tons of bananas in that same year. The top of the photo shows cleared land, but it is hard to tell whether it is planted with a crop.

Tea seeds appearing in the tea under the giant native trees in October 2004.

No basket and not a tea plucker, but Lucy Pontil.

The original 120-year-old tea in 2004

In 1959, small self-sown tea seedlings were uprooted from beneath the original abandoned tea trees – which at that time were 30 ft in height, growing up under tall forest – to start Australia's new tea industry on Nerada Plantation at Innisfail, Queensland.

Sometime after 1980 all the old tea trees – then about 45 ft tall – were cut down to ground level and have been allowed to grow up again into the healthy, vigorous bushes/hedges seen on this page.

Robert Pontil, present owner, with his son, standing next to Rod Taylor amongst the 120-year-old tea.

Tea hedges, bushes and palms beside a shady drive near the owner's house.

The graves of almost all the Cutten family stand on the edge of Bingil Bay Cliff, 100 feet above the sea.
The original tea that the brothers planted was not a success merely because the Aboriginal labour could not be relied upon to pluck the leaf regularly every week to ten days – going 'walkabout'. This same labour was, however, capable and reliable for picking the coffee berries during the comparatively short harvesting season once a year.

Early years at Nerada when all cultivation was done by hand.
(*Photo c1962, courtesy the Les Alexander Collection.*)

'Tea for Two'. Manager Mike Stephenson and his wife. (*Photo c1970, courtesy Les Alexander Collection.*)

The foundation for the tea industry in Australia is laid

Nerada, Glen Allyn Tea Estate

North Queensland

The first tea is planted on Nerada plantation in 1959 using self-sown tea seedlings taken from the Cutten Brothers' original plantings of 1884/85.
Nerada, Glen Allyn Tea Estate, North Queensland

The Manager's house, Queenslander style built on stilts with parts over 100 years old.
(*All colour photos, 2004, courtesy Rod J. Taylor and all black and white photos courtesy the Les Alexander Collection.*)

Tea mechanisation today on Glen Allyn from field to factory

Glen Allyn new factory built in 1992 with packing factory at Brisbane. Area under tea 556 acres – type of manufacture CTC.
During the cyclone in March 2006, with winds of 180 mph, Glen Allyn Tea Estate lost 70 tons of tea in storage and the estate was put out of production for two weeks owing to all the power lines being down.

A harvester discharging green leaf into 4 ton capacity bin in which it stays until processing.

General Manager, Bill Benson (blue shirt) and John Russell who was responsible for commissioning Glen Allyn Tea Factory.

Full bin being inserted in bin tipper.

The giant bin tipper with bin ready for tipping.

Bin being tipped by bin tipper; the green leaf is then automatically fed into the 'process line'. (Not shown here but see Evolution of Tea Machinery, India.)

A general view of factory showing driers and sorting lines. Steam is used as a heat source.

The manufactured tea is loaded at the factory in one ton bulk bags for shipment to the Brisbane Packing Factory.
(*All colour photos 2005, courtesy Glen Allyn Tea Estate.*)

Madura Tea Estate

Murwillumbah, New South Wales, Australia

The riding-type Harvester. This plantation-designed and locally manufactured machine harvests the green leaf between early October and the following July. Harvesting takes place once every three weeks at the start of the growing season but at weekly intervals at the height of the season.

A closer view of the small factory, left of which a tea harvester is seen cropping the green leaf from the original planting; these bushes are now 28 years old.

An early morning panoramic view of Madura, with mature tea, centre, factory at right and newly planted tea fields at left of photo. Established in 1978 by Mike Grant-Cook and his wife Norma, Madura blends its own product with imported high grown Ceylon teas and quality Assam teas to provide well balanced teas for the market in Australia.

Arriving from the fields, a harvester about to unload its wire-mesh hopper containing 300 kg of green leaf into a square bin...

...which is then lifted up to the withering loft.
(*All photos courtesy Madura Tea.*)

The company's tea plantations of almost 4000 acres are situated in the province of Corrientes and the tea produced at Las Marias is considered a high quality tea compared to that grown in the province of Missiones.

Argentina

Tea cultivation & manufacture Establishment Las Marias, Province de corrientes

The harvesting of green leaf is carried out by riding-type harvesters, the leaf then being loaded onto lorries for its journey to the factory. The leaf at this stage contains approximately 76% weight of water (moisture content).

A riding-type tea harvester is ideally suited to a flat terrain.

Single leaf and stem cuttings, each in its polythene compost-filled sleeve. The selection of clonal cuttings from high yielding mother bushes in the fields and subsequent vegetative propagation has been used at Las Marias since 1963.

One year old clonal cuttings ready for planting out in the fields.
(*All photos 1998, courtesy Establecimento Las Marias.*)

THE PLANTER

THE NEW ADMIRABLE CRICHTON — THE ESTATE ASSISTANT

"A rubber planter needs to be . . . a 'walking encyclopaedia' . . . He must have a . . . detailed knowledge of all branches of estate work. . . . He will have to acquire some knowledge of . . . agriculture, botany, chemistry hygiene, sanitary engineering, surveying, etcetera"—From *Rubber Planting* by C. Ward Jackson.

—(*From "The Planter", November* 1920)

Appendices

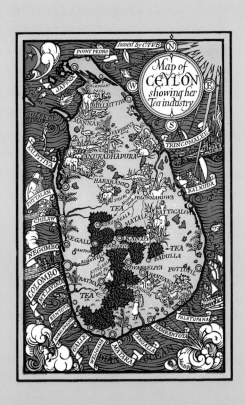

Tea - A Chronological History

2737 B.C. CHINA. Chinese legends ascribed the discovery of tea to the Emperor Shen Nung – first used as a medicinal drink.

493 B.C. Earliest written record on the tea plant published by the Chinese.

276 A.D. Tea plant described in the Chinese dictionary RH-YA by Kuo Po.

780 The famous *Cha Ching* (Tea Book) written and published by Lo Yu, describes the preparation of the leaf and its manufacture.

793 Tea becomes a common beverage in China rather than a medicinal drink.

960 A regular trade in brick tea was being carried on across China's borders into Mongolia and Tibet.

12th c. Japan. A Buddhist priest named Eisai brought tea seed from China to Japan; this was the commencement of growing tea in Japan.

1610 The Dutch East India Company is the first to bring China tea, via Java, to Europe in their 'Indiamen'.

1657 The first China tea is served to the general public in England in Garraways Coffee House, London.

1687 The English East India Company brings China tea direct to Britain in its 'Indiamen'.

1762 Attempts are made to introduce the tea plant into Europe.

1773 Boston Tea Party, Griffin's Wharf, Boston Harbour.

1788 The botanist Sir Joseph Banks suggests to the Court of the Honourable East India Company the possibility of growing tea in British India.

1823 INDIA. Major Robert Bruce reports on the existence of extensive tracts of tea plants growing wild in the forests of upper Assam; his brother Charles Alexander Bruce dispatches leaf and seed specimens to the Botanical Gardens in Calcutta; these are not recognised as belonging to the true tea plant of commerce. No action taken.

1827 JAVA. The Dutch Government imports, through its representative J. I. L. Jacobson, 500 tea plants from Japan.

1830 JAVA. From these Japanese plants the first 'samples' of black and green tea are produced and dispatched to Amsterdam. Over the next few years and at considerable risk to himself, Jacobson returned from China with Chinese tea artisans and yet more tea plants and seed.

1833 First consignment of chests of Java-grown tea received in Amsterdam.

1834 INDIA. Lieutenant Andrew Charlton finds similar tea plants in the forests around Sadiya to those found by Robert Bruce a decade earlier; he sends specimens to the Calcutta Botanical Gardens and this time Dr. Nathaniel Wallich is able to confirm they are indeed those of the true tea plant – *Camellia assamica*.

Lord William Bentinck proposes the formation of a 'Tea Committee' to investigate the possibility of growing tea in India. G. J. Gordon, Secretary of the 'Tea Committee', sails for China with a mission to procure tea seeds and to recruit Chinamen with a knowledge of tea cultivation and manufacture.

1835 JANUARY. A consignment of 80,000 tea seeds arrive at Calcutta; these are germinated in the Botanical Gardens, Calcutta, under the direction of Dr. Wallich.

Land is cleared in various trial regions in north, north-east and south India for the reception of the young China tea seedlings. Dr. Wallich, Dr. McClelland, a geologist, and Dr. W. Griffiths, also a botanist, journey to see at first hand the indigenous tea that has been discovered in upper Assam.

NOVEMBER. 20,000 young tea seedlings leave the Botanical Gardens in eight country boats bound for Assam. A further 20,000 China seedlings are dispatched to the Kumaon in north India and 2000 to the Nilgiri Hills in south India.

1835/9   C. A. Bruce is appointed Superintendent of Tea Culture in charge of the Government's tea tracts and trial nurseries in Assam.

1836   G. J. Gordon makes second visit to China to obtain more skilled tea makers, tea plants and seed.

1837   The first 'samples' of Indian tea manufactured from the leaves of the indigenous tea plants found growing at Chubwa, Deenjoy and Tingri tracts, are sent down river to Calcutta.

1839   The first consignment of 12 chests of Indian tea are auctioned at Mincing Lane, London.

The first tea company, the Assam Company, is formed. C. A. Bruce is engaged as Superintendent of the Company's Northern Division.

CEYLON receives its first importation of tea seeds (*Camellia assamica*) from the Botanical Gardens in Calcutta. Trial plantings are made at the Peradeniya Botanical Gardens, and on coffee estates in the hill districts.

1848   Robert Fortune returns from China to India with yet more tea plants, seed and cultivators for the trial region in the hills of north India.

1853   SOUTH INDIA. First tea estate opened.

1856   CACHAR. First tea estate opened.

1857   DARJEELING. First tea estate opened.

1860s   Introduction of the first tea machinery in India.

1862   TERAI. First tea estate opened.

1867   CEYLON. The first commercial planting of 19 acres of tea on Loolecondera Estate, by coffee planter James Taylor.

1872   The first consignment of Ceylon Tea (27 pounds) shipped from Colombo to Britain.

1874   DOOARS. First tea estate opened.

1877   AFRICA, SOUTH. The first importation of Assam-type seed from India.

1885   AUSTRALIA. The first tea is planted in Queensland.

1893   AFRICA, MALAWI. The first tea seed is sown on Thornwood and Lauderdale estates in Mulanji District.

1896   JAPAN. The National Institute of Vegetable and Tea Science started as a laboratory for tea manufacturing process under the Ministry of Agriculture, changing to a Tea Research Station in Kanaya, Shizuoka in 1919.

1903   AFRICA, KENYA. The tea industry is started with importation of Assam-type seed.

1911   Tocklai Experimental Station opened at Jorhat, Assam.

1925   The Tea Research Institute of Ceylon is established.

1932   The C.T.C. machine (crush-tear-curl) is invented by W. McKercher at Tocklai.

1949   Tea auctions commence in Cochin, south India.

1958   McTear invents 'Rotorvane' at Tocklai.

1959   AUSTRALIA. Self-sown tea seedlings and seed – taken from the Cuttens' original planting – is planted out on the Nerada Plantation, Queensland.

1964   Tea Research Association of India is formed.

There are many statistics from various sources regarding the chronology of tea, some contradictory. However, the foregoing is as near to the actual happenings as the writer can manage.

History seldom repeats itself, but historians repeat each other.

Ceylon's Plantation History

Embryo coffee estates that were to become the tea estates of today

These small coffee estates, each of some 200 acres, were carved out of the jungle by the early pioneers and form divisions within the tea estates of today; one example being the Scalpa and Louisa divisions on Great Western Tea Estate, Upper Dimbula.

Statistics of Ceylon coffee plantations in 1857, by A. M. Ferguson from the *Ceylon Observer* 11th July 1857.

A superior dwelling house! All that one could expect when opening out jungle for a coffee plantation during the pioneering years. No shops, no doctors but with a rifle there was no need for the former. The date of the photo is not known but it was probably taken during the 1860s.
(*Photo courtesy John Benst, planter, who found this and other photographs in Torrington Tea Estate bungalow, Agra Patanas, in 1939.*)

Number.	Names of Districts.	Number of Estates.	Bearing. Acres.	Not yet Bearing. Acres.	Total in Cultivation. Acres.	Average Crop last two Years. Cwt.	Crop per Acre. Cwt.	Average Cultivation on Estates. Acres.	Probable Crop in 1857-58. Cwt.	Labourers required during Crop time. Coolies.	Names of Estates to which the foregoing Statistics apply.
1	ALLAGALLA	14	1,900	400	2,300	7,000	3·7	164	8,000	4,000	Coodoogalle, Peak, Kirimittie, Allagalla, Oolankanda, Dekinde, Moragaha, Wyrley Grove, Amanapoora, Kadaganava, Gangarooa, Ingrogalla (?) (?).
2	AMBOGAMMOA	21	4,340	290	4,630	12,000	2·7	220	13,000	6,000	Imboolpittia, Hyndford, Wattewelle, Mount Jean, Inchyra, Trafalgar, Agrawatte, Wadiacadoola, Deekoya, Gangawatte, Templestowe, Woodstock, Galbodde, Koorookoodia, Atherton, Barcaple, Gilston, Henawella, Mookalana, Hangran-Oya, Dahanaike.
3	BADULLA	23	2,300	500	2,800	13,000	5·6	122	15,000	5,000	Wayvelhena, Ootoombye, Gourakelle, Passera Polligrolle, Kottugodde, Oodoowerra, Gongaltenne, Glen Alpin, Baddegamme or Spring Valley, Cannavarella, Nahavella, Weweise, Debedde, Dickhedde. Kahagalle, Happotella, Unugalla, Redipanne, Elizabeth, Cooroondokelle (?) (?) (?) (?).
4	DIMBOOLA, LOWER	7	1,590	370	1,760	8,500	5·3	251	9,000	3,000	Kellewatte, Bogahapatne, Niagara, Union, Hudson, Stoneycliff, Hunugalle.
5	DIMBOOLA, UPPER	7	1,110	330	1,440	3,500	3·1	206	4,200	2,000	Wattegodde, Scalpa, Louisa, Ratmalkelle, Radella, Palaradella, Hopewell.
6	DOLLASBAGE	18	2,900	370	3,270	9,500	3·3	182	10,400	5,000	Kooroondawatte, Paragalle, Hillside, Barnagalla, Raxawa, Madoolhena, Malgolla, Natakanda, Allakolla, Dorset, Windsor Forest, Penylan, Kellie, Kelvin, Kattaram, Hormusjie, Miroote, Oorakande.
7	DOOMBERE	9	1,520	250	1,770	16,000	10·5	197	18,000	3,500	Rajewelle No. 1, Rajewelle No. 2, Mahaberia, Ambecotta, Cangawatte, Deegalla, Teldenia, Kondissally, Palikelle.
8	HANTANNE	22	4,090	700	4,790	16,000	3·9	217	19,000	7,000	Doonomadalawa, Farieland, Hendrick's, Hantenne, Primrosehill, Peradenia, Govinda, Mount Pleasant, Dodangwella, Richmond, Shrub's Hill, Hindogalla, Amblamana, Gallaha, Ingrogalla, Ooragalle, Horagalle, Kitoolmoola, Oodoowella, Maha Oya, Dunally, Galoya.
	Carried forward	121	19,750	3,010	22,760	85,500			96,600	35,500	

Number.	Names of Districts.	Number of Estates.	Bearing. Acres.	Not yet Bearing. Acres.	Total in Cultivation. Acres.	Average Crop last two Years. Cwt.	Crop per Acre. Cwt.	Average Cultivation on Estates. Acres.	Probable Crop in 1857-58. Cwts.	Labourers required during Crop time. Coolies.	Names of Estates to which the following Statistics apply.
	Brought forward	121	19,750	3,010	22,760	85,500			96,600	35,500	
9	HEWAHETTE, LOWER	17	2,550	720	3,270	16,000	6·3	192	20,000	6,000	Charlemont, Medegamma No. 1, Medegamma No. 2, Bowlana, Maousakella, Belwood, Galantenne, Deltotte, Great Valley, Little Valley, Bopitia, Pattiagamma, Naranghena, Waloya, Lool-Condura, Codugalla, Kallogalpatne.
10	HEWAHETTE, UPPER	11	1,790	944	2,734	9,000	5·6	249	11,000	5,000	Gonavey, Hope, Mooloya, Nathoongodde, Yakabendakelly, Rickellegascadde, Wevatenne, Hangurankette, Pookeloya, Gallela, Cavinella.
11	HUNASGERIA	17	3,661	558	4,219	28,000	7·6	248	32,000	8,000	Galgawatte, Happoowidde, Nilocanda, Kittoolgalla, Hunungalla, Halgolla, Horagalla, Mahatenne, Dotallagalla, Elkadua, Algooltenne, Waygalla, Hunasgeria, Patampahi, Udogodde, Gavatenne, Ellagalla.
12	KADUGANAVA	20	3,976	1,651	5,627	17,000	4·3	281	22,000	8,000	De Soysa's, Mahabelongalla, Solomon's, Churchill, Franklands, Alpittykanda, Providence Mount, Prospect, Cottagalla, Kallagalla, Wackittiatenne, Gona-Adica, Gadadessa, Hunegalla, Ambelawa, Sinipitia, Ashbourne, Bokanda, Villakande, Kehelwatte.
13	KALIBOKKA	13	2,660	770	3,430	20,000	7·5	264	23,500	6,000	Religas, Hoolankanda, Deyanilla, Galheria, Nillomally, Hunnnagalla, Maousakelle, Madoolkelley, Hatella, Wattikelley, Malwattey, Ratnatenne, Lagallakanda.
14	KORNEGALLE	20	2,500	750	3,250	10,000	4·0	162	13,000	5,000	Handrookanda, Bulatvellekanda, Kattuwella, Moorootikanda, Dolangtalawa, Goongamma, Paragodde, Ambacoombra, Oodahena, Morrakanda, Katookitool, Dunira, Rockhill, Greenwood, Galgedera, Boldegalla, Tallatenne, Hatbowe, Doolwella, Belloongodde.
15	KOTMALIE	22	3,800	260	4,060	18,000	4·7	184	19,000	7,000	Bowhill, Kadianlena, Baharundra, Kataboola, Kooroowakka, Oonoocotooa, Telesangalla, Yallebende, Hennwelle, Oonoogalpatne, Harangolla, Tyspane, Bellevue, Queensberry, Doombegrastalawa, Habogastalawa, Doonuwille, Kolapatna, Gigiranoya, Gongolla Fettercairn, Cattoogalla.
16	KNUCKLES	16	2,045	792	2,837	12,000	5·9	177	16,000	5,000	Allakolla, Kandekettia, Leangolla, Madakelle, Katooloya, Kootooatenne, Tunisgalla, Dalookoya, Bellses, Bambraella, Battagalla, Middleton, Moraga, Goomera, Lebanon, Gouragalla.
17	MATELLE, EAST	27	3,291	1,712	5,003	26,000	7·9	185	37,000	8,000	Nagalla, Gammadua, Kensington, Mitchell's, Callagalla, Opalgalla, Ellagalla, Cattaratenne, Dankande, Midland Attgodde, Bambragalla No. 1, Cabroosa Ella, Bambragalla No. 2, Oodelamana, Nicholoya, Poengalla, Cabragalla, Pektianda, Sylva Kande, Kinrara, Damboolagalla, Kandenewera, Maousagalla, Wiriapolle, Godapolla No. 1, Godapolla No. 2.
	Carried forward	284	46,023	11,167	57,190	241,500			290,100	93,500	

Number.	Names of Districts.	Number of Estates.	Bearing. (Acres.)	Not yet Bearing. (Acres.)	Total in Cultivation. (Acres.)	Average Crop last two Years. (Cwt.)	Crop per Acre. (Cwt.)	Average Cultivation on Estates. (Acres.)	Probable Crop in 1857–58. (Cwts.)	Labourers required during Crop time. (Coolies.)	Names of Estates to which the following Statistics apply.
	Brought forward	284	46,023	11,167	57,190	241,500	7·4	183	290,100	93,500	
18	MATELLE, WEST	16	2,100	830	2,930	15,500	7·4	183	20,000	5,000	Kent, Amboka, Seligamma, Beradowella, Vicarton, Borders, Etta-polla, Berkshire, Wiltshire, Hampshire, Madua, Madewelle, Ancoombra, Ballacadua, Gorala Ella, Lagahaella.
19	MATURATTE	10	330	890	1,220	2,600	7·9	122	8,500	2,000	Goodwood, Gonapatna, Mormon Hill, Allakollawewa, Smith's Maduren, Newera, Manapitia, Seaton, Alma, Bartholomenz.
20	MEDAMAHANEW- ERA	9	895	450	1,345	4,500	5·0	149	6,500	2,000	Nugatenne, Gallakella, California, Ellen Maria, Alea Vittene, Dodangalla, Woodside, Watte Kelle, Hangrogamme.
21	NILAMBE	9	2,180	390	2,570	14,000	6·4	285	15,000	4,000	Wattegodde, Haaloya, Wariagalla, Nilambe, Vedehettia, Colgrain, Nawagalla, Galloway, Knowe, Goorookelle.
22	PUSILAWA	28	6,330	570	6,900	40,000	6·3	246	42,000	10,000	Moneragalla, Rothschild, Gouracodde, Waygahapittiya, Niapana, Harmony, Katookelle, Yattepiangalla, Doragalla, Dowategras, Peacock, Kalloogalla, Moragalla, Melfort, Blackforest, Delta, Glenlock Whyddon, Hallebodde, Kattookitool, Kandalawa, Stellenberg, Newmarket, Proprasse, Caragastalawa, Meegolla, Peak, and Peak Forest.
23	RANGBODDE	19	1,411	952	2,363	7,000	5·0	124	11,000	3,500	Condagalla, Labookelle, Pallagalla, Rangbodde, Bluepills, Rambodde, Weddemulla, Poojagodde, Wavendon, Eyrie, Willisford's, Sahonadiere's, Tavalamtenne, Poondelloya, Harrow, Eton, Robertson's, Neitner's, Meeriscotoakelle.
24	RANGALLA	8	1,095	820	1,915	9,000	8·0	239	15,500	3,500	Cotaganga, Girinde Elle, Lovegrove, Gallebodde, Ranwella, Battagalla, Rangalle No. 1, Rangalle No. 2.
25	SAFFRAGAM	7	1,200	500	1,700	5,000	4·2	243	7,000	2,000	Massena, Patigalla, Hatarebage, Springwood, Evarton, Barra, Palamcottah.
26	WALIAPANE	5	777	30	807	4,500	5·8	161	4,800	1,200	Alnwick, St. Margaret's, Tulloes, Kirklees, (?)
27	YACDESSA	8	1,430	580	2,010	3,500	2·4	251	4,500	2,500	Horagalla, Yacdesse, Dotola, Nagastenne, Burn, Galanudina, Bennetsfield, Stenshells.
	Totals & Averages	403	63,771	17,179	80,950	347,100	5·5	200	424,700	129,200	

Ceylon - Tea Manufacture - 100 Years Ago

TOP LEFT
Weighing up the leaf outside the factory.
(Courtesy Royal Commonwealth Society.)

CENTRE LEFT
Withering. When the leaf came in from the fields, it contained approximately 76 per cent weight of water. Having been weighed, it was carried up to the withering loft(s) to be spread thinly on the 'tats' and left to wither. The tats were wooden structures with loosely woven jute hessian stretched across. Withering allowed the moisture in the leaf to evaporate until the leaf became flaccid and, at the same time, susceptible to a good twist by the rollers in the next phase of manufacture. Depending upon climatic conditions and whether the withering was natural or artificial, by the use of fans which boost warm air – heated by the driers – through the lofts, the green leaf took between 18 and 24 hours to wither. By this time it was ready for the next stage of manufacture: that of rolling.

In the rolling room on the ground floor the noise level would have been deafening – the hollow grinding sound of the gyrating rolling machines, the whirring of the pulley wheels, the slap of the belting and, above all, the deep rythmic thump of the diesel engine. One had to shout to make oneself heard.

BOTTOM LEFT
Rolling. The withered leaf arrived by way of the shutes from the floor(s) above, to be placed in the rollers. In rolling, the leaf is crushed, broken and twisted, so as to break down the leaf cells and release the juices and oils which cover the surface of the leaf. As these juices come into contact with the air, oxidisation takes place and fermentation starts. The roller would rotate in one direction while its unfixed ribbed table base, on which the leaf rested, rotated in the other. When the leaf was sufficiently rolled, it was taken out, golden green in colour, and quite sticky and lumpy. The 'roll' was then put out onto a sloping, fine meshed machine called a roll-breaker which, whilst shaking backwards and forwards at high speed, broke up the lumps, letting the small leaf fall through onto the ground beneath. The large lumps were shaken to the end of the machine. The small leaf that came through the roll-breaker at each sieving was then ready for the next process of manufacture: fermenting. The rest was carried back to the roll-breaker, and the process was repeated three or four times. One rolling machine took the place of several old rolling tables, and did the work of about 60 hand-rolling coolies.

RIGHT
A roll-breaker inside the factory and a rolling machine to the left. (Photo 1900, courtesy Mrs Raffin.)

Fermenting. (For the lack of a suitable photograph, see watercolour drawing on page 184 'fermenting in India'.) It was in the cool, damp, and darkened fermenting room that the leaf, or 'dhool', was spread out on the fermenting beds of smooth polished concrete or cement. The process of fermentation – first started by rolling – now took place and, when the leaf assumed a bright copper colour, it was ready for lifting. Again, the precise time at which the fermentation should be stopped and the fermented leaf removed was crucial, and also depended on weather conditions. However, assuming all the tests had been carried out and the infusions tasted during the withering and again towards the end of the fermenting process, the fermented leaf was ready for lifting for the final stage: firing.

RIGHT
Firing. The fermented leaf was carried to the driers, or firing machines, where it was spread out onto an endless chain of wire trays. These circulated over a continual current of hot air which was drawn up from the stoves below by high pressure fans. Fermentation of the leaf was now arrested. The whole factory became filled with a glorious aroma and the tea, still hot, that emerged from the firing machine was now fully manufactured: it was black, dry, and brittle. One large drying machine – such as the one shown, manufactured by Davidson & Co. – does the work of about 35 coolies working over a line of charcoal-burning ovens. (Courtesy Royal Commonwealth Society.) The tea was now ready to be sorted into the different grades and then stored in large bins until a sufficient quantity had been accumulated for dispatch. From 1000 lbs of green leaf, 230 lbs of made tea is the result. (BELOW LEFT, AND RIGHT)

APPENDIX IV

The Tiger Affair
A Close Shave
Malaya 1920s

The year was 1929, and the place was Malaya. Although strictly speaking Malaya does not come within the confines of this book, the tiger affair had to be told, firstly because it happened on a plantation and, secondly, because it may help those readers who live in the concrete jungles of our cities to compare more vividly the hazardous life of a planter with that of a man who journeys to his office on the same train, at the same time, and even in the same carriage every day of his working life.

I was one-and-a-half years old. My father was a rubber planter out there and, at the time when the tiger first put in an appearance, he and my mother had been living on the estate for some three years. I had been born on the estate in the rambling old thatched bungalow; on one side, a strip of jungle came within a stone's throw of the house, whilst all around rubber trees came up to the garden boundary.

Although there were many tigers in the jungle up and down Malaya in the 1920s, they were rarely seen. The first reports from the alarmed estate coolies stated that a tiger had been seen on the fringes of the jungle adjoining the rubber trees. Not unnaturally, some of those whose tapping blocks lay along the estate boundaries became extremely nervous of tapping scores of rubber trees adjacent to the jungle. It was soon after the sightings that the tiger made its first human kill in the district. The victim was a Tamil woman who had been tapping her block of rubber trees on an outlying part of the estate; her partial remains were later found some distance into the jungle.

News travels fast in such circumstances, and my father and the other planters in the district were now on the look-out, for once a tiger has turned man-eater, it loses all fear of humans, and the sooner it is shot, the better it is for all who live in its path.

It is as well to say that humans are not the tiger's natural prey and there is usually some reason that makes it leave its customary hunting ground to frequent the habitations of man. This particular tiger could have received a gun-shot wound, or it could have been old and, being unable to catch its natural prey in the jungle, was seeking easier food. However, in most cases a tiger becomes a man-eater because of an injury of some sort; for instance, if a porcupine's long needle-sharp quills became embedded in the foot-pad or leg of a tiger, it would not be capable of catching its natural prey with such a wound. It is probably fair to say that man could pass quite safely through areas which are inhabited by tigers, unless the animals are cornered inadvertently in a ravine, or wounded in some way. I can do no better to illustrate this point than recount my uncle's experience of hunting peacock in Siam. He came face to face with a tiger at about 70 feet and, as he was only carrying a twelve-bore shotgun, he turned and beat a very hasty retreat. Having gone but a short distance, he looked back fearfully, only to see the tiger running too – in the opposite direction. By the laws of the jungle he had been reasonably safe and had no need to run, but sometimes that is easier said than done.

To return to the story. A day or so after the woman had been killed, the tiger paid its first visit to my parents' garden, carrying off their one and only goat which had been kept for milking. The goat had spent its nights in a lean-to shed at the back of the bungalow, next to another small shed that housed about a dozen chickens. The next morning the tiger's pug marks were clearly seen on the soft earth nearby. By now everyone on the estate was feeling a little nervous.

Under the bougainvillea tree were the pug marks of the man-eater; it had obviously been watching them.

A few evenings later, my parents and a friend from a neighbouring estate were sitting out on the verandah with their drinks – no doubt talking about the man–eater and its activities – when, in the fast fading light, my father saw, or thought he saw, a movement under a large Bougainvilia tree in the garden. He called for the boy to bring his rifle, but no one saw or heard anything further that night. The following morning at around six my father went across to the spot where he thought he had seen the dark shape and, close to the tree, on the round flower bed amongst the cannas, were the pug marks of the tiger. It had obviously been watching them.

The tiger paid its third visit a night or so later. It entered through the side of the bungalow, passed through a downstairs room, and then mounted the stairs that led to the bedrooms. My parents always slept upstairs on the right side of the house as one looks at the photograph,

RIGHT
Pontian bungalow and garden with bougainvillea tree on left of picture.

Either a baby or the dog would have made a tasty, if small meal for a man-eater. As things turned out, it was the dog.

whilst I was stowed away each night in a cot in the bedroom across the landing. It was the custom of our faithful dog Dunny to spend each night curled up at the entrance to my bedroom, lying just outside the open door on the landing. As I have already mentioned, my age was such that on that particular night I was blissfully unware of the entire proceedings and, as I came to learn later on, so were my parents.

Nothing was known of the tragedy until early next morning, when the boy came upstairs to call my father, as he always did around 5.45 am. On this occasion he burst into their bedroom to say that the tiger's pug marks were clearly to be seen all the way up the stairs and then on to my bedroom, and that Dunny was not there as usual. If Dunny had not

always slept outside my bedroom, the tiger in all probability would have carried me off instead. My parents had heard a noise of some sort during the night, probably a floor-board creaking under the animal's weight, but the cook and the boys who slept at the rear of the bungalow in an adjoining building had heard nothing.

Before the tiger had carried off the rubber tapper, my amah (nanny), a Javanese girl, had taken me for my daily outing in the pram along the cart road that ran through a patch of jungle at the approach to the bungalow. It was just a case of either being in the right place or wrong place when the man-eater first showed up. Countless humans have been taken by tigers up and down Malaya, India and other countries.

I have often wondered why there was no sound from Dunny, who either did not smell or hear the tiger's approach, or if he did, was petrified into silence, or at most a whimper of fright. My uncle who is now 86, and who was also out there planting at the time, can confirm the facts, but cannot add to what I have told you. A dog's life on an estate was often a short one; another of my parents' dogs fell down and died in a 'dead-fall' pit that had been dug in the jungle by some of the estate coolies to catch wild pig, and yet another just disappeared. As to the tiger, it was shot a few days later by another planter some miles away.

There was one other occasion when my parents came very close to a tiger, or to be more precise, the tiger came very close to them. They had been staying on Penang Island for a week end and were driving back to the estate through Ipoh when the incident occurred.

At times the road led through rubber estates and interconnecting jungle. It was while they were travelling along one such jungle stretch of the road that a tiger, which had been standing on the verge, rushed out at the car in much the same way as any pi-dog of the east will dash out at a motor cycle or car when it passes. It ran full tilt towards the car, which was veering off somewhat owing to my father taking as much avoiding action as he could while still staying on the none too wide road. The tiger undoubtably lost some of its momentum during its arc-like approach of the speeding vehicle, but for a few moments it bounded along by the side of the car before making an abortive attempt to jump on board.

My mother, sitting in the front passenger seat, had the best view of the proceedings as it was on her side that the tiger attempted to board. As the whole incident took only a few seconds, she was aware only of the beast running towards the car, and then of a sickening jolt as it landed on the running board and fell off all in the same moment. The car lurched, but sped on until my father pulled in about half a mile down the road to see

One of the women rubber tappers was the tiger's first victim; her tapping block lay along the jungle boundary on an outlying part of the estate.

what damage had been caused. There was no running board left, and there was quite a dent in the door. A few moments after the collison my father had seen the tiger scampering off the road into the jungle, having probably learnt that the fastest thing on wheels yet seen in the jungle was not to be trifled with.

Like my father, uncle and great-uncle before me, I became a planter – and duly went out to Ceylon in the *Chilka* BI cargo passenger vessel leaving Tilbury Docks in November 1950. We travelled via the Suez Canal and I and the other eight passengers on board enjoyed the trip so much that we were quite sad to leave *Chilka* and climb down the companion-way in Colombo, some five weeks later.

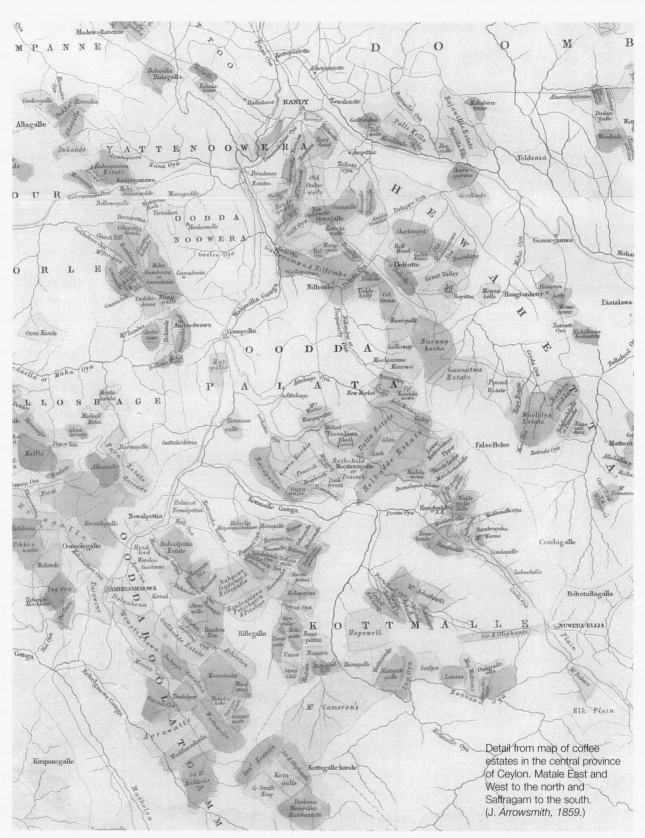

Detail from map of coffee estates in the central province of Ceylon. Matale East and West to the north and Saffragam to the south. (*J. Arrowsmith, 1859.*)

Bibliography

Bramah, E, *Tea and Coffee* (Hutchinson & Co 1972)

Brohier, Deloraine, *The Saga of the Colombo Club* (Colombo Club 2001) ISBN 955 9362 01 1

Brook-Smith, Charles, *Two Leaves & A Bud* (BlooZoo Ltd, Essex 2000) ISBN 1 903649 00 5

Bruce, C. A., *An Account of the Manufacture of Black Tea as now Practiced at Suddeya in Upper Assam, by Chinamen sent Thither for that Purpose*, Calcutta 1838 (British Library, O.I.O.C.)

Bruce, C. A., *Report on the Manufacture of Tea, and on the Extent and Produce of Tea Plantations in Assam, Calcutta 1839* (British Library, O.I.O.C.)

Campbell, Reginald, *Teak Wallah* (London Press Ltd., Warwick Square, 1951)

Corbett, Jim, *Man-eaters of Kumaon* (Oxford University Press 1944)

Crampsey, B, *The Kings Grocer*, The Life of Sir Thomas Lipton, 1955 Glasgow City Library

East India Company, MS F/41586 – 6457 (British Library, O.I.O.C.)

Forrest, D. M., *A Hundred Years of Ceylon Tea* (Chatto & Windus, 1967)

Griffiths, Sir Percival, *A History of the Joint Steamer Companies* (Inchcape & Co. Ltd., London)

Gupta, Sujoy, *Four Mangoe Lane, The First Address for Tea*, Williamson Magor & Co. Ltd. (Tata McGraw-Hill, New Delhi 2001) ISBN 0 07 043591 X

Handy, Elizabeth, *A Journey Through Tea* (Lawrie Group Plc) ISBN 0 9527549 1 6

Lindgren, Oscar, *The Trials of a Planter* (Privately printed, Kalimpong, India 1933)

Radford, John, OBE & Farrington, Susan, *Tombs in Tea Garden Cemeteries*, Sylhet and Bangladesh (B.A.C.S.A., Putney, London 2001)

Taylor, Rod, *The Lost Plantation*, A History of the Australian Tea Industry 1982 (Published by G. K. Bolton, Cairns, Australia) ISBN 0909920 16 8

Tea, Cultivation to Consumption (Chapman & Hall, London 1992, edited by Dr. K. C. Willson and Dr. M. N. Clifford) ISBN 0 412 33850 5

Ukers, W. H., *All About Tea* (Tea & Coffee Trade Journal, New York 1935)

Victorian India, Tea Garden of the World (British Library publication, 1996)

Weatherstone, John, *The Pioneers*, The Early British Tea & Coffee Planters and their Way of Life, 1825–1900 (Quiller Press, London 1986)

World Green Tea Association, *A Cup of Japanese Green Tea*, 2001 (www/o-cha.net/english/index.html)

Archive material used in support of the water-colour reconstruction drawings as under:

Map – Pioneer country north of Nazira, Ch II

- A contemporary map dated 1839 showing the Tea Tracts discovered by C. A. Bruce.

- Caption compiled from C. A. Bruce's Reports of 1838 and 1839

- Painted by Sidney Fever from my own rough vignette pencil drawings.

The Assam Company's H.Q. at Nazira, Ch II

- A contemporary pen and ink sketch made in 1841 by an unknown artist (depicted from ground level) showing the Station's buildings and part of the Dikhoo River. Painted by Sidney Fever from a rough plan by the author depicting an elevated view, together with early photographs showing labour lines, Tea House (factory) and staff bungalows typical of the period.

Sadiya nursery scene, Ch II

- A preliminary rough layout by the author (below) for figures, nursery beds, boats etc. Parts of E.I.C. MS relating to the river journey and transport of China tea plants, 1835.

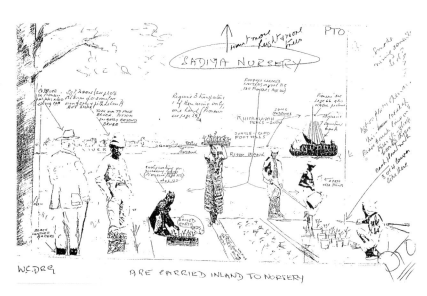

Index

Notes: The themes of the book are detailed in the contents pages vi and vii.
Pictue references are in italics

Map of North-East India

Tea pioneers.
(*Photo 1868, courtesy Royal Geographical Society.*)